31 Days Before Your CompTIA A+ Exams

Ben Conry

AUG   2009

Cisco Press ▪ 800 East 96th Street ▪ Indianapolis, Indiana 46240 USA

31 Days Before Your CompTIA A+ Exams

Ben Conry

Copyright © 2009 Cisco Systems, Inc.

Published by:
Cisco Press
800 East 96th Street
Indianapolis, IN 46240 USA

Printed in the United States of America

First Printing April 2009

Library of Congress Cataloging-in-Publication Data:

Conry, Ben, 1973-
  31 days before your CompTIA A+ exams / Ben Conry. -- 1st ed.
     p. cm.
  ISBN 978-1-58713-231-5 (pbk.)
 1. Electronic data processing personnel--Certification. 2. Computer technicians--Certification--Study guides. 3. Microcomputers--Maintenance and repair--Examinations--Study guides. 4. Computing Technology Industry Association--Examinations--Study guides. I. Title. II. Title: Thirty one days before your CompTIA A+ exams.
  QA76.3.C65675 2009
  004.165--dc22

                                        2009010757

ISBN-13: 978-1-58713-231-5

ISBN-10: 1-58713-231-1

Warning and Disclaimer

This book is designed to provide information about preparing for CompTIA A+ certification exams (2006 objectives). Every effort has been made to make this book as complete and as accurate as possible, but no warranty or fitness is implied.

The information is provided on an "as is" basis. The authors, Cisco Press, and Cisco Systems, Inc., shall have neither liability nor responsibility to any person or entity with respect to any loss or damages arising from the information contained in this book or from the use of the discs or programs that may accompany it.

This book is part of the Cisco Networking Academy® series from Cisco Press. The products in this series support and complement the Cisco Networking Academy curriculum. If you are using this book outside the Networking Academy, then you are not preparing with a Cisco trained and authorized Networking Academy provider.

For more information on the Cisco Networking Academy or to locate a Networking Academy, Please visit www.cisco.com/edu.

CISCO.

The opinions expressed in this book belong to the author and are not necessarily those of Cisco Systems, Inc.

Trademark Acknowledgments

All terms mentioned in this book that are known to be trademarks or service marks have been appropriately capitalized. Cisco Press or Cisco Systems, Inc., cannot attest to the accuracy of this information. Use of a term in this book should not be regarded as affecting the validity of any trademark or service mark.

Corporate and Government Sales

The publisher offers excellent discounts on this book when ordered in quantity for bulk purchases or special sales, which may include electronic versions and/or custom covers and content particular to your business, training goals, marketing focus, and branding interests. For more information, please contact:

U.S. Corporate and Government Sales   1-800-382-3419   corpsales@pearsontechgroup.com

For sales outside the United States please contact: **International Sales**   international@pearsoned.com

Feedback Information

At Cisco Press, our goal is to create in-depth technical books of the highest quality and value. Each book is crafted with care and precision, undergoing rigorous development that involves the unique expertise of members from the professional technical community.

Readers' feedback is a natural continuation of this process. If you have any comments regarding how we could improve the quality of this book, or otherwise alter it to better suit your needs, you can contact us through e-mail at feedback@ciscopress.com. Please make sure to include the book title and ISBN in your message.

We greatly appreciate your assistance.

Publisher: Paul Boger	**Business Operation Manager, Cisco Press**: Anand Sundaram
Associate Publisher: Dave Dusthimer	**Manager Global Certification**: Erik Ullanderson
Executive Editor: Mary Beth Ray	**Copy Editor**: Keith Cline
Managing Editor: Patrick Kanouse	**Technical Editors**: Sharon Hain, Matthew Newell
Development Editor: Dayna Isley	**Proofreader**: Sheri Cain
Project Editor: Seth Kerney	
Editorial Assistant: Vanessa Evans	
Cover and Interior Designer: Louisa Adair	
Composition: Mark Shirar	
Indexer: Ken Johnson	

CISCO

Americas Headquarters	Asia Pacific Headquarters	Europe Headquarters
Cisco Systems, Inc.	Cisco Systems (USA) Pte. Ltd.	Cisco Systems International BV
San Jose, CA	Singapore	Amsterdam, The Netherlands

Cisco has more than 200 offices worldwide. Addresses, phone numbers, and fax numbers are listed on the Cisco Website at **www.cisco.com/go/offices.**

About the Author

Benjamin P. Conry graduated from Oberlin College in 1995 with a bachelor's degree in music education with an emphasis in composition. He earned a master's degree in instructional technology from Johns Hopkins University in 2002. Currently, he holds CCNA, CCAI, and A+ certifications and is the lead instructor for Information Technology Essentials, PC Hardware and Software in Baltimore County Public Schools. Ben Conry consistently takes disadvantaged and minority students and sees them through their A+ certification and into college and careers. He has received awards and citations for his commitment to educational excellence and for preparing students for college and the workforce. Ben Conry lives with his wife and two children in Lutherville, Maryland.

About the Technical Reviewers

Sharon Hain has been an active high school and community college educator for more than 40 years, teaching at both levels in Illinois and Arizona. She has been an innovative leader in education through her affiliations with educational leadership opportunities and organizations. She holds both a bachelor's degree and master's degree in business education. She is a certified A+ and CCNA instructor.

Matthew Newell has been with TRECA (Ohio CATC) since 2000, splitting time between systems administration in TRECA's enterprise data center and as an instructor for the Cisco Networking Academy. Matt teaches instructor-level courses (train-the-trainer) for the CATC in IT Essentials (A+), CCNA, Wireless, and PNIE (Copper and Fiber Optic Cable Installation), and often visits Cisco Networking Academies across the region to speak to IT students. Over the years, he has gained extensive experience in LAN/WAN hardware, network design, and multiplatform server administration. Matt has acquired various certifications during his IT career from Microsoft, Cisco, and CompTIA, and is currently the technical contact for TRECA's Microsoft Certified Partner Program.

Dedication

This book is dedicated to my wife, mother of my children, and life-long best friend, Marisa, and to Daniel and Eli, for their patience and understanding when Go-Boys time was met with their least favorite phrase, "After Dad's deadline." Now, it's Go-Boys time!

Acknowledgments

Mary Beth Ray is the best, forward-thinking, encouraging, honest executive editor ever, anywhere, and truly among the most genuine and kindest people I know.

Dayna Isley has the patience of a saint and the unique ability to turn my unintelligible techno-mumble into coherent statements. Thank you.

Special thanks to Sharon Hain, Matt Newell, and Lloyd Allen. They are defenders of facts, slayers of uninformed statements, and champions of accuracy.

Thanks also to Keith Cline and Seth Kerney for their excellent copy editing. Without them, my murder of the English language would be public knowledge.

Contents at a Glance

Contents

Command Syntax Conventions

The conventions used to present command syntax in this book are the same conventions used in the IOS Command Reference. The Command Reference describes these conventions as follows:

- **Boldface** indicates commands and keywords that are entered literally as shown. In actual configuration examples and output (not general command syntax), boldface indicates commands that are manually input by the user (such as a **show** command).

- *Italic* indicates arguments for which you supply actual values.

- Vertical bars (|) separate alternative, mutually exclusive elements.

- Square brackets ([ ]) indicate an optional element.

- Braces ({ }) indicate a required choice.

- Braces within brackets ([{ }]) indicate a required choice within an optional element.

Introduction

31 Days Before Your CompTIA A+ Exams is a bridge between the Cisco IT Essentials: PC Hardware and Software v4.0 course and the CompTIA A+ exams. You stand ready to make your knowledge official, provable, to become a professional computer technician. Every day for the next 31 days, you will cover a small area of the exams. The divide-and-conquer strategy allows you to focus on the topics at hand and not be overwhelmed with the massive amount of tested material.

Professional certifications have been an important part of the computing industry for many years and will continue to become more important. Many reasons exist for these certifications, but the most popularly cited reason is that of credibility. All other considerations held equal, the certified employee/consultant/job candidate is considered more valuable than one who is not.

Goals and Methods

The goal of this book is to provide you with a step-by-step method of study and preparation for the CompTIA A+ exam that is mapped directly to the Cisco Networking Academy course IT Essentials: PC Hardware and Software. In this book, you will find the following:

- Short summaries of topics, definitions, and diagrams of important concepts
- Numbers that map topics in this book to pages in the IT Essentials: PC Hardware and Software v4.0 course
- Tables, figures, and examples of devices, directions, and commands you might find on the CompTIA A+ exams
- References for further study and exploration
- Occasional attempts at nerd humor

This book can also serve as guide for instructors to review the IT Essentials: PC Hardware and Software v4.0 course and prepare an entire class for the A+ exams. You can use this book to fit certification exam preparation into a busy schedule, because it is a little bit of study each day.

Who Should Read This Book?

This book is for students who are about to take the CompTIA A+ exams and are either currently enrolled or a recent graduate of Cisco Networking Academy IT Essentials: PC Hardware and Software v4.0 course.

Strategies for Exam Preparation

Find a distraction-free area: no kids, no siblings, no pets, no headphones, no radio or TV. (A cup of coffee and a fireplace are recommended, however.) Dedicate about an hour every day to study in this refuge. It can be difficult at first to find the time and place, but it is time and effort well spent. To that retreat, bring this book, your attention, and preferably access to the Cisco IT Essentials PC Hardware and Software v4.0 online course. A set of A+ flash cards are a great resource, too. InformIT offers a great set that you can find at http://www.informit.com/title/0789739208.

How This Book Is Organized

This book is organized differently than most. The A+ exam has three paths to completion. Everyone takes the A+ Essentials exam. Then you choose one of three specialization exams to take. Sucessful completion of either the 220-602 Field Technician, 220-603 Remote Technician, or 220-604 Bench Technician exam will earn your A+ certification.

This book begins with the Essentials exam coverage in Day 31 to Day 15. After that, you choose which exam to take based on your scores in the eight domains covered on the Essentials exam. (Refer to the CompTIA website, http://www.comptia.org, for more information about the eight domains.) You will then continue on to the part of the book that covers that exam and work through Day 14 to Day 1 of that specific part.

To aid in your exam preparation, use the calendars printed on the tearout card to map out each day of study. Also, before you take the Essentials and specialized exams, use the checklists printed on the inside front and back covers of this book to ensure you have a firm grasp of the exam topics.

Part I

Taking the Essentials Exam (2006)

Hardware Concepts: Part 1 of 2

A+ Essentials Exam Objective

Objective 1.1: Identify the fundamental principles of using personal computers

Key Points

Today you will cover topics from Chapters 1 and 3 in the IT Essentials v4.0 course. Specifically, you will review the names, purposes, and characteristics of storage devices, adapter cards, motherboards, central processing units (CPU), and power supplies. Today is the first half of two challenging days. It does get easier. The internal devices have many details, all of which are fair game on the CompTIA A+ exam. Today you will cover the devices, and tomorrow you will review some of the technologies and installation procedures. Remember that 21% of the CompTIA A+ Essentials exam comes from these first two days. Faced with entering a cold swimming pool, a running-start, closed-eye, tucked-knee cannonball is a great way to get in the water (and impress your friends). So take a big breath and hold your nose.

Storage Devices

1.4.6: Storage devices include hard drives, floppy drives, nonvolatile random-access memory (NVRAM), tape drives, optical drives (CD and DVD drives), and network drives.

Hard Drives

The hard disk drive (HDD) has been a mainstay of PCs for a long time. Because of its widespread use, it is a big part of the A+ exam. Traditionally, the HDD stores the operating system and the bulk of data in the PC. It is mounted in a 3.5-inch bay, and connects internally through a parallel advanced technology attachment (PATA) channel. PATA interfaces are sometimes referred to as advanced technology attachment (ATA) or integrated drive electronics (IDE). Jumpers are used to determine the HDD's designation either as master or slave.

Most new PCs use a controller called serial ATA (SATA) for HDD and optical drives. SATA does not use jumpers or designations. Instead, SATA uses one header and one cable per drive.

All HDDs work the same way. Arms move read/write (R/W) heads over the surface of spinning magnetic platters. These R/W heads either align molecules to create a positive charge (a 1) or leave it neutral charge (a 0), thus making the binary code. When reading, the heads float above the disks and feel the positive charges or no pull from the neutral.

Floppy Drives

In many ways, a floppy disk drive (FDD) is like a HDD. It spins a disk, moves R/W heads across the surface, and stores data magnetically. There are two important differences: Capacity is limited to 1.44 MB, and the disk is removable by the end user. A classic A+ question involves an FDD status light that stays lit all the time. The cable is oriented backward. Turn off the PC, unplug the FDD cable from the drive, flip it over, and plug it back in. Normally, the colored wire on the ribbon cable (pin 1) is closest to the Berg power connector. On the motherboard end, it should be oriented based on the numbers printed around the FDD cable header. Because there are 34 wires in an FDD cable, it is narrower than a PATA ribbon.

Solid-State HDD and NVRAM

Ranging from small external universal serial bus (USB) devices to larger-capacity HDDs, solid-state drives are in reality NVRAM storage devices. NVRAM, often referred to as flash memory or flash RAM, is slower than RAM but still faster than traditional magnetic storage media. Unlike RAM, NVRAM can maintain its data when not powered. Solid-state drives are especially good for laptops where portability, performance, durability, and low power consumption are valued over price and drive capacity.

Tape Drives

A magnetic tape is drawn across stationary R/W heads, but the same magnetic process takes place. The tape is removable by the user, but the drive remains mounted and connected to the PC. Tape capacity is large, comparable to HDDs, but access time is slow because of the sequential nature of tape media. These are primarily used as server backups.

CD and DVD Drives

The basic optical drive is a compact disc read-only memory (CD-ROM). This CD-ROM drive reads premade discs and cannot write (burn) CDs. The CD can hold 650 MB or 700 MB of data. The CD-ROM drive mounts in a 5.25-inch bay and connects to the motherboard via a PATA or SATA interface.

Digital versatile disc (DVD) has many more variations. The basic read and write letters still apply, but there are two formats: + and –. For our purposes, they are the same. Just note that they are not compatible with each other. Plus drives only read/write plus CDs. Newer +/– hybrid drives can read and write both. Generally speaking, DVD drives are backward compatible and can use CDs. A typical DVD holds 4.7 GB of data or 8.5 GB for double layered (on the same side).

Table 31-1 compares CD and DVD drives.

Table 31-1   Optical Drives

CD Family	DVD Family	Need to Know
CD-ROM	DVD-ROM	Can only read premade discs.
CD-R	DVD+/-R	(Recordable) Write a disc once, and it is read-only after that.
CD-RW	DVD+/-RW	(Rewritable) Read and write a disc repeatedly.
CDRAM (not an optical drive)	DVD-RAM	("Endlessly" rewritable) Used primarily as surveillance-camera footage.

Network Drives

These drives are often referred to as remote, shared, or mapped drives. This means that the storage device resides on another computer, server, printer, or other network device, not on the end user's (local) PC.

Interfaces and Cables

1.4.7: All storage devices in the computer are connected to the motherboard through cables. For your A+ exam, you just need to know a few basics about each cable. The term *hot swappable* means the drive can be connected and unplugged while the PC is running. Pin 1 is always the pin with the blue, red, or pink stripe. Both the device and the motherboard will specify (usually with inhumanly small numbers) which side is pin 1. If there is no indication how to orient the cable, put pin 1 closest to the Molex power plug.

Table 31-2 compares the features of different drive interfaces.

Table 31-2   **Drive Interfaces**

Interface	Drives per Channel	Number of Pins	Hot Swappable	Need to Know (In Order of Importance)
PATA, ATA, IDE, EIDE	2	40 80	No	Old standard. Two drives per channel. Jumpers assign master and slave drives.
SCSI	8 or 16	50 68 80	Yes	Typically found on servers. Drives are arranged along a bus-like cable with terminators on both ends. Jumpers or dip switches assign drive numbers in binary.
SATA	1	7	Yes	Small cable improves air cooling. Faster than PATA. One drive per channel No jumpers, no master, and no slave.
FDD	1	34	No	Only for the FDD. Pin 1 is usually oriented closest to the power connector, but look for the red strip e. Some old FDD cables support multiple FDDs. They have a twist in the middle of the ribbon connectors.

Adapter Cards

3.6.1, 3.9.2: Adapter cards convert binary communication into a format that other devices or humans can understand. There is always an adapter card between an external port and the motherboard. Many fundamental adapter cards are built (integrated) into the motherboard. A driver is a small piece of software that explains to the OS how to use the device, not unlike a translation guide or instruction manual. It is common to install an OS and then need to install additional drivers afterward, even for commonly integrated devices such as sound cards and network interface cards (NIC). USB is an external port and is a common interface for external adapter cards. The devices that connect through an adapter card also need drivers.

Daughter Boards Versus Riser Boards

A classic A+ exam question focuses on the difference between daughter and riser boards. Daughter boards and risers are essentially the same device. They are smaller boards that plug into the motherboard that expand the number of expansion slots, ports, or in some cases, add devices. If the board is used solely to add extra PCI slots or turn the angle of adapter cards to fit into smaller cases, then it is a riser. The two exceptions are Audio Modem Riser (AMR) and Communications Network Risers (CNR). They are an evolutionary missing link between true integrated devices and full-fledged expansion cards.

Adapter Card Interfaces

1.4.5: Whereas there are countless ports and external devices, there are a finite number of expansion slots though which adapter cards and motherboards connect. What you need to know about adapter cards and interfaces is explained here in order of learning importance. Check out the Cisco IT Essentials v4.0 course curriculum for great photos of these cards. You should be able to identify them by sight and description.

Table 31-3 describes internal side of the cards and the kinds of expansion slots. Table 31-4 describes the external aspects, such as which devices or ports are commonly supported by specific cards.

Table 31-3   Expansion Slots

Adapter Card/ Bus Name	Bus Width	Need to Know (In Order of Importance)
PCI	64 64 32	Current standard, 32 bit and 64 bit, shorter than ISA. Usually white. 32 bit have two in-line slots; 64 bit have 3.
AGP	32	Dedicated graphics card slot, 32 bit, shorter than PCI. Brown.
PCIe	x1 x4 x8 x16	Full duplex lets data be sent and received simultaneously. Measured in throughput as a multiple of 250 MBps. For example a x4 PCIe slot and card can transfer data at 1000 MBps. (250 MBps × 4 = 1000 MBps)

Table 31-3   **Expansion Slots** *continued*

Adapter Card/ Bus Name	Bus Width	Need to Know (In Order of Importance)
EISA	32	Old technology, slot 8- and 16-bit versions (32-bit EISA).
ISA	16	Black.
	8	Common in older PCs.
MCA	32	Old proprietary IBM version competitor of 32-bit EISA.

Table 31-4   **Adapter Cards**

Adapter	Uses These Buses	Need to Know (In Order of Importance)
NIC	PCI, PCIe, or USB	Connects the PC to a network.
Wireless NIC	PCI, PCIe, or USB	Connects a PC to a wireless network.
Video adapter	PCIe, AGP, or PCI	Translates data into video signal for the monitor.
USB	PCI	Is an adapter in this case. Like a SCSI, it forwards data onto another kind of bus. It often provides both internal and external USB ports.
FireWire	PCI or PCIe	Is similar to USB but nearly twice as fast. Commonly used to transfer video or other data-intensive applications.
Sound/audio adapter	PCI or PCIe	Translates data into audio signals for speakers.
SCSI adapter	PCI or PCIe	Is an additional bus link, like a transfer station. It forwards data to and from the PC to SCSI HDDs and devices.
RAID adapter	PCI or PCIe	Controls the spreading of data across multiple HDDs. Commonly used for SCSI but can also be used for SATA.
Modem	PCI or USB	Is like a combination NIC and sound adapter. It connects the PC to an audio/telephone-based network.
Parallel port	PCI	Connects peripheral parallel devices to the PC. Although somewhat rare today, it was the predominant method to connect to printer, scanners, and fax machines. The distinctive cable has a 25-pin D plug on the computer end and a 36-pin Centronics port on the other. Moves data along multiple channels simultaneously (parallel).
Serial port	PCI	Connects peripheral parallel devices to the PC. Not commonly used today. Moves data along one channel, bit by bit (serial).

Motherboards

1.4.1: Motherboards are the unsung heroes in the PC. They are responsible for practically all the communication and physical connections. The vintage advanced technology (AT) and Baby AT motherboards of the 1990s are not a major focus on the A+ exam. You need to know that they supported mostly ISA expansion cards and have 66-MHz busses.

Advanced technology extended (ATX) motherboards have been continually upgraded and modified over the past 15 years. There have been letter designations along the way to thicken the alphabet soup. The ATX and its offspring make up the majority of the current marketplace. Table 31-5 describes the different motherboard form factors.

Table 31-5   Motherboard Form Factors

Motherboard Name	Need to Know (In Order of Importance)
ATX	Introduced riser boards and daughter boards. Integrated keyboard, mouse, and video. Single 20-pin power-supply connection.
BTX (balanced technology extended)	This progeny of the ATX is the most common motherboard on the market today. First to integrate SATA, PCIe, and USB 2.0.
NLX	Integrated AGP, NIC, and USB support.
Mini ATX	Smaller and fewer expansion slots than ATX.
Micro ATX	Even smaller than Mini ATX.
LPX	Expansion cards run parallel to motherboard and can therefore fit in to a smaller case. Proprietary designs complicate repair. Typically must use original equipment manufacturer's (OEM) parts.
Mini LPX	Smaller and fewer expansion slots than LPX.

The chipset and buses on the motherboard determine a great deal about the computer that is built around it. The general architecture of motherboards is a great source of A+ questions.

Figure 31-1 shows the map of a motherboard, which is hierarchal. That means that it is organized from top to bottom in order of importance. Basically, the farther away a device is from the CPU, the less priority it has. Like the human body, the really important organs (devices) are inside, close to the core, and protected.

Figure 31-1   Motherboard Map

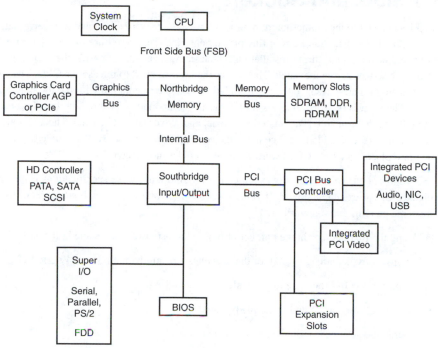

The CPU is only a processor, fast but not able to do anything but follow instructions. It uses a clock like a metronome to keep everything synchronous (on the beat), just as a marching band uses drums to stay together. The clock rate is the actual speed of the processor. The speed of this clock is measured in gigahertz (GHz) and is either set by jumpers (like those on PATA drives) on older systems or in the basic input/output system (BIOS) in newer PCs. The front-side bus (FSB) is the front door to the CPU. The width of the FSB determines whether the chip is a 32- or 64-bit processor. The speed of this bus is critical to the performance of the PC. All too often, novice technicians or manufacturers trying to save money will build and sell super-fast processors on cheap motherboards that have very slow FSBs. This is akin to driving a race car on a one-lane dirt road.

The northbridge controls two of the most important tasks on a PC: It sends instructions from RAM to the CPU, and it sends graphic data to the video card. The video card is a fast, dedicated card very much like a small motherboard complete with RAM and a graphic processing unit (GPU). Video cards often have their own cooling system. This allows the PC to worry about tasks other than constantly redrawing the monitor 60 or more times a second. RAM often has its own group of devices to support ever-faster access times and increasing capacities.

The other requests and data that are not RAM or video are forwarded on to the southbridge. That is where storage devices, adapter cards, and ports are located. This is collectively referred to as the input/output (I/O) controller. If your PC is using the integrated video, all that data must be processed by the southbridge. It is often busy with HDD and CD data, network traffic, and so on. Using AGP or PCIe cards tied into the northbridge used for video greatly increases the overall efficiency of the machine.

CPU Slots and Sockets

1.4.2: CPUs connect to the motherboard in only two ways. A socket is designed to receive flat, square, tile-like CPUs with hundreds of tiny pins on one side. The socket uses zero-insertion-force (ZIF) to avoid bending pins during installation. The latching lever sits alongside the socket. Pull it away from the socket to free the catch. Then move the lever upward to release the CPU. The CPU sets into the pin grid array (PGA). During installation, note the orientation with the missing pin in the corner. The lever is returned to its position. Thermal compound is used to help transfer heat from the CPU to the heat sink. This material is toxic, and gloves should be used. The slot-style CPUs are built to receive a blade that contains the contacts. They simply slide in guided by posts and snap into place. Slot-style CPUs were common on older motherboards.

Table 31-6 shows CPU socket and slot specifications. Memorizing these specifications is universally disliked by A+ exam candidates. If you are good at memorizing, enjoy. For the rest of us, here are some patterns and a few tricks:

- PGA and the first number in the number of pins is almost always the same in the early CPUs.

- PGAs are always square (21 × 21), or the new ones are simply a number (949 grid PGA).

- Slots don't use PGAs (because they are slots).

- Socket 6 is not used at all and is not likely tested.

- In general, the newer the CPU, the less voltage it uses.

- The names of the later connectors include the number of pins (socket 370, for example).

Table 31-6   CPUs

Connector	CPU	Pins	Voltage
Socket 4	Pentium 60/66	273 pins 21 × 21 PGA	5V
Socket 5	Pentium 75/90/100/120/133	320 pins	3.3V 37 × 37 SPGA
Socket 7	Pentium MMX, AMD KS, Cyrix M	321 pins 37 × 37 SPGA	2.5V to 3.3V
Super Socket 7	AMD KS-2, AMD KS-III	321 pins 37 × 37 SPGA	2.5V to 3.3V
Socket 8	Pentium Pro	387 pins 24 × 26 SPGA	3.3V
Socket 370 or PGA 370 Socket	Pentium III FC-PGA, Celeron PPGA, Cyrix III	370 pins 37 × 37 SPGA	1.5V or 2V
Slot 1 or SC242	Pentium II, Pentium III	242 pins 2 rows	2.8V and 3.3V
Slot A	AMD Athlon	242 pins 2 rows	1.3V to 2.05V

Table 31-6   CPUs *continued*

Connector	CPU	Pins	Voltage
Socket A or Socket 462	AMD Athlon and Duron	462 pins SPGA	1.1V to 1.85V
Slot 2 or SC330	Pentium II Xeon, Pentium III Xeon	330 pins 2 rows	1.5V to 3.5V
Socket 423	Pentium 4	423 pins 39 × 39 SPGA	1.7V and 1.75V
Socket 478	Pentium 4	478 pins micro PGA (mPGA)	1.7V and 1.75V
Socket PAC418	Itanium	418 pins	3.3V
Socket PAC611	Itanium 2	611 pins	3.3V
Socket 603	Xeon DP and MP	603 pins	1.5V and 1.7V
Socket 754	AMD Athlon 64, Sempron, Turion 64	754 pins PGA	0.8V to 1.55V
Socket 775 or Socket T	Pentium 4, Celeron D, Pentium 4 Extreme Edition, Pentium D, Pentium Extreme Edition, Core 2 Duo, Core 2 Extreme	755 pins LGA	
Socket 939	AMD Athlon 64, Athlon 64 FX, Athlon 64 X2, Opteron, Sempron	939 pins PGA	0.8V to 1.55V
Socket 940	AMD Athlon 64 FX and Opteron	940 pins PGA	0.8V to 1.55V
Socket AM2	AMD Athlon 64, Athlon 64 X2, Athlon 64 FX, Sempron	940 pins PGA	1.35V

The reality is technicians always refer to the documentation to verify compatibility before purchasing CPUs and motherboards. A quick lookup is well worth avoiding a pricey mistake.

RISC and CISC

There are two families of CPUs: Complex Instruction Set Computing (CISC) and Reduced Instruction Set Computing (RISC). When asked to multiply 4 x 5, a CISC chip will spend more time looking for the multiplication tool among the many possible methods than completing the task quickly. A RISC will quickly find the addition tool among the fewer options available to it and add 4 + 4 + 4 + 4 + 4. The calculation will take longer, but locating the tool took less time. RISC is outstanding for repetitive tasks such as packet routing in Cisco routers, display adapters, servers. CISC chips are great for multipurpose PCs that face many different kinds of requests. Most CPUs are CISC, but only recently did Macintosh switch. For many years, it used RISC chips by Motorola. Today, Intel and American Micro Devices (AMD) dominate the PC CPU market.

Power Supplies

1.3.2: Power supplies switch alternating current (AC) power from the wall to direct current (DC) power for the PC. There is a switch on the outside of the power supply that chooses 115 volts (V) AC in North America versus 230, the European standard. A switch near the power plug allows power supplies to accept U.S. or European standards. Power supplies are measured in watts (W); the more watts, the better. You need to provide more watts than the PC consumes. A 500-W supply is about standard. Gaming systems and other high-end graphics applications tend to use more than that.

The standard form factor for power supplies is the ATX. A 20-pin block connects the motherboard. Another small block of 4 to 8 pins lets the BIOS and OS control the power supply. The communication between computer and power supply is called advanced configuration and power interface (ACPI). All the other devices in the PC are powered by 12V yellow, 5V red, and a black ground wire. There are two sizes of plugs: Molex and Berg. Molex is bigger than Berg. An easy trick to remember this is that the name Molex (five letters) is longer than the name Berg (four letters). Newer power supplies provide special 15-pin power connectors for SATA drives. You can power SATA HDDs with either, but not both.

Use a multimeter to test the DC output. Set the multimeter to read volts DC (20V DC on older, non-auto-ranging multimeters). Put the common lead on the black ground wire or directly on the chassis (metal frame). The chassis is the electrical ground. Use the test lead to contact the other colors on a plug. The colors should read as shown in Table 31-7.

Table 31-7	Power-Supply Voltages	
Color	**Voltage**	**Mnemonic**
Yellow	12V	**Y**ou
Red	5V	**R**eally
Orange	3.3V	**O**ughta
Black	0V	**B**elieve
White	–5V	**W**arren
Blue	–12V	**B**uffett

Green, gray, and purple are signal wires and standby features, so they are not a major focus on the A+ exam.

To test the wall outlet, the multimeter must be set to read volts AC. Connect the black common lead on the round ground hole or the large (neutral) slot, and put the test lead in the small (phase) slot. A properly functioning outlet should read 110 to 120 VAC. In the absence of a multimeter, use a working lamp or appliance to test the outlet.

WARNING: These colors are not standard among all electrical systems. The black ground in DC should never be confused with the black wire in AC systems that carry 110V, usually at 20 amps or more, which is more than enough to kill you.

A technician should never, ever open three specific PC components: the power supply, laser printers, and cathode-ray tube (CRT) monitors. These contain capacitors and charges that are still "live," even when unplugged. The A+ exam uses these as distracters.

If you are not fully confident about electricity, find an experienced electrician and ask for a fuller explanation. You need to "own" this knowledge to be a PC technician.

Uninterruptible power supplies (UPS) are an external battery-powered device that supply power to computer and network devices during a power outage. Battery UPSs are frequently used on mission-critical devices like servers and routers. UPS power is usually limited to about 30 minutes and is normally designed to provide enough power to automatically shut down the PCs. For extreme cases, diesel generators are used to generate "unlimited" electricity (provided unlimited fuel is available) for banks, air traffic control, hospitals, and so on.

Homework

1. Practice drawing the motherboard map for memory.

2. Practice the power-supply mnemonic until you can re-create the chart from memory.

3. Wiki the ATX and BTX motherboards.

4. Have someone quiz you on the PCI, PCIe, AGP, and ISA need-to-know details.

Funwork

There are several build-a-PC activities in this book. You don't need to actually purchase the equipment. These activities are like fantasy football or using a website to customize a car or shoe *without* actually buying it. These activities are designed to immerse you in the details and force you to "speak" your future language.

The first build-a-PC exercise is for a high-end, money-is-no-object, over-the-top (imaginary) game system. Start by reading online techie forums about video cards and motherboards. Immerse yourself in geekspeak, and it will get easier to understand. Ask techies questions, but watch out for IT bravado. Many hard-core techies are not kind to newbies. Also understand that these dream machines are not really tested on the A+ exam. State-of-the-art expert opinion and the A+ exam seldom line up. It is like asking a NASCAR driver how to parallel park for your driver's license exam.

"Purchase" a motherboard, CPU, HDD, and CD drive. Keep in mind that the motherboard determines the kind of storage interfaces, adapter cards, and RAM you can use in the future. Hint: The FSB and video adapter and RAM bus are common bottlenecks. Choose carefully. Next, figure out what kind of case and power supply best suits your needs. Tomorrow, we will add RAM and install the devices. Good luck and have fun. Check out computers by Alienware and other game-oriented PCs to see how the pros build them and to check your work.

Hardware Concepts: Part 2 of 2

A+ Essentials Exam Objective

Objective 1.1: Identify the fundamental principles of using personal computers

Key Points

Today you will continue to cover topics in Chapters 1 and 3 in the IT Essentials v4.0 course. You will review purposes, characteristics, and kinds of memory, ports, and input/output (I/O) devices (including keyboards, mice, and monitors). This is the second of two challenging days. At the end of today, you can finish designing the king of all gamer PCs.

System Resources

1.8: Interrupt request (IRQ), I/O address, and direct memory access (DMA) are system resources. Initially, these were set manually. Since Plug-and-Play (PnP) was introduced in 1995, however, we no longer need to manually set these system resources unless using a vintage device that is not PnP compatible. Table 30-1 lists the IRQ values, Table 30-2 lists the I/O port address values, and Table 30-3 lists the DMA channels.

Table 30-1   IRQ

IRQ	Value
0	System clock
1	Keyboard
2	Cascaded with IRQ 9 (free)
3	Serial communication port 2 and 4
4	Serial communication port 1 and 3
5	Sound card or parallel port 2 (LPT 2)
6	Floppy disk
7	Parallel port 1 (LPT 1)
8	Real-time clock
9	Cascaded with IRQ 2 (free)
10	(Free)
11	(Free)
12	Mouse

continues

Table 30-1   IRQ *continued*

IRQ	Value
13	Math coprocessor
14	Primary IDE channel
15	Secondary IDE channel

Table 30-2   I/O Port Addresses

I/O Address	Value
Com1	03F8
Com2	02F8
Com3	03E8
Com4	02E8
LPT1	0378
LPT2	0278

Table 30-3   DMA Channels

Channel	Use
0	Sound
1	Sound
2	Floppy disk
3	LPT1
4	Cascade to DMA 0–3
5	Sound
6	(Free)
7	(Free)

Memory

1.4.4: Memory is the third part of the "trinity." The processor, motherboard, and memory make up the heart of the PC. In fact, if those were the only things in a computer, it would go about its business just fine. Granted, there would be no way to store data or communicate with other computers, let alone humans, but who would want to do anything like that? Like the various adapter cards and slots, there are many different kinds of memory, each with its own capabilities and unique slots.

There are two families of RAM: dynamic (DRAM), which loses its data when unpowered; and static (SRAM), which maintains it data regardless of power supply. The standard RAM for many years was called SDRAM. In this case, the *S* stands for synchronous (in step with the system clock), not static.

Cache

Cache is a small piece of memory that is a temporary storage place where frequently used commands are stored like a quick reference guide.

Cache is organized in three levels. Level 1 (L1) is located on the CPU. L2 is located on the motherboard. L3 is additional cache that can be added via chips similar to adding RAM. These are the traditional locations and descriptions of cache.

Note that many processors like Intel's dual-core and quad-core series are actually multicore CPUs. In that case, the lines are blurred about exactly where the cache is located. L2 is frequently included on the CPU. Today, L3 is really used only in very high-performance PCs and servers.

RAM

RAM is a special storage device in almost every way. It is volatile, which means when the power is off, the data is lost. This might seem like a problem, but it lets the computer restart and recover from software errors. If the RAM were nonvolatile, the errors would still exist after a reboot. Therefore, RAM really isn't a storage device; it is more of a short-term memory, a place for the CPU to do its work.

To correct a common misperception, RAM does not make the PC run faster unless the reason it was slow was due to a lack of RAM. The computer runs faster only by increasing the clock rate of the CPU, increasing the motherboard bus speed, or if you replace the CPU with a faster one. More RAM allows the computer to run more software simultaneously. However, when your computer has "minimal" RAM, adding more will improve overall performance.

There is a 4-GB memory maximum for 32-bit processors. That limitation is more a hardware issue than an OS issue. Vista and Macintosh OS X and many Linux distributions have 64-bit versions that can run 64-bit processors. A 64-bit CPU and supporting system can address more than 4 GB of RAM.

The highest-capacity, fastest RAM chip should be seated in the first RAM slot. The computer always measure RAM in bytes (with no multiplier). We speak of RAM with multipliers. Actual amount of RAM will vary slightly from the amount specified on the actual chip that is specified in bytes and multipliers. Table 30-4 lists different styles of RAM.

Table 30-4   RAM

Memory Type or Technology	Need to Know (In Order of Importance)
DRAM	Dynamic RAM means no power = no data.
SRAM	Static RAM keeps its data regardless of power. More expensive and slower than DRAM. Is the basis for solid-state HDDs and flash memory.
SDRAM	Synchronous DRAM is the standard for most PCs today. Should not to be confused as static DRAM (which shouldn't make sense anyway).
DDR	Double data-rate is the standard for good PCs today. DDR 2 and 3 are faster versions of DDR.
Parity	Parity adds a bit to each byte so that they all equal an even number. A technique for checking for corrupt data. Slower and more expensive than regular RAM but more reliable.
ECC	Error correction code detects and fixes corrupt data in RAM. Slower and more expensive than regular RAM but more reliable.
EDO	Extended data output is an older technology that made more efficient use of the RAM.
FPM	Fast page memory is an older technology that transfers data more quickly.

Virtual RAM

Virtual RAM is a copy of the contents of RAM on the HDD to aid in reliability and data recovery. Unless there is a good reason to, let the OS set the amount of virtual RAM it needs. The amount of virtual RAM is usually twice the amount of installed RAM. Because the virtual RAM is memory copied to the HDD, it must be in the form of a file. The copied RAM data appears in HDD as page files or swap files. In other words, page/swap files and virtual RAM are the same.

ROM

ROM is reliable and always there regardless of version, flashing, power on or off, and so on. The problem with ROM is if the technology grows beyond the capabilities of the permanently written instruction set, you must upgrade (replace) the complementary metal-oxide semiconductor (CMOS) chip/the entire motherboard. ROM instruction sets therefore are kept to a minimum.

EEPROM

Although manufacturers burn ROM into chips, erasable programmable read-only memory (EEP-ROM) is memory that you can flash via software and rewrite. This allows the BIOS to grow and adapt as newer, faster, and bigger devices are developed. A classic troubleshooting question involves a client with a new much larger HDD that the BIOS does not recognize in spite of the correct jumper and IDE settings. Use the software on CDs that came with the HDD or that you downloaded from the BIOS/HDD manufacturer's website to flash the BIOS (EEPROM) with an updated version.

NVRAM

Nonvolatile RAM (NVRAM) is used for instructions that will change over time. The best example of this is the size of the HDD. (Note that the A+ exam refers to size as capacity, not physical volume.) RAM is used as a fail-safe. In the event of some BIOS failure, you can reset the RAM parts of the BIOS by jumper or by removing the battery, but the NVRAM will not change until it is flashed. (Don't forget, data stored in RAM requires power to stay there, hence the battery.) These include the IDE settings, time and date, system password, and other features of the BIOS. A combination of RAM and NVRAM allows for a stable, editable, and flashable BIOS chip. Classic A+ exam scenario: If you have a computer that forgets information when it reboots, such as where the boot sector is or the time and date, you might need to change the battery. To expedite the reset, remove the battery and use a screwdriver to gently connect the battery leads, which drains the capacitor.

Memory Slots

1.4.4: The motherboard dictates which CPU and memory the system uses. There are many different kinds of memory, and each requires its own kind of slot.

Single inline memory modules (SIMM) are the old standard (pre-1999). There is a 30-pin version and a 72-pin version. RAM modules are always used in pairs. SIMMS, therefore, need to be installed in pairs: literally two identical RAM chips installed side by side.

Modern RAM uses dual inline memory module (DIMM) technology. The contacts are printed on both sides of the RAM chips, eliminating the need for pairing.

Table 30-5 compares the different types of memory slots.

Table 30-5   **Memory Slots**

Slot Type	Need to Know (In Order of Importance)
DIMM	Most common form factor for RAM. Contacts on both sides of the module. SDRAM and DDR RAM use DIMMs. Many different variations of DIMMs, none compatible with another.
SODIMM	Small outline DIMM (SoDIMM) is a smaller form factor designed for laptops.
MICRODIMM	Very small, used in sub-notebooks.
RDRAM	RAMBUS dynamic RAM (RDRAM), also called RAMBUS inline memory module (RIMM). Used in game systems because of its speed. Today it is rare, fast, expensive, and comparable to DDR3. On a RDRAM motherboard, empty RAM slots need to be filled with modules called a continuity RIMMs (CRIMM).
SIMM	Very old; requires installation of RAM in pairs.

Input and Output

1.5: Peripherals are devices that connect to ports. Note that even wireless devices still connect to ports wirelessly, but are ports nonetheless. Peripheral devices fall into two categories: input and output. An output device presents binary data in a form that humans can understand. An input device enables us to communicate with a binary-speaking PC.

From the PC perspective, outgoing is output, and incoming is input. Input and outputs are often found in opposites (for example, scanners and printers, video cameras and monitors, microphones and speakers). Combinations of these technologies create hybrid I/O devices. A networked printer/scanner is an all-in-one office printer. A touchpad/monitor is a touch screen. A cell phone is a wirelessly networked, video camera/monitor microphone/speaker device.

Mouse and Touchpad

A mouse is an input device that connects to the PC through USB, wireless infrared (IR) or radio frequency (RF), or PS/2 port. They come in many styles, but the two most common are trackball and optical mouse. Trackballs get dirty and need to be cleaned with alcohol and cotton swabs. Optical mice tend to work better on patterned surfaces. Wireless devices drain batteries quickly or they need a recharge cradle of some kind. The touchpad is ideal for laptops. Touch-screen monitors are basically a clear touchpad in front of a monitor.

Keyboard

A keyboard connects to the PC in the same ways as a mouse. Keyboards have different technologies that make them more comfortable, spill resistant, small, and so on. Nonetheless, they all function by actuating buttons that translate into binary codes.

Some very exotic keyboards exist. There are some that fold out from personal digital assistants (PDA). Another shines onto any tabletop surface and senses when your fingers hit the squares. With some touch-screen keyboards, the letters and symbols can change depending on the language, or game, or specialized input scenario. Some flexible keyboards can even be rolled up and are essentially unbreakable. No small amount of creativity has gone into designing the keyboard.

Video Input Devices: CMOS Versus CCD

1.6: There is much debate over the merits of CMOS and charged coupled device (CCD). (This is not the same CMOS chip mentioned earlier that contains the BIOS.) CMOS is cheaper, consumes less power, and has lower picture quality than CCD. They are found in laptops, PDAs, and cell phones.

CCD is more expensive, larger, and consumes much more power, but has a better picture quality. They are used in scanners, security cameras, and digital cameras and video cameras.

Cables and Ports

1.5: It might seem obvious, but the first step in troubleshooting any peripheral is to make sure it is connected and has power. Many computer geeks have been foiled by this simple fact even if they do not own up to it. The writers of the A+ exam know this common oversight and often include it in a check-all-that-apply kind of question. Watch for it.

USB

Today's PCs have hot- and cold-running USB ports: internal, external, in the front, in the back, on monitors, printers, keyboards, projectors, car dashboards, practically everywhere. There are equally various USB devices: wired and wireless network interface cards (NIC), modems, printers, phones, audio devices, HDDs, optical burners, even LED lights, cell phone chargers, and tiny missile launchers (no kidding).

USB is an example of the entire computer industry agreeing to work together on a standard interface. We should count ourselves lucky because USB is fast, easy to configure, and provides its own 5-volt (V) power supply. The cables can be up to 5 meters long (almost 16.4 feet). There are four wires in a USB cable, as shown in Table 30-6.

Table 30-6   USB Pinout

Pin	Color	Name	Description
1	Red	VCC	5 volts (just like in the PC)
2	White	D–	Data
3	Green	D+	Data
4	Black	GND	Ground (just like in the PC)

NOTE: The shell around the pins is electrically grounded to the case. Therefore it should considered 0 volts.

The two ends of the USB cable are different from each other. Type A is the standard rectangular shape most closely associated with USB. The other end, type B, is more box-like, with two tapered corners sometimes referred to as "trapezoid like." There is a mini version of the USB that has smaller and skinnier plugs. These mini USB cables also have an additional wire that is used to communicate to the PC what kind of device it is. Hubs allow for up to 127 devices to be controlled from 1 USB channel. To be specific, 1 USB controller actually supports 128 devices, but 1 of the devices is the controller itself. If you really must have that last 128th device, you will need to install an additional USB controller.

Just in case you are planning on such an endeavor, be aware that powered USB hubs plug into the wall and provide electricity to downstream devices that draw power directly from the cable. Unpowered hubs do not do this because it would cause too much draw on the tiny wires. It is the same principle about daisy chaining power strips. Too much draw through too narrow wire causes resistance, makes heat, melts wire insulation, and starts fires. Not a good day.

USB 1.1 transferred data at 12 Mbps. Today's standard 2.0 looks and acts exactly the same as its older counterpart, but it transfers data at 480 Mbps. A common A+ exam question involves a USB 2.0 device plugged into a USB 1.1 port. It will recognize the device but communicate with it at the 12-Mbps speed. Update the drivers to 2.0 if the motherboard can support it. If it still does not work, add USB 2.0 ports via a PCI card. Note that the opposite (a 1.1 device in a 2.0 port) would not be a problem because of backward capability.

FireWire

Apple trademarked the name FireWire, and although the company might not like its brand name dragged into public domain use (much like Xerox, Band-Aid, and Ziploc), *FireWire* is the term you will see on the A+ exam. Sony and Texas Instruments (TI) also jumped on the trademark bandwagon with I.link and Lynx, respectively. Technically on a PC, the port is called IEEE 1394, so there are actually four names for the same port.

FireWire is fast becoming the primary method of connecting external storage and video devices to PCs. FireWire can stream video directly to the PC. Unlike its brother USB with 127 printers, FireWire can connect only a mere 63 devices.

FireWire comes in two flavors: 1394a four wire, 400 Mbps; and 1394b six wire, 3000+ Mbps. Both are hot swappable, have a maximum length of 4.5 meters (about 14.5 feet), and use addressing that can support a version of networking. The USB architecture is one host with many devices. FireWire can have many hosts with equal importance and a variety of devices shared among them, similar to an Ethernet environment.

The FireWire plug on the PC side is rectangular, with one of the short legs bowed out to form a half octagonal shape. The other side is much smaller and shaped like an ottoman. The mini1394 looks like a tiny high definition media interface (HDMI) connector on one end and a tiny ottoman shape on the other. They are primarily used on laptops.

PS/2

PS/2 was the de facto standard for keyboards and mice until the early 2000s when everything finally went USB. PS/2 ports are female, with six pins arranged in a circle and surrounded by a metal ring. Often, the mouse port is green and the keyboard purple. It is easy to inadvertently switch these, which generates missing keyboard errors on power-on self test (POST) or an unresponsive, or "dead," mouse. In addition to color, remember that the keyboard is more important than the mouse and is closer to the motherboard. PS/2 ports and devices are not hot swappable and require a restart after making the physical connection.

Serial

Serial ports are easy to spot. They are usually the only male port on the back of the PC. A morbid way to remember that the male port is serial is that most serial killers are male. Serial ports send data 1 bit at a time.

They have two rows of pins in a trapezoid-shaped band. These are the classic COM ports, the old-school I/O ports. Sometimes, these are referred to as RS232 or DB9 ports. Like USB today, the serial port was the universal, go-to connection for everything, most commonly used for mice, keyboards, and modems. Today, serial ports are used for configuring other devices, such as routers and switches, uploading and downloading programs from microchips, and for some data-collection devices.

Parallel

IEEE 1284, the parallel port, is almost always used for old printers, scanners, and backup devices. It looks like an elongated, female serial port with 2 rows and 25 pins. Almost all parallel ports are bidirectional, although some early ones were not. Printer cords have a Centronics port on the printer side. It is a trapezoid shape, but it is rather large and has wire "ears" that fold into place securing it into the printer. The mini-Centronics connection is about the same shape and size as a parallel port side, but it has blades like a SATA header. Parallel ports transmit multiple bits at a time, usually 4 or 8. Because some data transmissions are in serial format and some in parallel, Universal Asynchronous Receiver/Transmitter (UART) processing uses buffers to switch between the two.

SCSI

Small computer system interface (SCSI) cables connect daisy-chained drives together and must be terminated at each end, either by a terminator or a drive. These old but fast ports are found almost exclusively on servers and some high-end workstations. Like USB, it is common to find ports both internally and externally. Not surprisingly, SCSI is also rapidly being replaced by USB and FireWire.

Display Adapter Ports

Video graphics array (VGA) ports contain three rows of five pins. They are female on the computer side and are often colored blue. VGA is the standard video port. If a customer complains of weird colors or a "tinted" monitor, check the physical connection of the VGA connector. A partially connected one causes some odd effects.

Digital video interface (DVI) bypasses the need to convert digital video data into an analog signal for the old CRT monitors and then lets the LCD screens reconvert the analog signal back into a digital format. This is quickly gaining popularity as LCD screens become ubiquitous.

DVI ports are often white and have three rows of eight pins and a larger slot on one side. It is one of the only asymmetric ports in existence. Video ports are the only ones with three rows, because there are three primary colors in light.

HDMI is designed to stream uncompressed digital video and audio signals from computers and game console systems to high-definition monitors and TVs. HDMi supports very high-resolution and -quality images

S-video uses a four-pin mini-DIN port. It is almost exactly the same size and shape as a PS/2 port, with a slightly different pin arrangement. Another difference between the PS/2 and S-video is that the plastic rectangle that orients the plug is in a different position. S-video plugs are typically yellow, whereas PS/2 are normally purple and green. S-video sends the intensity information and the color signals on different wires. Composite video sends them together. Component video takes it a step further and separates each color onto its own cable using multiple RCA jacks.

Audio

The standard round jacks for line in, microphone in, and speaker out work fine for the majority of applications. However, an increasing number of people and businesses are moving to music, video, TV, and phone on PC. These applications demand a higher-quality sound output than the small underpowered speaker port can provide.

Digital audio connections are not yet standardized and come in a variety of shapes and configurations. Sony Philips Digital Interface (S/PDIF) sends a digital audio signal to speakers that are designed to receive such signals. Optical audio ports allow for a fiber-optic cable to carry data to remote speakers without electromagnetic interference (EMI).

Network

Category 5 cable is the standard network cable; however, categories ranging from 1 to 6 exist. Network cables plug into an RJ-45 jack that looks like a large phone jack with eight contacts inside. Very old networks like cable TV use cable called coaxial (also just called coax). We cover more about network cabling on Day 20.

Cooling Systems

1.4.3, 3.3.1: There is an expression among the PC gamers: "There is no such thing as overheating, just inadequate cooling." A heavy processing load makes the CPU/GPU draw more power, and that generates more heat. Servers, multimedia-providing computers, and laptops are typically the most common PCs to have heat issues. In the case of laptops, overheating is often caused by a lack of air flow because they are used in extreme environments and they tend to sit on warm laps or blankets that smother air vents.

The biggest cause of heat in a normal desktop or tower case is lack of air flow because of dust. Dust is slightly statically charged and sticks to everything inside a PC, especially the heat sink. This creates a thick layer of insulation exactly where you need it least. When asked about this issue the A+ exam, the correct response is to use a can of compressed air (right-side up) to blow out the dust bunnies. If you actually need to do this, stand way back, or better yet get the rookie to do it (because it will soon rain dusty bits all over the place). Specialized vacuums designed to work around computers *do not*. Note that household vacuums generate a great deal of EMI and ought not be used in or around PCs.

The fan is necessary. Without the fan, the air will flow only by convection, which the cases are not designed for. Visually look at the spinning fan and make sure it is pushing air through the heat sink and that the power-supply fan is blowing air out of the case. Also make sure cables are not resting alongside the blades, because if they are they will make a whining or lawn mower noise.

On most motherboards, the CPU's temperature is measured, and the BIOS will shut off the PC if it gets too hot. A classic A+ question asks why a PC would turn on and shut off automatically after running for a few minutes. Check the cooling fan. Higher-end motherboards will monitor the temperature and scale the processor speed (clock rate) so that it is the highest possible without getting too hot.

When done correctly, water-cooled systems are highly effective. However, if there is air in the lines, or not enough fluid in the reserve, it will heat up and burn an otherwise great computer. Further, we tempt fate when we mix water and electronics.

A Day in the Office

Let's summarize Day 31 and Day 30 with an analogy. There are surprising similarities between the devices in a PC and an office, as shown in Table 30-7. Your task is to complete the rest of this table, to put everything you've learned in these two days into perspective. The answers can be found in Table 30-8.

Table 30-7   Office-PC Analogy

PC Component	Office Analogy	Explanation
CPU	You	Measured in speed.
RAM	Your desk	Bigger desk = more projects working simultaneously.
Motherboard	Physical office space	Better arrangement = more efficient work. It is how you move around your office.
Keyboard/mouse/any input device		
Monitor/printer/any output device		
Hard drive		
Floppy/USB flash drive		
CD-ROM/DVD-ROM		
CD/DVD writer		

Table 30-8   **Office-PC Analogy Self-Check**

PC Component	Office Analogy	Explanation
CPU	You	Measured in speed.
RAM	Your desk	Bigger desk = more projects working simultaneously.
Motherboard	Physical office space	Better arrangement = more efficient work. It is how you move around your office.
Keyboard/mouse/ any input device	Inbox	Stuff enters your office.
Monitor/printer/ any output device	Outbox	Stuff leaves your office.
Hard drive	Filing cabinet	Well organized, large capacity, "nonremovable" storage place.
Floppy/USB flash drive	Briefcase	Small, removable storage place "hot swappable."
CD-ROM/DVD-ROM	Dictionary, phonebook, encyclopedia	Removable, read-only, reference.
CD/DVD writer	Printer or pen	Printed once, read-only after that.

Homework

Review all the tables from yesterday and today.

Funwork

Continue the funwork from yesterday and "pretend to buy" the remaining pieces of your dream gaming PC. Check out the forums, and make sure that you're designing the best available. Remember in our fantasy PC project, cost is no object, but performance is.

Hardware Installation

A+ Essentials Exam Objective

Objective 1.2: Install, configure, optimize and upgrade personal computer components

Key Points

Now that you know more than any sane person should about different hardware, let's take it a step further and add installation and configurations. Today covers the installation of internal storage devices. You can find more information on these topics in Chapters 2, 3, 5, 11, 12, and 14 in the IT Essentials v4.0 course. Installing and configuring drives is a critical part of the computer tech's job, and the authors of the A+ exam know this. Study these topics carefully.

SATA Installation

3.7.2: Installing a serial advanced technology attachment (SATA) drive is straightforward. Just don't tell your customers. Because the SATA drive provides its power via the cable, simply connect the hard disk drive (HDD) to the lowest-number channel available, check the BIOS to confirm the system recognizes it, and boot the operating system or partition and format the drive in preparation to install the OS.

The A+ exam will likely ask a question about powering a SATA drive. SATA drives have a power port. They can also draw power from the data cable. Use either the power provided in the SATA cable or the Molex port, not both on the same drive. If you are opting for the Molex-powered drive, you use the seven-pin SATA cable. A standard SATA power cable has 15 pins: Three pins carry 3.3 VDC, three carry 5 VDC, three carry 12 VDC, five pins carry ground, and one pin coordinates staggered spin-up. The staggered spin-up is important only when you have many drives that start up simultaneously, as in awaking from sleep mode. It helps reduce the sudden draw on the power supply. Again, it cannot be stressed enough: Use one source of power for a SATA drive, not two.

PATA Installation

3.7.2: Parallel ATA (PATA) is more complicated. The BIOS manages PATA configurations. There are typically two PATA channels: primary and secondary. Each of those can contain two drives: master and slave. The master/slave or cable select (CS) settings must also be set by jumper on the drives. The cable select allows the drive at the far end of the cable to be master. It is worth noting that in some cases in both 80- and 40-pin PATA environments the CS simply cannot work. Set the jumpers to reflect the master on the end and slave in the middle. If still no luck, consider an HDD failure or PATA controller failure. Put together, any given PATA drive (HDD or optical) has one of the assignments shown in Table 29-1.

Table 29-1   Typical PATA Settings

PATA Designation	Number	Typical Assignment	Jumper Setting	BIOS Setting
Primary master	0	Main hard drive	Master	Auto Detect
Primary slave	1	(Available)	N/A	None
Secondary master	2	Main optical drive	Master	Auto Detect
Secondary slave	3	(Available)	N/A	None

Each PATA channel has its own PATA cable. Tiny writing on the motherboard identifies which port goes to which channel. PATA plugs are usually keyed and will only go in one way. The system PATA ports will have a tiny 0 on one side indicating the location of pin 1. Pin 1 is the pink or blue wire. PATA cables have three ends: one end goes to the motherboard; the other end goes to the master drive; and the third, which is in the middle (closer to the motherboard), connects to the slave drive.

NOTE: FDDs and SATA HDDs do not use jumpers.

SCSI

11.3.6: Some basic small computer system interface (SCSI) concepts are likely to show up on the A+ exam. Conceptually, SCSI is a small network of devices controlled by a SCSI controller. This is a card that plugs into a PCI or PCI-e slot and has one of many different kinds of SCSI-style ports on the outside and several internal ribbon cable connections. One way to spot a SCSI cable is its width. It will always be the widest (most pins) in the PC, markedly wider than PATA 40, FDD 34, and SATA 7. Another way SCSI cables differ from other cables is that they have nine connectors to support the card and eight devices. A SCSI array requires unique IDs, created using a binary code (3 bits for SCSI1, 4 bits for Wide SCSI). This code is set by jumper, dip switch, push button switch, or can be configured with a separate SCSI BIOS. SCSI arrays also need a common medium (SCSI cable), termination at each end, and a controller card.

The A+ examiners love to ask questions about SCSI devices with identical names. Remember, each SCSI device needs its own unique ID number. You also need to know that old SCSI systems require terminators that absorb the signal. Both ends of the cable need to be terminated so that the messages don't reflect and get sent back like an echo. This is normally done by putting a device at each end and enabling termination so that a device acts as both HDD and terminator. Today, SCSI is used almost exclusively in servers. It is almost always used to support hot-swappable redundant arrays of independent (or inexpensive) discs (RAID) or old-school, high-end gaming servers.

RAID

11.4.5: Redundant array of independent (or inexpensive) discs (RAID) has several defined levels, but the most common are 0, 1, and 5. RAID 0 writes the data across two drives. This increases speed but does not provide any protection. Think: "Zero" provides "zero" protection from data loss. *Striping* is the technique used to write the data across multiple disks. Consider that the processor is usually faster than the HDD, so it uses multiple HDDs simultaneously to handle the load. *Mirroring* simply copies one HDD to the other. Think of looking at "one's" self in the "mirror."

Parity, as it does in RAM, adds 1 bit to the bytes to make everything either even or odd. It reduces access time but identifies data loss and corruption and is therefore more reliable. In RAID 5, there are at least three HDDs. This is so that all the parity can be kept separate from the data. RAID 5 also stripes data, and so it does enhance performance somewhat, and it spreads out the data in case of failure. However, the constant parity updating lowers overall performance. RAID 5 is the most common implementation. Hybrids such as RAID 1+0 and 0+1 exist, and they require at least four HDDs because they are either two striped disks that are mirrored to two others, 0+1, or they are two mirrored disks striped to two others, 1+0.

Flashing the BIOS: A Closer Look

14.4.4: If the new HDD is too big for the BIOS to recognize, you will need to upgrade, or flash, the BIOS. This is always done by following the manufacturer's recommendations. It usually involves downloading a program from their website and running the program on the computer. Classic A+ exam question: I added a new 200-GB (or higher) HDD, but it shows in the BIOS as only 137 GB. 137 GB is the dead giveaway. When you see that in a question about HDDs, know the fundamental problem is that the BIOS is not running 48-bit (or higher) large block access (LBA). Solutions: Verify that the motherboard can handle large drives, flash the BIOS, and/or download and run XP Service Pack 1 (XPSP1). Some BIOS upgrades can be done from within the operating system; others are ROM packs and must be downloaded to a bootable media, such as floppy disk, bootable USB device, or CD (enabled in BIOS), and run as a separate program.

Preparing the HDD for an OS Installation

5.4.1: Before installing the OS, you need to prepare the HDD. It must be partitioned into at least one logical drive. That partition needs to be formatted. Last, run Scandisk to detect errors. Then you are ready to install the OS on a clean slate.

Partitioning

12.2.3: When an HDD is new or when you are performing a "clean" OS install, you must partition the HDD. Applications that enable you to do so include Fdisk, Partition Magic, or native software in the OS installer package. Note that the Disk Manager in Administrator Tools in the Control Panel is generally the place where you make partition changes after the OS has been installed. There are two kinds of partitions: primary and extended. In Windows-based PCs, the primary partition contains the boot files and needs to be active in order to boot. This what we refer to as the C: drive. Extended partitions can be divided further into logical drives, D:, E:, and so on.

Essentially, a partition is a fence that marks where data will be written or "planted." Like a piece of property, you can map many logical partitions (up to 23) on 1 HDD. Likewise, a partition can extend across multiple physical drives. The C: name is actually the logical drive on the primary partition, not the actual entire HDD.

Formatting

5.4.2: If the partition is the fence, formatting is plowing in preparation to write or "plant" the OS. Formatting sets up the kind of file allocation table (FAT). The FAT is a map of the HDD that the OS uses to locate and retrieve stored data. There are dozens of kinds of FATs. Fortunately, the A+ exam focuses on only a few.

FAT32 is used in Windows 98/Me and it is an option in XP and Vista. NTFS is the standard used in XP/Vista. The only time FAT32 is preferred in XP/Vista is if you need to provide network file sharing (NFS) for 98/Me PCs or to view FAT32 partitions. Upgrading from FAT32 to NTFS is fine. Converting back is not really possible. By most measures, NTFS is superior to FAT32 and should be used if given the option. Among the advantages of NTFS are security, sharing, disk quotas, and compression. Note that low-level formatting (LLF) is not at all the same as formatting. HDD manufacturers have programs for download that enable you to wipe the HDD clean. LLF erases all partitions, data, everything. It is even difficult for forensics programs to reconstruct the data once an LLF has taken place.

Scandisk

2.2.2: Sometimes, the molecules get tired and are reluctant to hold a polarity. These areas are known as *bad clusters*. The HDD will compensate for this and write around those areas. Besides adding to fragmentation, this slows down the access time and is serious enough to reduce the capacity and reliability of the HDD. A program called Scandisk or CHKDSK will find these sectors and attempt to "exercise" them. Often, writing back and forth 0s and 1s will make that sector more flexible and able to again store data.

Drive-Related Best Practices Found on the A+ Exam

Keep in mind the following best practices:

- Set all drives to CS and plug in the largest drive at the end, making it the master.

- Connect drives on separate PATA channels to improve data transfer.

- Upgrade to SATA by adding a controller card or newer motherboard.

- Don't use the entire drive for one partition.

- Create a dedicated partition for the OS and leave lots of extra room for updates. Make another partition for user data. Even better, put all the user data on a separate drive. Better yet, spread it across a RAID. This simplifies backups and network file sharing.

Homework

You can expect a question or two about PATA (IDE), installing a USB device, RAID, partitioning, and formatting an HDD. It is reasonable to assume you will need to identify problems that can be fixed with Scandisk, disk cleanup, and defragmentation. Review these sections.

Funwork

Let's build the unsinkable ship. You are going to "purchase" and "build" the most fantastic redundant server system ever. Your system has the largest capacity of any server, the fastest disk access time, multiple power supply, multi-CPU, multi-NIC, multi-HDD, RAID 5, the safest backup system, uninterruptible power supply (UPS), the works. This might be less cool than a game system, so let's add a twist of motivation. Consider that this computer contains your family's bank records. Your life savings are tied directly to the infallibility of this server. Are you going to use tried-and - true SCSI, fast-but-cheaper SATA, or FireWire? What kind of cooling system will you use for this leviathan of data? Will it mount on 19-inch racks or use a tower? Is dust an issue? Electromagnetic interference (EMI)? Once you have "built" this server, compare the specs to a top-of-the-line Dell server.

Hardware Troubleshooting

A+ Essentials Exam Objectives

Objective 1.3: Identify tools, diagnostic procedures and troubleshooting techniques for personal computer components

Objective 1.4: Perform preventive maintenance on personal computer components

Key Points

Troubleshooting is an art. Every art is a combination of skill, intuition, and experience. Experience comes with time. Intuition is a natural ability. Great troubleshooting skills separate true technicians from the hobbyists and wannabes. This is your art. It is why people call on you and why they pay you for your time and expertise. Chapter 4 is one of the best and most important in the IT Essentials v4.0 course. Today also touches on topics discussed in Chapters 2 and 3 of the course. Become intimately familiar with it. Keep in mind that as a new technician, you will likely troubleshoot PCs over the phone.

CompTIA conducted extensive surveys before the development of 2006 objectives. Overwhelmingly, companies voiced the need for employees with "soft skills" as well as technical ability. As a result, questions about etiquette and people skills frequently appear on the A+ exam.

Troubleshooting Process

4.2: The troubleshooting process consists of six steps:

Step 1   Gather data from the customer.

Step 2   Verify the obvious issues.

Step 3   Try quick solutions first.

Step 4   Gather data from the computer.

Step 5   Evaluate the problem and implement the solution.

Step 6   Close with the customer.

Gather Data from the Customer

4.2.2: Asking the customer open-ended questions does two important things. First, it gives the customer the ability to tell you valuable information. And second, it allows the customer to feel listened to, respected, and part of the solution. Remember that computers don't pay you, customers do. Having good data-gathering conversations is critical to quality customer relations, not to mention repeat business. Possible questions to ask include "So, what is the computer not doing?" or "Show me what it does" or "What was going on right before the problem began?" In seconds, you can eliminate broad areas where the problem isn't.

It might seem perfectly obvious, but you don't want to create more problems by going down wrong roads. You want to efficiently isolate the fault. If the person is talking about printers, it's not a boot problem, network problem, display problem, and so on. The problem could be the OS, drivers, cable, connections, paper, ink, and so forth.

During the data-gathering phase in the process, you should get name and contact information. You also need to know what kind of system you are troubleshooting. At the very least, you should know the manufacturer and model, OS (including the service pack in use), antivirus (AV), and networking setup. You also need to note anything unusual, such as whether the customer is using a touch screen monitor, a remote-access server, and so on. When you have a general direction, begin to narrow the field by using closed-ended questions.

Verify the Obvious Issues

4.2.3: Continuing from collecting customer data, introduce closed-ended questions to isolate the fault and really get into the heart of the problem. Possible questions might be "Does this happen only in Internet Explorer (IE) or in all programs?" or "Are the lights blinking?" or "How long has it been doing this?" You are narrowing your search.

Try Quick Solutions First

4.2.4: Often, information gleaned from the initial questions lead to obvious issues that solve the problem. Possible quick solutions might include saying "Let's just check quickly to see whether it is plugged in correctly," "Can you plug in a lamp or appliance to verify that the wall outlet is working?" or "Will you verify that the printer has paper and all the ink cartridges are correctly installed?" You wouldn't believe how often printer complaints are the result of no ink.

Gather Data from the Computer

4.2.5: Visually check for damaged cables, devices plugged in incorrectly, bent pins, noises, blue screens of death, burning smells, and so on. Watch the computer boot, note any error messages, and reproduce the problem. Determining the problem is like playing the board game Clue. The fault is hidden somewhere, and between the data gathered from the customer and gleaned from the PC you can identify the fault correctly. This step is where you hone your skills.

Evaluate the Problem and Implement the Solution

4.2.6: Pure troubleshooting identifies the problem. Usually, your job also includes fixing it. Some of the fixes seem daunting, but consider this: Do you really think you have found a completely new, original, never-been-seen-before computer problem? Probably not. Surely others have come across this before. If they were disciplined techies with good documentation skills, they probably posted it on a forum, wrote an article, or blogged about it. Consider this, too: It is in every manufacturer's best interest to make sure their products work and are supported by people just like you.

The point is that we as techies have the best informal support networks anywhere. There is a general feeling among the techie community that information should be free and collaboration is a good thing, especially if you give credit where it is due. If someone posts a solution to your problem (even if you posted the problem three years ago), add a thank you to the forum. E-mail a blogger and say thanks. The quickest way to diffuse IT bravado is to add a little praise and thanks.

Close with the Customer

4.2.7: An oft-missed step, this is the layman's explanation of the problem, the solution, and how to prevent it in the future. This is a critical step to develop confidence and generate repeat business. It also helps justify the amount that you charge. Documenting your work is critical because you may come across the problem again. The A+ exam will likely ask you a question about documentation. Remember that in the troubleshooting process, you need to document everything, early and often.

Troubleshooting Best Practices Found on the A+ Exam

Remember these best practices for the A+ exam and for real-world troubleshooting:

- Back up the data before making any critical changes.

- When changing the amount of RAM, document the current amount either in the OS or BIOS, make the change, and then document the change.

- Wear an antistatic wrist strap and use grounded mats when working inside a PC.

- A field replaceable unit (FRU) is the component that is replaceable. We don't fix RAM because it is an FRU. We replace it. In fact, practically every internal component falls into the FRU category: CPU, HDD, CD, DVD, fans, cables.

- Blow dust out of the PC with compressed air.

- Use isopropyl alcohol and cotton swabs to clean the rollers inside ball mice.

POST and Boot Problems

3.9.1: If your PC has LEDs, the HDD spins, the fan blows, the monitor LED is amber because of no signal but nothing else happens, it failed to power-on self test (POST). The most common POST failure is something wrong with the RAM. Older PCs had lots of manual settings with jumpers; incorrect settings will cause POST problems. Most ATX motherboards have few jumpers, and almost everything is set in BIOS.

Some PCs have internal speakers and beep codes that can be deciphered by the BIOS or motherboard documentation. These are far from standardized among manufacturers. If the PC won't POST and there are beeps, start with the RAM and work out from there to the motherboard and processor. Chances are really good it is a problem somewhere in the "trinity" (RAM, motherboard, and CPU) and any failure there is a catastrophic problem that usually involves replacing core components. If you are fortunate to actually get a number on the screen, you can precisely identify the problem. For example, a 147 error code is a motherboard issue, error 304 is a keyboard issue, and so on. There are many mnemonics for memorizing the error codes. Table 28-1 shows one example.

Table 28-1   POST Error Codes

Range	Faulty Device	Mnemonic
100–199	Motherboard	M
200–299	RAM	R.
300–399	Keyboard	Keys
400–499	Monochrome (video)	Makes
500–599	Color (video)	Colorful
600–699	Floppy (drive)	Fried
1700–1799	Hard (drive)	Hotcakes

Another boot problems is the BIOS being set to boot to a media (floppy, CD, USB drive, and so on) that has no boot files in it. This is the "missing operating system" error. Errors in IDE configurations also prevent a boot. A BIOS password could prevent a boot. Both the password that protects the BIOS info and the password that restricts access to the computer at boot can be disabled by jumper on the motherboard.

Resolving Resolutions

Video cards have a basic resolution, usually 640x480 or 800x600, with 256 colors. Sometimes, it is as low as 8 or 16 colors. In any case, it is enough to see what you are doing while you install the correct drivers. When the drivers, and by extension the OS, control the video card, resolutions can go much higher depending on the quality of the card and capabilities of the monitor. Table 28-2 shows the resolutions you need to know for the A+ exam. (How many QXGA-capable video cards does your dream game system have?)

Table 28-2   Monitor Resolutions

Name	X Pixels Wide	Y Pixels Tall
VGA	640	480
SVGA	800	600
XGA	1024	768
XGA+	1152	864
SXGA	1280	1024
SXGA+	1400	1050
UXGA	1600	1200
QXGA	2048	1536

These all are 4:3 aspect ratios. Many new computers and laptops use a 16:9 aspect ratio (HDTV/widescreen). After the correct drivers are installed, an LCD screen really should be run in its native mode. There are many exotic, nonstandard resolutions as well, including on a cash register, a cell phone, or a dashboard display in a car. 4:3 screens are measured diagonally. All others are measured by width. Projectors typically have low resolution. Most will not exceed 800x600. Seldom does a need arise for huge screens with postage-stamp-size icons in a presentation environment.

Troubleshooting Tools

2.2.1: Physical tools for troubleshooting are few. A Phillips screwdriver and a multimeter are really the main ones. Make sure the screwdriver does not have a magnetic tip. Some experienced techs do use magnetic tips for convenience. Absolutely avoid touching the magnetic tips to HDDs, tapes, flash drives, and floppy disks and any other magnetic media. Keep in mind that screws and screwdrivers conduct electricity. Yes, many techs operate on live PCs to save time, but they run the risk of dropping the tool or screw onto a live circuit board. You should never have to explain to your customer (and employer) why you accidentally shorted out a $300 motherboard because you were in a hurry.

Multimeters were addressed on Day 31. In a pinch, you can troubleshoot wall outlets with a desk lamp. You can use known good internal devices to test the DC side of the power supply. Systematically connecting a device to every lead and feeling the vibration or seeing lights indicates that it works. This is a tedious method, but works. If a power supply fails in any way (even if it is just a gut feeling), it should not be trusted and ought to be replaced. A $50 fix is well worth the piece of mind.

Antistatic wrist straps, magnetically shielded bags, and grounded mats are used to reduce electrostatic discharge (ESD). ESD is worst in a cool, dry environment, which paradoxically, is an ideal environment to store printer paper. Most important, make sure the machine is powered off before removing or adding any hardware.

Software tools are many. Techies all have their favorites. The A+ exam focuses almost exclusively on those built in to Windows, such as DEFRAG.EXE, SCANDISK.EXE, Disk Management, Internet Connection Firewall (ICF), Windows Explorer, and so on.

Preventive Maintenance

4.2: An OS is complicated, is built by committee, has a little bit of everything, and makes for an odd-looking, cumbersome system. There is no shortage of criticism of the Windows family of operating systems. Some is legit, most is not. Because of the complexity and constant flood of new devices to support, you need to think of operating systems as organic and constantly changing. Updates are issued almost daily to patch errors and security holes. Periodically, Microsoft groups a bunch of updates together and makes a large download called a service pack (SP). A few service packs later and the OS has changed so much that they give it a new name. For example, 2000(2K) was updated with 2KSP1, then 2KSP2, and 2KSP3. Enter: Windows Experience (XP) XPSP1, XPSP2, and so on.

This constant improvement model is true for all software: AV, drivers, BIOS, everything. The first step in maintaining the PC is update, update, update. Get new AV and spyware definitions when available. Uninstall unused programs and delete temp files using the Disk Cleanup utility. Using Scandisk, check the HDD for errors. Then run Defrag to create more contiguous files. Beyond that, specifically which utilities you use is just personal preference.

The A+ exam and your customers will ask about the benefits of preventive maintenance. It increases the longevity, efficiency, and reliability of the components; it reduces future repair costs; and it better protects the data.

Homework

Review the monitor resolutions and six troubleshooting steps.

Pick a troublesome part of Days 31–28 and learn about it online. Ask a friend. Read what how others study for that part of the A+ exam. Really master that content and own that knowledge.

Funwork

Google "funny helpdesk stories." It is a great way to see very funny, real-world examples of troubleshooting. Remember, we can joke about these among ourselves in the IT community, but when the customer is present, we are all business and give friendly service.

Laptops and Portable Devices: Part 1 of 2

A+ Essentials Exam Objectives

Objective 2.1: Identify the fundamental principles of using laptops and portable devices

Objective 2.2: Install, configure, optimize and upgrade laptops and portable devices

Key Points

After four straight days of hardware, we are going to focus on a simpler and more fun domain for a while before we start headlong into operating systems. You will primarily focus on Chapter 6 from the IT Essentials v4.0 course today.

Portable computing is truly a landmark turning point in our culture. Just consider life without a cell phone, e-mail, or iPod. The A+ exam follows major IT trends and does not especially care about what is trendy. The latter drifts into history like 8-tracks, portable game consoles, and Tamagotchi pets. What does not change are the fundamental principals behind these portable devices. That is where the A+ exam focuses.

Batteries

6.3.3: Batteries have come a long way over the past 20 years. Ask someone who had an early laptop or cell phone. It is not uncommon to find batteries that power laptops for more than six hours, although the kinds of usage affect the charge life. DVD and HDD disk access and wireless networking draw more power than normal.

All batteries have "bad" chemicals in them, and local governments regulate how to dispose of or recycle batteries.

Lead-acid, alkaline, and NiCd batteries tend to develop memories. A *battery memory* is a decrease in the time between charge cycles. In other words, it holds a charge for less time and takes longer to charge. Exercising the battery helps reduce the memory. To exercise a battery, you must charge it slightly above the normal voltage and then use it until no charge is left. Do this regularly and the memory will not be as much of an issue.

Table 27-1 describes different types of batteries.

Table 27-1   Batteries

Battery	Characteristics	Usage
Nickel-cadmium (NiCd)	Heavy, long life, develops a memory over time	Power tools, cordless phones, camera flash, motorized toys, anything that draws a big load and does not live long outside the charger
Nickel metal hydride (NiMH)	Moderate weight, moderate life expectancy	Cell phones, GPS systems, digital cameras, flashlights; most things that are meant to be carried around for a while but don't have a large electrical load
Lithium-ion (Li-ion)	Light, long lasting, will catch fire if overcharged or experience too much draw	Cell phones, laptops, medical devices such as pacemakers and monitors
Lithium-ion polymer (LiPo)	Quick recharge, small, light, expensive, medium lasting, medium life span	PDAs, laptops, MP3 players, gaming devices, radio-controlled toys

ACPI Power Management

6.3.3, 6.4.1: Advanced configuration and power interface (ACPI) is found in the Power Management applet in the Control Panel. On a historical note, advanced power management (APM) is the predecessor of ACPI and is supported in Windows 9x, 2000, and XP. Vista and Windows 7 do not support APM. It must first be enabled in the BIOS like an integrated device. There are six power states, as shown in Table 27-2.

Table 27-2   ACPI Power States

State	CPU	RAM	Description
S0	On	On	PC fully on
S1	On	On	Power saving mode
S2	Off	On	More power saving
S3	Off	Slow	Standby mode
S4	Off	Off	Hibernate mode
S5	Off	Off	PC fully off

Laptops and Projectors

6.2.2: When using a projector, practice first. Nothing screams newbie more than arguing with a projector during a presentation. Laptops save energy by not sending a signal to the external video port. To use the projector, external monitor, or TV, use the manufacturer's keystroke combinations or buttons to redirect the video signal. Usually, it is the function key F8, but it varies by manufacturer. Resolution on projectors is often much lower than laptops. Change the resolution to SVGA 800 by 600 or VGA 640 by 480 so that you provide a good, simple signal to the projector.

Memory and Expansion Slots

6.3.4: Small outline dual inline memory module (SoDIMM) is the standard laptop memory. It is accessed by a panel on the bottom of the laptop. Mini-PCI expansion allows for some additional functionality of laptops. Personal Computer Memory Card International Association (PCMCIA) cards can be use if the laptop is designed for them. Another, more modern expansion slot for laptops accommodates ExpressCards. They look and act very much like PCMCIA cards, but they are actually a tiny bit narrower. (On a fun note, some say that PCMCIA really stands for People Can't Memorize Computer Industry Acronyms.)

Table 27-3 compares the laptop expansion buses.

Table 27-3   Laptop Expansion Buses

Bus Type	Thickness	Usage and Description
PCMCIA Type I	3.3 mm	SRAM flash (like a USB flash drive).
PCMCIA Type II	5 mm	Standard PCMCIA, used for modem, NIC, WIFI.
PCMCIA Type III	10.5 mm	Double thick, primarily used as an HDD.
ExpressCard /34	5 mm	The name notates the length in millimeters (34 mm).
ExpressCard /54	5 mm	Usually used for card readers and sometimes the cutest little HDD ever made. (Stick with solid-state flash drives.)

Homework

Review the batteries, ACPI levels, and the PCMCIA types. These topics are an A+ exam favorite.

Funwork

If you have access to Vista, check out Windows Journal in the Accessories or under Tablet in the Start menu. It is the application that supports tablet PC handwriting recognition. You can use a mouse to "hand write" something even if you are not using an actual tablet. Select the text and convert to text. Lots of fun.

Go find three laptops: One for less than $400, one around $2000, and one for more than $4000. Compare and contrast them component by component and determine why the disparity in price exists for essentially the same device. If you want a real challenge, go find out what a Tamagotchi digital pet is.

Laptops and Portable Devices: Part 2 of 2

A+ Essentials Exam Objectives

Objective 2.3: Identify tools, basic diagnostic procedures and troubleshooting techniques for laptops and portable devices

Objective 2.4: Perform preventive maintenance on laptops and portable devices

Key Points

Today, we talk more about the topics in Chapter 6 of the IT Essentials v4.0 course. Laptops and portable devices are quite possibly the future of computers, just as the microcomputer (micro compared to mainframes) of the 1980s became the modern PC. Familiarizing yourself with the care, maintenance, and troubleshooting of these devices is definitely time well spent.

Cell Phones

6.5: There are industry protocols behind cell phones. The names of these protocols are sometimes lost in the mire of brand names, marketing, and constant advertising. The cell phone world is going through adolescence. Every new technology is trying to outpace the others. It is an exciting time, but confusing as well.

We are starting to see the arrival of robust, all-inclusive protocols that will likely develop into widely adopted standards, much like TCP/IP is for networking. Until that takes place, you need to familiarize yourself with the many protocols. Table 26-1 lists the cell phone protocols found on the A+ exam.

Table 26-1   Cell Phone Protocols

Protocol	Generation	Description
SMS	All	Text messaging protocol
MMS	All	Video- and file-transfer protocol
Packet Switching	All	Internet access
iDEN	2G	Push-to-talk (walkie-talkie)
GPS	2G	Global positioning
GSM	2G	Global call coverage
GPRS	2.5G	Better, faster GSM

continues

Table 26-1   Cell Phone Protocols   *continued*

Protocol	Generation	Description
EDGE	2.5G	Adds data transfer to GPRS
CDMA	2.5G	Digital voice and data
1xEV-DO	3G	Better, faster CDMA
UMTS	3G	Better, faster GSM

Cleaning Laptops

6.6.1: To do any work, even cleaning, you absolutely must unplug all peripheral devices (some devices, such as a camera, might have their own power supply), unplug the laptop from the wall outlet, and remove the battery. Some laptops have more than one battery. Spray cleaning solution on a soft lint-free cloth, and then wipe the laptop. Do not spray anything onto the laptop; they don't swim very well. Never use a paper towel on an LCD screen. It will permanently scratch it.

Repairing Laptops

6.4.2: Portable devices are surprisingly tough, but because they live in the world rather than in a climate-controlled, secured server room, they tend to take extreme abuse. Repairing a laptop is simple. The parts that break have their own access panel: RAM, battery, HDD, and expansion slot devices. Parts that break and cost more to replace than the value of the laptop are difficult to access: CPU, motherboard, and LCD screen. It is imperative that you explain this to your customers before you commit to a major repair on a laptop (considering their very short life span).

Troubleshooting Laptops

6.7.2: Unfortunately, repair of many common problems, such as cracked LCD screens, battery failure, water damage, and overheating, is often an economic death sentence. First check to determine whether the laptop is still under warranty. Many laptops come with a three-year warranty under the condition that it gets fixed by the manufacturer. You do not want to be the one who voids it on behalf of your client. Table 26-2 shows some common laptop problems, all of which are fair game on the A+ exam.

Table 26-2   Common Laptop Problems

Symptom	Troubleshooting
Blank screen.	Check for LED, heat, vibrations, or other signs of life. (It might not be turned on.) The video might be redirected to the auxiliary port for a projector. The brightness or contrast might not be set correctly. The video drivers or resolution might not be set properly. Test the battery with a multimeter.
Dim screen.	Check for a brightness option in the BIOS, Control Panel, or Power Management; sometimes a button controls this manually.
Black border.	Adjust the resolution in display properties. Check the BIOS for monitor settings. Reinstall or roll back the video drivers.
Battery won't charge.	Check the power adapter with a multimeter to determine whether it is producing the right voltage. Visually inspect the power adapter port on the laptop. Many laptops die because the power adapter was plugged in as the laptop pushed against something. It could be that the battery's life has ended. They don't last forever.
Battery drains rapidly.	The battery has a memory and will need to be replaced soon.
No networks detected.	Check on the outside of the laptop for a WIFI (and often Bluetooth) on/off switch. Verify that a properly working wireless local area network (WLAN) is available and it is set up to allow more PCs. Start the basic troubleshooting process of enabling the device in the BIOS and installing correct drivers in the Device Manager. In the case of a network interface card (NIC), make sure the network settings are correct. (More of this on Days 19 and 20.)
Touch screen won't respond.	Treat it like any other input device: Enable it in the BIOS; install correct, updated drivers in the Device Manager; and ensure the touch screen application is running. Calibrate it using the application. If necessary, train the user how to use the touch screen.

Homework

Search online for information about troubleshooting laptops and laptop repair. Many good flow-charts and videos are available. Note what kinds of tools are used, where the devices are located, and what they look like inside a laptop.

Funwork

Find the lightest laptop and the heaviest laptop. Who makes the toughest laptop? Hint: If it doesn't have a solid-state drive, a sand/waterproof keyboard, and a really long warranty, it isn't that tough (no matter how "ruggedized" it looks). Why are smaller laptops often more expensive?

Go see a really neat use of laptops by searching for "OLPC" on Google.

Operating Systems Concepts

A+ Essentials Exam Objective

Objective 3.1: Identify the fundamentals principles of operating systems

Key Points

The operating system (OS) is the lifeblood of the computer. It is also the way we communicate with an otherwise inanimate box of electronics. Microsoft Windows XP is by far the most widely installed OS in the world. Apple and Linux operating systems make up the small remaining market, and they compete by specialization. Linux is very stable, small, and perfect for servers. Apple's Macintosh OS X is very user friendly, perfect for home users willing to pay a little extra for the convenience. XP dominates the business world, gamers, and many home PCs. You will focus primarily on XP because it is the main focus of the A+ exam. Learning some basics of the other operating systems helps your knowledge of XP, just like learning a foreign language helps solidify concepts in your native tongue. You will spend most of today in Chapter 5 and just a little in Chapter 12 of the IT Essentials v4.0 course.

Operating System and the Layered PC Model

5.1.1: It is important to see where the OS fits into the bigger picture. This Layered PC Model maps the interactions among the devices and ultimately the user. Figure 25-1 shows the Layered PC Model.

Figure 25-1   Layered PC Model

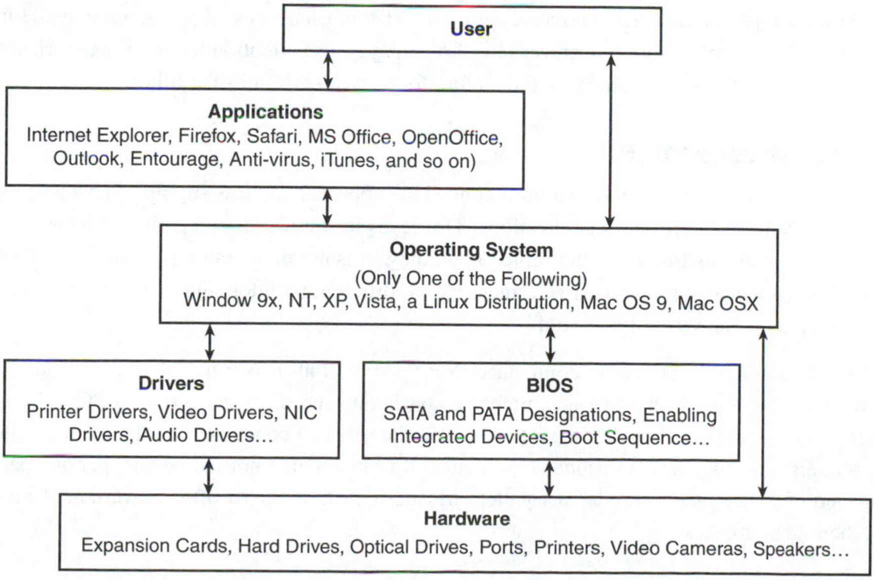

Follow the model as the user surfs the web. The user uses the OS to navigate to the icon to launch Internet Explorer (IE). The application uses several subsystems in the OS to call on the network interface card (NIC), which is at the hardware layer. But the OS does not understand how to talk to the NIC without the driver. The NIC then begins to send signals based on the driver's instructions. The driver was told what to do by the OS that was told what to do by the application that was controlled by the user. A less-micromanaged way to look at this is each layer provides services to the layers above it.

You use this model in troubleshooting. For example, if a printer will not print, you check the hardware first: paper, ink, online, cable. Then you move up to the BIOS and driver layer. Is the USB port enabled in the BIOS? Do the USB drivers work in the Control Panel? When these are yes, yes, and yes, then you look at the OS. Does the OS know that there is a printer installed in the Printer part of the Control Panel? If yes, the application might have some issue with the printer, such as the margin settings or fonts. Otherwise, the issue could simply be an operator error. Chances are that along the way the problem will be found and solved.

Desktop Operating Systems

5.2.1: Nothing in the computer world is more contentious than the Mac versus PC debate. Linux is not in the public eye, but it too is a major player. If you are going to be a computer technician, you need to understand this debate so that you can correctly advise customers. Their needs should determine the choice of OS, not really good commercials, not your familiarity with a particular OS, and certainly not "because you said so."

Apple OS X

Apple carefully chooses hardware to avoid any compatibility issues within its computers. Then, it designs an OS to make the most efficient use of that hardware. As a result, Apple seldom, if ever, has any hardware or software compatibility issues. Further, it can tweak the software to maximize performance. The disadvantage with this strict relationship between the hardware and software is limited upgrade potential. Users tend to "outgrow" a Macintosh because they cannot upgrade it very much. Because of this high turnover rate, Apple pays close attention to the user experience, the look, and image of their products and therefore foster an almost cult-like following.

Microsoft Windows

Microsoft (MS) makes operating systems that need to support an endless supply of new and old devices and countless third-party applications. This leads to significant compatibility issues. However, it also allows for almost unlimited upgrading. It is not uncommon to find a 4- or 5-year-old PC that has a new burner, larger HD, more RAM, different monitor, and even a newer MS operating system than when it was sold.

Another MS attribute is its market dominance. Nearly 90% of all PCs run a MS OS. Windows is a very robust OS that works hard to accommodate conflicting and disparate uses of a PC. It is the ultimate compromise, like making a car that can handle off-road conditions, haul a tractor trailer load, seat eight people, have surround sound, but still fit nicely in a normal garage, parallel park easily, and of course, get 130 miles per gallon. Most criticism of Microsoft is unwarranted considering their daunting task.

The A+ exam likes to ask about upgrading from one Windows OS to another. Any MS OS can upgrade to any other, except 9x cannot be upgraded to NT. You would need to reformat the partition as NTFS and perform a clean install of NT. Downgrading is tricky, and you really ought to perform a clean install to use an earlier version.

Linux

Linux is only for the geek at heart. It is the skinniest, most efficient OS. Linux is unique because it is open source. That means that anyone can modify it, and it is owned by no one. We pay not for Linux itself, but for the effort put into new research, development, and compatibility with new hardware. Companies such as RedHat, SuSE, Caldera, and Ubuntu sell Linux in this manner. They provide technical support and updates. Many Linux aficionados download a free copy of Linux, called a Distro (short for distribution), such as Slackware or FreeBSD, and customize it to their needs. This is not for the computer novice and certainly not for the end user. One major problem with Linux is its insistence of using the terminal (command-line interface [CLI]) to make any system changes. End users often have allergic reactions to anything CLI. Hardware support is challenging even to seasoned Linux people.

OS System Requirements

5.3.2: Table 25-1 compares the system requirements of the major OS players. Remember these are the absolutely bare minimum requirements found on both the MS site and the A+ exam. The CPU, RAM, and HDD numbers need to be at least doubled to achieve any kind of acceptable performance. You should focus your memorizing on the Microsoft information.

Table 25-1   OS System Requirements

Operating System	CPU	RAM	Hard Drive	Video	Other
Microsoft Windows 2000	133 MHz	64 MB	2 GB	VGA	N/A
Microsoft Windows XP	233 MHz	64 MB	1.5 GB	SVGA	N/A
Microsoft Vista	1 GHz	1 GB	40 GB	WDDM Driver 128 MB graphics RAM	DVD-ROM Internet connection
Mac OS X	867 MHz	512 MB	9 GB	Only proprietary video card	DVD-ROM Internet connection
Linux RedHat 9	400 MHz	192 MB	5 GB	Practically any video card	DVD-ROM Internet connection

The Windows Display Driver Model (WDDM) is a new model of drivers for graphics displays that gives the OS much more control of the video content. The Internet connection is used for verification of authenticity and for providing support for integrated programs such as instant messaging (IM), Really Simple Syndication (RSS) feeds, widgets/dashboard, and the seemingly constant updates. Some subtle differences exist between XP Home and Pro, Media Edition, and the 64-Bit Edition and among the many Vista versions. As their names suggest, they are customized for different roles. Home offers more support for peripherals, Pro offers more security and stability, Media provides better sound and video support, and 64-Bit is for 64-bit CPUs.

Network Operating Systems

5.2.2: A more significant differentiation is between desktop operating systems and network operating systems (NOS). A NOS acts as a server and provides services, data, files, application, access, authentication, and so on to other PCs on a network. Even "desktop" operating systems can provide network services such as sharing files or a printer. A true NOS is designed to maximize those kinds of services instead of supporting local applications like Word, PowerPoint, and so on. NOSs have applications like e-mail servers, web servers, authentication, printing, and naming services. All of these are dedicated resources to other network devices. Popular NOSs are Linux Server, OS X Server, the many Windows Servers, and Novell.

Linux makes up a majority of server-side operating systems. Almost every website is hosted by an open source server called Apache, and almost all of those are installed on a Linux operating system.

The "Multi" Terms

5.1.2: Table 25-2 compares and contrasts five terms, the "multi-somethings," you will likely see on the A+ exam.

Table 25-2   The "Multi" Terms

"Multi"	Description
Multiuser	Many users log on to one OS. Users could use local or remote logon. Accounts are managed and permissions assigned to each.
Multitasking	The operating system can handle more than one application at a time (which would be all the operating systems on the A+ exam).
Multiprocessing	A computer doing more than one task simultaneously. In reality, it can't, but it gives the appearance that it can.
Multithreading	A technique that allows multiprocessing to take place. It actually buffers threads (tasks for the CPU to do) and manages the input by alternating the threads to give the appearance of multiprocessing.
Multicore	Is not an OS concept but is a "multi" term. Many CPUs on a single physical chip. This actually allows for true multiprocessing. Still, at some point (the front-side bus, the display, cache, someplace), multiple threads need to stop and take turns.

Modes

5.1.2: Some aspects of the OS domain of the A+ exam are not relevant to real-world techies. Nonetheless, know that programs can run in different modes. Real mode lets an application have direct access to the hardware. This is fine, unless there is a problem. Then the entire PC is stuck and needs to be rebooted.

Protected mode lets the OS manage RAM and virtual RAM and choose where to put the programs to avoid one program from writing over another in RAM.

Virtual real mode lets the application (even ones written for real-mode access) work in a virtual environment (a virtual copy of the RAM and other hardware that fools the application into thinking it has real control of the computer). It asks the virtual hardware to do something. The OS analyzes the request. If the request is deemed not dangerous, the OS will allow it to happen. Otherwise, the OS will crash that session, not the entire machine. When that occurs, you can use Ctrl-Alt-Del to open Task Manager and see that a program is "not responding." Only that program does not work. Chances are good the rest of the PC is fine and will recover.

Compatibility mode builds on virtual real mode, and the CPU queries the application to determine for which OS it is designed. Then a virtual machine creates and supports the application as if it were on another OS.

Logical Memory

5.1.2: The first megabyte of memory or RAM is divided into sections: Conventional (0–640 KB), Upper (640 KB–1 MB), and Extended (anything above 1 MB).

Registry

5.4.7: The Registry is bound to be on your A+ exam. Like the DNA of the PC, every little detail is answered somewhere in the five hives of the Registry. Each hive supports different things. These files and all other significant Windows system files are stored in the System32 folder. The Control Panel is where we make changes to the Registry. For finer control of individual keys, we use REGEDIT.EXE. Be very careful when using REGEDIT.EXE. It is like toying with your own genes. One misstep and bad things happen, like losing the ability to understand what a file is, not remembering the name of the CPU, or other critical errors necessitating the need for a complete OS reinstall.

Table 25-3   Registry Hives

Registry Hive	What It Contains
HKEY_CLASSES_ROOT	File-extension mapping
HKEY_CURRENT_CONFIG	All devices in current use
HKEY_CURRENT_USER	User environment
HKEY_LOCAL_MACHINE	All devices regardless of current usage
HKEY_USERS	Settings that affect all users

GUI Versus CLI

5.1.1: A graphical user interface (GUI) is easy to use but uses a lot of system resources, including RAM, video, sound, and HDD space. You might ask, "In these days of mice, 4-GB RAM, and beautiful monitors and so on, why do we still have the command-line interface (CLI)?" Two reasons: It keeps inexperienced end users out of the inner workings of the OS. (This also increases job security for those who speak CLI.) A better reason is script files. You can automate tasks by making a file in Notepad (explains why we still have Notepad, too) that is a list of the commands that you would enter in the command prompt. The script will execute those commands in that order. This is not really possible in a GUI, although some rather sophisticated third-party applications can record your motions and then save them like a script to automate tasks in a GUI.

Command Prompt Command Syntax

All command prompt statements follow the same syntax (grammar): command (space) argument switch. In other words, verb, object, modifier (see Table 25-4).

Table 25-4   Command Prompt Syntax

Command	Argument	/Switch
Do this	To this	Like this

Let's take apart some commands.

Table 25-5 breaks down the command **FORMAT A: /S** and then explains what it means.

Table 25-5   Syntax Example: FORMAT A:/S

Command (Space)	Argument	(Space) /Switch
FORMAT	**A:**	**/S**
Make ready to receive data…	A floppy disk…	And put system files on it to make it bootable

Table 25-6 breaks down the **DIR /P** command and then explains what it means.

Table 25-6   Syntax Example: DIR /P

Command (Space)	Argument	(Space) /Switch
DIR	(Nothing here means "do it right here.")	/P
Show…	The contents of this directory…	Per page

Table 25-7 breaks down **COPY A: C:\New Folder**.

Table 25-7   Syntax Example: COPY A: C:\New Folder

Command (Space)	Argument	(Space) /Switch
COPY	A: C:\New Folder	
Copy…	Everything on the floppy disk to the New Folder on the HDD. Notice the space between the two arguments. Notice also the backslash is used to notate "down a level."	(Nothing here means that nothing is modified.)

Command Prompt Commands

There are hundreds of command prompt commands. Fortunately, you only need some to get by in most CLIs. This is a good start. Like a foreign language, the more time you spend immersed in it, the more proficient you become. In the Windows CLI, the command prompt has a built-in translation guide, a command aptly named **HELP**. Table 25-8 shows common command prompt commands.

Table 25-8   Command Prompt Commands

Command	Explanation (In Order of Importance on the A+ Exam)
HELP	Truly one of the most useful commands in CLI, type **HELP** and then the command; the syntax and list of switches appears.
/?	To get CLI help in Vista, type the command first then use a ? switch. For example: **EDIT /?.**
C:	Moves to the C: drive.
CD	Change the directory (also called folder). **CD** Moves to the top of the directory tree. **CD** *DirectoryName* moves to that directory.
CD..	Move one level up the directory tree.
ATTRIB	Change file attributes. + adds an attribute, and - removes it. **A** = archive; **R** = read only; **S** = system; **H** = hidden. **ATTRIB -R +A -S -H** *IMPORTANT.DOC* will flag this document to be backed up.
DIR	Display the contents of a directory (folder). To show the hidden files in the CLI, use **DIR /AH**. **A** = all and **H** = hidden.
MD or MKDIR	Make a new directory.
RD or RMDIR	Remove a directory. This cannot be used to delete files. In fact, the target directory must be empty before this command will work.
COPY	Copies files to a new location.
XCOPY	Copies directories and all the subdirectories to a new location.
*	Wildcard is anything, any length.

continues

Table 25-8 **Command Prompt Commands** *continued*

Command	Explanation (In Order of Importance on the A+ Exam)
?	Wildcard is anything, just one character.
Using wildcards	**DEL *.mp3** will delete all MP3s. **DEL lost*.mp3** will delete any MP3 that begins with the characters *lost*. **DEL lost??.mp3** will delete any song that begins with *lost* and end in two characters. What do you suppose **DEL *.*** does (every file)?
DEL	**DEL** *UNIMPORTANT.DOC* deletes this file. Delete one or more files in the current directory. Can be used with the * and the ? wildcards. This will delete *all* files in the current directory. *Use with caution.* (Note that **DEL** cannot be used to delete directories. Use **RD** to remove a directory.)
RENAME	Rename a file. Be sure to include the filename and the extension when doing this.
CLS	Clear the screen.
EDIT	Edit a file with a rudimentary word processor.
PRINT	**PRINT** *LETTER.DOC.* Prints whatever the argument file is. Most modern printers do not support this.
TYPE	Display the contents of a file. This command almost always uses an additional piece, **|MORE**. The | symbol is pronounced "pipe." **TYPE** *FILE.TXT* **|MORE**.
>	This redirects the output to a file. This is used to create reports and logs. This is also used in lieu of a printer. *SWEEP > SWEEPLOG.TXT* makes a log of all virus-infected files.

Users and Permissions

5.4.4: All modern operating systems allow for multiple users to log in and use the PC, each with different levels of permissions. Limiting an end-user's privileges is not necessarily a bad idea. In FAT32 partitions, permissions are assigned at the partition level. This user can or cannot access this or that drive. This is not a secure environment. In an NTFS EXT2 and EXT3 partition, any given user can be assigned any of the following permission to any given folder:

- Full Control

- Modify Contents

- Read & Execute

- List Folder Contents

- Read

- Write

Windows administrator is essentially the same as Linux and Mac OS X root. In XP and Mac OS X, users can run a program from a restricted user account if they provide the correct login credentials as the administrator when prompted. In Linux, this is called *sudo* (super user, do…). This technique greatly simplifies the logistics of logging off as restricted user, logging on as administrator, making the change, logging off as administrator, and logging back on as restricted user to verify the change.

Windows Vista Administrator Account

In Windows Vista and Windows Server 2008, the administrator account is by default disabled. To enable the administrator account, you must follow these steps:

Step 1   Open the MMC console, and choose **Local Users and Groups**.

Step 2   Right-click the **Administrator** account and choose **Properties**.

Step 3   On the General tab, clear the **Account Is Disabled** check box.

To disable the administrator account, go to **Start > Run**, enter **SYSPREP / GENERALIZE**, and then reboot.

File Extensions

5.4.9: All files have an extension, which is three to five characters and acts as a "last name." The filename associates files with the appropriate application. Sometimes this gets mixed up, and suddenly users complain that another application has "hijacked" all their movie files or documents. To change a file extension in XP, choose **Control Panel > Default Programs > Associate File Type or Protocol with a Program**. From there, you can reassociate the extension back to the original application.

Anytime you see an extension with an underscore (for example, .do_), it is a backup copy. NTOSKRNL.EX_ is a duplicate and the backup copy of NTOSKRNL.EXE. Because it is unrecognizable as a file, it is ignored. By simply editing the file extension, you can make the file active.

NTOSKRNL.EXE is a good example of the 8+3 or 8.3 naming convention. Operating systems pre-95 and -NT used only eight characters (dot) and three characters for the extension. This led to some creative abbreviations. New Technology Operating System Kernel (dot) Executable becomes NTOSKRNL.EXE. Today's operating systems use long filenames (up to 255 characters) that support names like Documents and Settings and have extensions like .html. Table 25-9 shows a list of common extensions.

Table 25-9   Common File Extensions

Extension	Explanation
.exe	An executable file, also called a program
.bat	Script file
.doc	Text document with complex formatting, usually associated with MS Word
.txt	Very simple text document
.ppt	PowerPoint file
.xls	Excel spreadsheet

continues

Table 25-9   **Common File Extensions**   *continued*

Extension	Explanation
.jpg	Picture
.mpeg	Movie
.avi	Movie
.wav	Short audio file
.html	Web page
.zip	A file-compression software
.rar	Another file-compression software called RAR, found in all three major operating systems
.tar	Linux version of file a compressed file (A tarball is a group of files compressed into one tar.)
.mp3	Music file (Note that MP4 is a movie format, not, as some end users insist, an upgrade to MP3.)

Plug-Ins, Players, and Viewers

Some extensions require third-party software called plug-ins or viewers. This is a list of the most common extensions that require such software. Even though Windows Media Player comes standard on Windows PCs, it is still a standalone application with its own associated file extensions. Table 25-10 lists extensions that require third-party software.

Table 25-10   **Common File Extensions That Require Third-Party Software**

Extension	Third-Party Software
.pdf	Adobe Acrobat Document
.mov .qt	QuickTime Movie
.ram	Real Audio Music
.rm	Real Movie File
.swf	Adobe Shockwave Animation
.fla	Adobe Flash Animation
.wmv	Windows Media Viewer
.wma	Windows Media Audio

File Attributes

5.4.9: Remember the acronym RASH: **r**ead-only, **a**rchive, **s**ystem, **h**idden. These are the four file attributes that can be changed with the CLI command **attrib** or by right-clicking Properties in a Windows GUI. Read-only is just that: The file can be read but not modified, and read-only is useful for ad-hoc templates and documents that you don't want to accidentally change. Archive is flagged to be backed up. System is a file that needs administrator privilege to modify (although depending on the OS, this is negotiable), and hidden is hidden from normal view. Going to **Folder Options > View** will provide options to be viewed, including Show Hidden Files. Hiding files is not a security feature. It is so that end users don't explore or modify sensitive files. It is the same reason car manufacturers make it difficult to look inside of a car's transmission. Doing so might be really neat, but they don't want end users messing with it.

Virtual Memory

12.2.4: The process of copying the contents of RAM on the HDD is called *paging*. Operating systems do this automatically with lesser-used applications running in RAM to free up RAM for the active programs. In short: Virtual memory (often called virtual RAM) = swap files (often called page files). This technology is also used for crash recovery. Remember, RAM loses its data when the PC has no power. In a secure environment, it may be wise to eliminate the virtual RAM because the HDD has a copy of what was last in RAM before it was turned off. RAM calls this area of the HDD virtual RAM. The HDD calls this data swap files. In general, you should let the OS determine how much of the HDD to allow for this. If you set it up manually, it should be at least equal to the amount of RAM in the PC.

Homework

Review CLI commands and explore them on your PC (remember the **HELP** command). Review the extensions, minimum requirements, and the Registry hives.

Funwork

Write a script that automatically copies your Documents folder to a USB drive. This might prove more useful than you realize. It is not uncommon for administrators to write short scripts to accomplish tedious or mundane tasks.

If you haven't yet found a newbie friendly forum, try Computerhaven.info. They are dedicated, helpful, and considerate IT professionals who remember what it was like to be new to the computer world.

Operating Systems Installation

A+ Essentials Exam Objective

Objective 3.2: Install, configure, optimize and upgrade operating systems

Key Points

Installing an operating system is deceptively simple. In fact, Windows XP, Mac OS X, and Linux are rather goof-proof. Simply boot to the CD and "next" your way through the questions. As a tech, you cannot just "next" your way through. You need to understand the significance of questions about when to use NTFS versus FAT, how many and what kinds of partitions are needed, and what additional programs should be installed after the OS. We will spend more time in Chapter 5 from the IT Essentials v4.0 course.

Hardware Compatibility List

5.3.2: Microsoft has a process by which manufacturers send their hardware to be evaluated and tested. If Microsoft finds the product to be compatible with one (or all) of its OSs, it is "certified" and listed on the online hardware compatibility list (HCL). The HCL is an important resource if you are making large purchases. If you buy 400 new HDDs to upgrade your network, for example, it is in your best interest to verify that they will work with your OS first. A similar process is used for applications, drivers, peripherals, and adapter cards.

Boot Process

5.4.7: An unbootable PC that says "Missing Operating System" or "Missing NTLDR" means the BIOS cannot find the boot files and it is time to check the boot sequence in the BIOS. The boot process does not stop there. Here are the steps in order. Be sure you learn this process for the A+ exam:

1. POST (power-on self test).

2. BIOS reads MBR (master boot record).

3. MBR takes control and loads NTLDR (new technology loader).

4. NTLDR reads BOOT.INI to know which OS and which partition to boot.

5. NTLDR uses NTDETECT to detect and install hardware.

6. NTLDR loads NTOSKRNL.EXE and HAL.DLL.

7. NTLDR reads the Registry and loads device drivers.

8. NTOSKRNL.EXE loads WINLOGON.EXE.

Clean Operating System Install

5.4: Every techie has memorized the process of installing Windows (after installing it over and over). It is likely going to be one of your first tasks to prove your worth in a shop. They will hand you a PC and an OS and say, "Install this." Failure is not an option. Your reputation is on the line. First check the inside of the PC to make sure everything is connected properly, make sure it POSTs, and then follow these steps:

Step 1   Set the boot sequence in BIOS to boot to CD.

Step 2   Boot to the OS CD or DVD.

Step 3   . Create a partition. Let Linux and Mac OS X create their own suggested partitions.

Step 4   Format NTFS (or FAT when 9x systems). Use Linux's and Mac OS X's recommended formatting.

Step 5   Install the OS.

Step 6   Install drivers (Device Manager).

Step 7   Update the OS.

Step 8   Update drivers.

Step 9   Install printers and other devices.

Step 10   Deal with driver issues.

Step 11   Update all drivers.

Step 12   Install applications (Office, for example).

Step 13   Update applications.

Step 14   Defrag.

Step 15   Install antivirus (AV) spyware-removal software and other utilities.

Step 16   Create a restore point.

Add New Hardware Wizard

5.5.2: In the unlikely chance you find a legacy (very old), non Plug-and-Play (PnP) device that must be installed in a PC, use the Add Hardware applet in the Control Panel. It will find a spot for the legacy device among the newer and more negotiable devices. There was a day pre-PnP that all devices were manually assigned interrupt requests (IRQ), direct memory access (DMA), memory input/output (I/O) addresses. It is for these legacy devices that these areas are still tested on the A+ exam.

Add/Remove Software

5.5.4: One rookie mistake is deleting a shortcut (or worse, program files) without uninstalling the program first. When a program is installed, pieces of it are scattered around the PC so that it can be integrated and work seamlessly with other apps. To get rid of a program completely, all of these pieces *and* the main program files need to be rounded up and removed. To remove an application, select it from the list of installed programs, click **Remove**, and let the OS do the rest of the work.

Problem: At any given moment, the doomed application is sharing resources with many others. Ripping out the main files leaves fragments (ghosts) wandering around and wreaking havoc. Those (living) programs continue to rely on shared resources that no longer exist. These programs will generate errors and fail in some way. Many times, the errors will freeze the application. Task Manager can provide a clue, but it is sometimes cryptic and unhelpful.

Missing dynamic link library (DLL) files is the opposite problem: Pieces of the program are missing, but the main program is still there looking for them. This missing DLL problem is known as *DLL hell*. Instead of having duplicate reference files for each application, many programs can share common resources called DLLs. Removing one program might take with it a shared library and leave another program looking for something it can't find.

An important piece of the Add/Remove Software utility is the Add/Remove Windows Features tab. This is where you add or remove support for local services, networking components, Telnet, messaging, and support for obsolete network protocols and print services. You will usually need the OS CDs to add one of these Windows features.

Device Manager

5.4.5: Device Manager is a critical tool. It lists of all the devices in the PC, their associated drivers, and what resources they use. You mainly use it to manage drivers. When a problem occurs, a yellow exclamation point (!) and question mark (?) will indicate a missing or misunderstood driver. Right-clicking the device gives you the option to remove or reinstall the driver. Removing the driver prompts you upon reboot that a driver is missing for that device. Either will result in you ultimately reinstalling the driver or removing the hardware. You have two other options: disable the device in the Device Manager, or if it is an integrated device it can be disable it in the BIOS. Watch for questions about the Device Manager on the A+ exam.

Homework

Review and memorize the OS install and boot sequences. Consider how a sequence might change if you have a redundant array of independent (or inexpensive) discs (RAID) or if you're dealing with a dual-boot system.

It is time to begin your driver collection. Start collecting every OS, support, drivers, and restore CDs that come with your computers. Make a backup copy of the restore CDs or DVDs. Continue your collection by downloading the drivers for the current hardware. You will thank yourself during the next OS install. The best place to get drivers is the manufacturer's websites. If the device is no longer supported, check out sites like Opendrivers.com or just Google the name of the device, the OS, and the word *driver*. Your collection CD or flash drive will become a go-to resource for you in the future.

Funwork

What if you have to go through the entire clean install process for 40 computers in a new office? Maybe there is an easier way. Google the phrase *imaging an HDD and ghosting it*. Imaging and hosting an HDD is a much more efficient way to install an OS on multiple identical PCs.

Operating Systems Troubleshooting

A+ Essentials Exam Objectives

Objective 3.3: Identify tools, diagnostic procedures and troubleshooting techniques for operating systems

Objective 3.4: Perform preventive maintenance on operating systems

Key Points

There is no such thing as a small operating system (OS) problem. It's like having a small problem with air breaks on a truck or a slight issue with the landing gear on a plane. It may seem fatalistic, but you can pretty much count on a catastrophic OS problem at some point in time. The best way to deal with this is frequent backups and to be ready to reinstall the OS. Typically, a clean reinstall and copying the backups to the PC is much quicker (and much less frustrating) than actually troubleshooting the problem.

Memory Dumps

12.5.2: If the RAM has a problem, the system crashes. It produces the blue screen of death (BSoD) and displays a stop code. True ubergeeks can read this and figure out which memory block failed, where, why, and so forth. For the fledgling tech, write down the stop code and the explanation. Go to a working PC and Google the stop code and explanation. Many great sites provide information about stop codes. The cause is often badly written or corrupt software and drivers. Sudden restarts are often BSoDs followed by an immediate restart. (Not to be confused with sudden shutdowns, which are usually caused by overheating.) BSoDs are not exclusive to Windows. The diversity of hardware and applications written for Windows makes it more susceptible.

ERD and ASR

5.6.2: An emergency repair disk (ERD) is a copy of the master boot record (MBR). If something goes horribly wrong and the boot files are corrupt or missing (you get "missing OS" errors, for example), a copy of the MBR will allow you to boot and probably save the data. The OS CD also has this ability. By putting the CD in and acting like you are going to reinstall, you can actually use the CD to repair the OS. This is called automated system recovery (ASR). This is just a temporary fix, however. Be sure to get what you need off the drives, and then plan on reinstalling the OS for real.

Not Enough HDD Space

2.2.2: One of the most troubling messages involves low memory or disk space. Savvy users will check My Computer and see they have several gigs left and that should be more than enough. What this error is really saying is this: "There is not enough room for the HDD data *and* the virtual RAM. Something has to give." The best thing to do is run Disk Cleanup. This eliminates the temporary and useless things on the HDD. This buys you time to back up and remove pictures, music, and other big-ticket items. It is time to recommend the user add, upgrade, or otherwise increase the storage. Chat with the user and learn his or her PC needs. Maybe the user plays a lot of games. Many games sit unused and can be uninstalled, freeing up lots of room. Maybe they can't help but download every MP3 that exists. Teach them how to store MP3 files on an external drive or CD. There are many options, and customer service is important for the A+ exam and in the working world.

Last Known Good Configuration

5.4.8: One of the truly great inventions with Windows XP is Last Known Good Configuration. There was a time when we booted to safe mode by pressing F5 during the splash screen. This was a driver-light version of Windows that allowed the administrator to adjust the display properties back down to a reasonable resolution or to remove a troublesome driver. Now when something in the OS causes the system not to boot properly, XP asks whether you want to Boot Normally or enter the Last Known Good Configuration. You can initiate this during any system boot by pressing F8.

Event Viewer

4.2.5: When things go wrong, there is always a record of it. Learning where to find these logs and understanding what they mean separates tech newbies from alpha-geeks. The Event Viewer in Administrator Tools explains what happened, the date and time it occurred, the severity, the source, and who was logged in at the time.

MSCONFIG

5.4.8: MSCONFIG is truly one of the most used and loved utilities. It can improve performance by not loading unused startup items. This is done using the System Configuration utility. This can be run from the command prompt by entering **msconfig** and using the Startup tab to uncheck items. The System Configuration utility also is a quick way to manage services and edit BOOT.INI, SYSTEM.INI, and WIN.INI. Those can be manually edited in Notepad, too. MSCONFIG also contains shortcuts to the commonly used tools normally found buried deep in the menus of the Control Panel. System Information provides accurate, detailed information about your PC. In the unlikely event you have an interrupt request (IRQ) conflict or a memory address issue, this is the place to see what is really going on. It is also a way to inventory the hardware without opening the PC, which is a time and equipment saver.

Change File Extension Associations

5.4.9: In Windows XP, navigate to **Control Panel > Folder Options**. In Vista, go to **Control Panel > Default Programs > Set Default Programs > Set Program Associations**. From there, you can assign a program to open with (or associate with) a specific program (in other words, map the file extensions to an application). Earlier versions of Windows used the command-line interface (CLI) **assoc** command or the technician directly edited the WIN.INI file.

Install a Program on OS X, Windows, and Linux

5.5.4: Mac OS is almost exclusively a graphical user interface (GUI); therefore, you just drag the application to the HDD Application folder. This launches an installer package much like Windows Installation Wizard.

In Windows, either run the install program provided by the software publisher, or open Add or Remove Software in the Control Panel and follow the wizard.

In a Linux terminal, navigate to the application and run it.

View the CLI on OS X, Windows, and Linux

To view the CLI on a Mac, go to **HDD > Applications > Utilities > Terminal**.

On a PC, go to **Start > Run > CMD** or **Accessories, Command Prompt**.

NOTE: The A+ Exam often displays paths like this: The > means "go to" or "trace to."

Linux almost always has an icon nearby to launch a terminal. Often, a true server-style Linux distro will not be booted to the GUI and run entirely on the CLI. This cuts down on the RAM usage and dedicates more resources to providing services to other PCs.

Disk Management and Utilities

To access disk management utilities on a Mac, go to **HDD > Applications > Accessories > Disk Utilities**.

On a PC, go to **Control Panel > Administrator Tools > Computer Management**. This opens a Microsoft Management Consol (MMC), which is a customizable interface where administrators can manage multiple PC capabilities. Disk Management is an MMC. Other examples include Event Viewer and Performance Monitor. To launch System File Checker from the CLI, use the command **sfc /scannow**.

Microsoft Backup Utility

5.6.3: The Microsoft Backup Utility is graphic look at your HDD. Just check what you want backed up. A wizard then asks you where and when or how often you want it backed up. The A+ exam often asks question about the different kinds of backups. Table 23-2 lists the different backups.

Table 23-2   Backups

Backup	Description
Normal or full	Everything gets copied.
Copy	Makes a backup but does not mark files with the archive bit. (See **ATTRIB** in the CLI.)
Differential	Backs up anything that has changed since the last full backup. Does not change the archive bit.
Incremental	Same as a differential backup, but it clears the archive bit.
Daily	Backs up the files that changed that day, but does not change archive bit.

Homework

Consider all the reasons an OS won't load, try to find at least 10 reasons (be creative: boot sequence, missing MBR, power-supply problems, and so on). Install a program using Add or Remove Programs in the Control Panel. Familiarize yourself with this alternative to just running the CD.

Explore MSCONFIG on your PC by going to **Start > Run > MSCONFIG**.

Back up your own PC data.

Update your OS and antivirus software, and then run Scandisk.

Visit TechNet, Microsoft's big-dog forum. This is not the place to ask dumb questions. It is the place to glean answers from others' questions and answers. These people have forgotten more about Windows operating systems than most people ever learn.

Funwork

Download and burn a live CD copy of Ubuntu or Knoppix. Boot a Windows PC to the Linux CD and view the files on the HDD. You will be able to view them even though they are password-protected in Windows. You can use a USB drive and copy files. This should not be confused with hacking or stealing data from a PC—it's called data recovery, a subtle but significant difference. If you don't own the PC in question, make sure you have permission first.

Printers

A+ Essentials Exam Objective

Objective 4.1: Identify the fundamental principles of using printers and scanners

Key Points

Today and Day 21, "Scanners," are intentionally easy to give you a break between two big sections about operating systems and networking. So enjoy the break. You are on the downhill side of preparing for the A+ Essentials exam, with only one more hill to climb: networking. Today you will spend time in Chapter 7 of the IT Essentials v4.0 course.

Printer Measurements

7.1.1: There are many kinds of printers. The A+ exam focuses on a few common ones: laser, inkjet, impact (dot matrix), solid ink, thermal, and dye sublimation. The following is a list of common printer measurements:

- **Pages per minute (PPM):** Measures printer speed.

- **Characters per second (CPS):** Measures printer speed of impact (dot-matrix) printers.

- **Dots per inch (DPI):** Measures quality.

- **Mean time between failures (MTBF):** Measures reliability.

- **Cost per page (CPP):** Measures the price of each printed page. A proper measurement of CPP takes into consideration the cost of ink, paper, electricity, and scheduled printer maintenance.

Types of Printers

7.1: Printers are available in black and white or color; the difference is cost and speed. Color is slower and much more expensive. Let's take a closer look at printer technologies.

Laser

7.1.3: Laser printers are a good balance between cost and quality. They are quiet, reliable, and produce high-quality printouts. Laser printers are not cheap, and toner can be pricey. Except for the initial costs, the actual CPP is quite low. Table 22-1 outlines the six steps of the laser-printing process.

Table 22-1   Laser-Printer Process

Step	Details of Each Step	Mnemonic
1. Cleaning	The drum is cleaned by a wiper or in some cases an electrical charge can drop excess toner from the drum.	California
2. Conditioning	Puts uniform charge of –600 volts direct current (VDC). This phase is also called charging.	Cows
3. Writing	Laser traces the image on the charged drum and changes the voltage to –100 VDC in those areas the laser touched.	Won't
4. Developing	Negatively charged toner is applied to the drum and sticks to the areas with altered voltage.	Dance
5. Transferring	The secondary corona wire charges the paper. The toner is statically attracted to the paper.	The
6. Fusing	Rollers melt the toner and embed it into the paper.	Fandango

Inkjet

7.1.5: Inkjet printers include either thermal or piezoelectric nozzles. Thermal nozzles boil the ink, and jets of steamed ink are shot out onto the paper. Piezoelectric nozzles energize crystals that vibrate and control ink flow. In either case, the nozzles get clogged and misaligned. Routine self-testing and calibration is recommended to maintain high-quality print output.

Photo paper allows the ink jets to produce very high-resolution "photo-quality" pictures. Inkjet printers are usually inexpensive, but the ink can cost upward of $1 per full-color page. In many inkjet printers, all the ink cartridges must be installed and full even if you are printing a black-and-white document.

Impact Printers

7.1.4: A dot-matrix printer uses a group of pins that strike a ribbon against the paper. When the pins are used in combination, they create shapes of letters. A daisy wheel looks like a flower, and each petal has a letter, number, or symbol on it. It spins to the right letter and is whacked against the ink ribbon, printing the character onto the paper. Impact printers are measured in characters per second (CPS), not PPM. Near letter quality (NLQ) is the best quality a dot-matrix printer can have. Impact printers are used on carbon copy paper.

Solid Ink

7.1.6: Solid ink printers are like a hybrid laser and inkjet. The solid ink is melted and sprayed (written) to a drum and is then transferred onto the paper. These printers are used for posters and other large-format, high-quality photos.

Dye Sublimation

7.1.7: Another high-quality printing technology is dye sublimation. This process prints the page four times, each with a different color of ink. This produces long-lasting, high-quality images. These printers and supplies are quite pricey.

Thermal

7.1.7: Used on point-of-sale systems, thermal printers print receipts and other inexpensive continuous-feed outputs, such as those produced by electrocardiograms, label makers, and old fax machines. The paper is stored on rolls and is treated so that heat will darken it.

Printer Connections

7.1, 7.2.2: The three primary ways to connect to a printer are

- Directly connected to a PC via USB, parallel, FireWire, or infrared (IR)

- Directly connected to a remote networked PC that acts as a print server for the network

- A networked printer that has a network interface card (NIC) and is a fully capable network device

Regardless of the physical connection, the drivers must exist on the PC from which the print job is sent. Start the process by selecting **Control Panel > Printers > Add New Printer**. This wizard searches for directly connected PCs or searches for print servers on the network. If it doesn't find the printer, check the obvious things first: Is the printer plugged in and turned on? Does it have paper and ink? If it is a network printer, check whether the network settings are correct. (See Days 20 and 19.) Is the printer "online," meaning is it ready to receive print jobs? Is there a job stuck in the queue? The queue is RAM on the printer that stores multiple jobs in the order they were received. If the printer stops working, end users have a terrible habit of repeatedly clicking the Print button in an effort to motivate the printer back into service. Be sure to clear the queue before printing a test page.

TCP/IP printers are controlled by a printer server. Print jobs are sent to the print server, and are then forwarded to the printer. It is important to note there are two styles of print servers. One is a standalone PC with a NIC connected to the network and a USB directly connected to the printer. The other print server is built in to the printer. These network printers connect directly to the network, and the printer manages the print services with no need for a dedicated PC.

Printer Troubleshooting

7.6: Table 22-2 lists common printer problems and their solutions. Note that you never protect a printer with an uninterruptible power supply (UPS). It will damage the UPS. Besides, who needs to print in the dark?

Table 22-2   Common Printer Problems

Problem	Solution
Streaks or lines on the paper.	Replace the toner cartridge.
Consistent tick marks.	Clean or replace the drum.
Prints gibberish characters.	Reinstall the drivers or clear the printer queue, turn off the printer, and reboot the computer.
More than one sheet of paper enters the feeder at the same time.	Humidity causes paper to "clump." Store paper in cool, dry area.
Printer will not pick up the paper.	Clean the grip wheel with a cotton swab and 70% isopropyl rubbing alcohol. Replace the pickup roller if it is "smooth."
Paper tray does not push paper up high enough.	Check the spring tension in the tray.

Homework

Think back over the subjects, tables, and descriptions discussed in the past nine days and pinpoint the subjects you struggled with the most. Review those sections in this book and in the IT Essentials course. Use HowStuffWorks, TechSpot, Cnet, TechRepublic, *PC Magazine*, ZDNet, or other good resources to explain the topic to you in a different way. You have an exam in a week. Be sure that you're ready.

Funwork

Find an appropriate printer for each of the following clients:

1. An advertising agency that produces poster-size, full-color ads for store windows (prints on plastic film)

2. A college student who will move frequently over the next 4 years (small, light, and tough)

3. A small home/small office (SOHO) wireless network for a real estate firm (legal-size paper a must)

Answers: (There are many correct answers, but these are a good start.)

1. HP DesignJet Large Format series or Epson Stylus Pro Large Format series with static cling vinyl material rather than paper

2. Canon i70 or i80 or HP DeskJet 460 series

3. Brother SOHO-class series or HP Laser All-in-One series, preferably with built-in network support

Scanners

A+ Essentials Exam Objectives

Objective 4.2: Identify basic concepts of installing, configuring, optimizing and upgrading printers and scanners

Objective 4.3: Identify tools, basic diagnostic procedures and troubleshooting techniques for printers and scanners

Key Points

Today's topics relate mostly to Chapter 7 and a little to Chapter 1 of the IT Essentials v4.0 course. You will learn about different types of scanners, optical character recognition (OCR), and how to maintain scanners.

Handheld, Flatbed, and Drum Scanners

7.3: All scanners read the light reflected off a paper with charge-coupled devices (CCD). The image is sent to the PC through a USB or other cord. The user saves the image most often in the form of a JPG file. The difference in scanners is how the scanner and the paper interact. A handheld scanner is dragged along the paper, a flatbed scanner drives the scanner across the paper that is laid flat, and the drum scanner rolls the paper past a stationary scanner. They are essentially the same device. Images from handheld scanners tend to be distorted because of the human-driven element. However, they are more portable than the other two. Flatbed scanners are good for bound books but are cumbersome if you need to scan multipage documents. Drum scanners can process loose-leaf paper only and can jam, but are the best way to scan multipage documents. Listen to your clients' needs to determine which is best for them. Table 21-1 offers a quick comparison of scanners.

Table 21-1   Scanner Comparison

Scanner	Features	Portable	Scans Multiple Pages	Scans Bound Books or Thick Paper
Handheld	Scanner is dragged along the paper.	Yes	No	Yes
Flatbed	Drives the scanner across the paper that is laid flat.	No	No	Yes
Drum	Rolls the paper past a stationary scanner.	No	Yes	No

All-in-one devices are perfect for residential settings and the small office/home office (SOHO) because they function as a printer, copier, fax, and scanner. The biggest drawback is if the all-in-one breaks, then everything goes with it. There is no redundancy.

Optical Character Recognition

7.3.1: Optical character recognition (OCR) is an application that looks at a picture file and recognizes letters, symbols, and numbers as text. That text can be saved as a document, completing physical-to-virtual transformation of a piece of paper. OCR works well with printed words but struggles with handwriting.

One application of this proves beneficial for the visually impaired. For example, blind people can use a combination scanner/OCR/text-to-speech/speaker device to hear written words. This device enables a blind person to read a menu, an airplane ticket, a train schedule, and make change with paper money.

Maintaining Scanners

7.5: Scanners and printers have many similarities: same ports, same cables, required drivers, some are networked, and some are directly connected. A printer prints from an application, whereas a scanner scans and imports that image to an application. To maintain a scanner, clean the glass, maintain the condition of the paper-handling surfaces, and keep the drivers and firmware updated. Some high-end scanners have calibrations that increase accuracy.

Other Scanners

1.6: A barcode reader shines a laser at a barcode and reads the reflecting light. It serves the same function as radio frequency identification (RFID) chips and readers. These devices are often used in inventory management and tracking. Retinal patterns, fingerprints, palm prints, and facial characteristics are inputs scanners read to determine whether they recognize a valid (allowed) pattern. Then an application maps those patterns to a password, which is used to authenticate a logon. Biometric devices are supported like any other peripheral, whether integrated or not.

Homework

This is the second easy day in a row. Enjoy it. Tomorrow we start the last big hill: networking. Tonight, your assignment is to use YouTube. Search there for PC repair or a specific aspect of PC repair you still don't understand. You will find many homemade, how-to, and DIY videos about computers. Watch them. Some are well done, some are not. Search for reviews of printers, scanners, OCR, and handwriting recognition. YouTube lets you observe computer geeks in their natural habitat, as you would penguins in a nature documentary. Most important, you will be reinforcing the A+ exam terminology and concepts.

Funwork

If you have access to a scanner, experiment with it and become familiar with an OCR application. Many OCR applications are free online. Try to get the OCR to read your handwriting.

Networking: Part 1 of 2

A+ Essentials Exam Objective

Objective 5.1: Identify the fundamental principles of networks

Key Points

When CompTIA introduced the 2006 A+ exam objectives, networking became a big part of the new test. This can be a surprisingly difficult part of the A+ exam, and many future techies get discouraged and unwisely dismiss it as unimportant. Question: When was the last time you saw a completely standalone, non-networked PC? Today, even calculators and kitchen appliances communicate on a network. By enabling automatic updates, your computer, your refrigerator, or your car run a self-diagnosis, find a problem, "call" home for advice on how to fix it, download a fix (an update), install it, and run just fine without you (or the customer) even knowing there was a problem. It truly is a connected world. Networking is just as important as motherboards, drivers, printers, and security. Today, you will cover topics in Chapter 8 of the IT Essentials v4.0 course.

LANs, WANs, and WLANs

8.2.1–8.2.3: A network is a group of PCs and devices that serve different functions. In a local area network (LAN), devices are close by (within a building, campus, or house) and include use of upper-layer protocols. LANs are end-user oriented.

Wide area networks (WAN) are full of Layer 2 and 3 devices (switches and routers) and contain few actual computers. WANs connect LANs to each other and can extend enormous distances around the world, and literally beyond into space, using wireless technologies.

Wireless LANs (WLAN) are commonly known as WIFI. These "spots" allow portable devices such as PDAs, phones, laptops, heart monitors, alarm systems, and others to connect to each other and to the Internet. The physical layer of a WLAN is the antennas and radio signals.

OSI Model

8.8.2: The seven-layer OSI model reduces complexity, ensures interoperability among devices, and simplifies learning. Table 20-1 describes the layers of the OSI model. It is important to memorize this table.

Table 20-1   OSI Model

Layer	Name	Mnemonic	Description
7	Application	**A**ll	This layer is the actual application (for example, e-mail, browser, IM client). The "layer" above this is the user.
6	Presentation	**P**eople	This layer is all about how data is presented to the application. Is it compressed? It will need WinZip or another utility in the application layer. Is it a PDF file? It will need Adobe reader. Don't have it? The user will see a file with a nonassociated extension.
5	Session	**S**eem	This layer establishes, maintains, and terminates communications.
4	Transport	**T**o	This layer deals in flow control. If someone is talking too slowly, you might ask him to speed up. The opposite is also true. If something is missed because the speed is too fast, the receiver asks the sender to send it again, just as you would in a conversation. This is error checking and correction.
3	Network	**N**eed	IP addresses are assigned in this level. An IP address is considered logical because it can be assigned by the administrator or given out by a Dynamic Host Configuration Protocol (DCHP) server. Routers make routing decisions here based on the name and network information.
2	Data link	**D**ata	Media Access Control (MAC) addresses are in this level. They are permanently burned into the network interface card (NIC) and are therefore considered physical. Do not assume that the physical address is in Layer 1. Tip: Layer 2 has two words in the name. Devices in Layer 2 are switches and bridges. A switch has many ports, and a bridge has few. Both perform switching, but bridges are nonexistent in the real world.
1	Physical	**P**rocessing	This is the actual wire, light impulses, or radio waves that carry the data. Devices here include hubs and repeaters. Hubs have many ports, and repeaters have few, usually two.

Layer 1 devices cannot make decisions. They just retime, regenerate, and reproduce the signals they receive.

Layer 2 devices make up the majority of networking traffic. Layer 2 devices read and determine whether they recognize the MAC address. If not, they send it to everyone to see whether the others have heard of the address. If they have heard of the destination MAC address, Layer 2 devices forward it down that port only. This is called *switching*. The name comes from switching locomotive trains, and from old-school telephone operators who actually connected and disconnected, or switched, wires to make connections.

Layer 3 is where routing decisions are made. Routers direct packets using routing protocols to determine the best path for each packet.

Simplex, Multicasting, Half Duplex, Full Duplex

8.3.1: Simplex, often called broadcast, is a standard TV- or radio-style signal. One transmitter to everyone, and no one talks back to the transmitter.

Multicast requires a naming scheme. One sender, many receivers, and everyone hears the message. If receivers hear their name as one of the many destination addresses, they actually pay attention to the signal and pass it up to other layers.

Half duplex is like walkie-talkies: One person talks, and the other listens. Then they switch roles. This turn taking is initiated by first listening to confirm that no one else is talking. That is called carrier sensing, which is a critical part of carrier sense multiple access collision detect (CSMA/CD), which we will discuss in a moment.

Full duplex is like a phone conversation. The sender and receiver work independently of each other.

Network Addressing

8.3.2: Network devices have two names: the MAC address and the IP address. The MAC address functions in the data link layer (Layer 2), and the IP address is a network layer (Layer 3). MAC addresses are used in communicating with the closest device (a hop), and the IP addresses are used when communicating with other computers on the LAN or Internet.

MAC

You can't help but have a unique MAC because the first half of its 48-bit address, the first three octets in a hexadecimal address, is the Organizational Unique Identifier (OUI). Every NIC manufacturer gets one. The last half is assigned by that company, like a serial number. The MAC address 00-0C-41-68-B2-85 means that it is made by Cisco Linksys (68-B2-85 is the number that Cisco Linksys gave that NIC).

IP Address

An IP address is one of the two names assigned to every network device. IP addresses are a logical aspect of networking because they are changeable. There are four octets in an IP address. It is actually four, 8-bit binary numbers, but we read them as "normal" numbers, where each octet can be any number from 0 through 255. 192.168.0.4 is an example of a standard IP address, but 192.256.0.4 is not because the 256 is too big for that octet.

Subnets

A subnet divides a network into smaller groups of related addresses. It accomplishes this by ignoring or masking parts of the IP address. A subnet mask such as 255.255.255.0 is actually 11111111.11111111.11111111.00000000. The IP address contains two parts: the network name and the host name. The host portion of the address is identified by 0s and the network portion is identified by 1s. Network designers move the line that separates the network from the host portion to create subnetworks, much like subdividing a piece of land into smaller sections.

The following is an analogy relating the way the postal system reads and forwards an envelope to IP and subnet masking on a network. A letter enters the mail system. The mailroom reads the state, city, and Zip Code. The actual street and house numbers are masked (ignored) because they are unimportant at that time. The focus is to get the envelope to the right area (network). Once inside the destination area, the letter carrier is not concerned with the city, state, and Zip Code. The concern now is exclusively with the street and house number (host number).

Network Class

If the first octet (the number before the first decimal or "dot") is between 1 and 126, it is a Class A address, a Class B address is 128 to 191, and Class C is from 192 to 223. The addresses 224 to 255 are special classes not within the scope of the A+ exam. 127.0.0.1 is the loopback address. Pinging 127.0.0.1 tests your NIC regardless of the actual assigned IP.

Network Topologies

8.5.1: A network is a physical collection of devices that share data and resources to increase efficiency and reduce duplicate devices, such as printers, Internet connections, and file storage. It provides centralized points for backups and management, but also provides centralized points for failure.

Physical Topology

Physical topology defines the layout of the physical connections. Star/extended star means a central point allows and controls flow to the rest of the network. Rare is a true star. Usually, the pattern is an extended star with branches off of other branches in a tree-like pattern. This pattern is referred to as *hierarchical*.

A physical bus topology is also rare. It looks like one common cable with transceivers that tap into that line for each node. This topology is used mainly as a logical concept, not so much as a physical one.

Physical ring topologies are also rare, but they do exist. The most common example is a fiber-optic cable. Picture a circle with data flowing along that ring between two computers. Picture an inner circle with information that flows in the opposite direction between the same two computers. Now squeeze that circle into long inner and outer ovals and eventually into four straight lines. That is how data on a fiber-optic cable flows.

Logical Topologies

The most common topology is a star/bus topology. That means a physical star and logical bus. Logical bus means everyone hears everyone else and only pays attention when they hear their name. The other and less-common kind of network is a star/ring. That means the token is passed from one computer back to the device that looks like a switch or hub but actually functions a little differently. The multistation access hub (MSAU) looks just like a switch, but it is not a star topology. The MSAU sends the token down the first port to whatever device is on the other end, and that device sends it back. The token is sent down the next port and sent back by the next device, and so on. If any device has something to send, it waits for and then attaches the packet to the token and sends it back to the MSAU. Taking turns like this prevents collisions, but is slower.

Client/Server Versus Peer to Peer

8.2.4 and 8.2.5: Another topology that functions in the upper levels has to do with the roles and relationships among the network devices. Client/server networks are centralized, hierarchical, and easy to grow. Dedicated servers provide resources to client PCs. This topology is used when authentication and security is important or the network is highly dynamic. It is also used to help organize large networks.

Peer to peer means any PC can be a client or server at any time or all the time. Peer-to-peer networks are good for small environments (for example, residential or small office/home office [SOHO]). Management is more difficult because the resources are not centralized.

Network Architectures

8.5.2: As if groups, topologies, addresses, subnetting, and dedicated roles are not enough micro-management, we also need important-sounding names to define the physical layer concepts. Because "stuff goes from here to there" will not be good enough on the A+ exam, you need to memorize the official names for these protocols. The standards organizations will be spelled out tomorrow. For right now, just focus on memorizing these next few tables. Table 20-2 lists the different network architectures and the organization that defines each.

Table 20-2   Network Architectures

Architecture	Standards Organization	Memorization Tips
Ethernet	IEEE 802.3	"Threee" sounds like "Eeethernet."
Token Ring	IEEE 802.5	A pentagon has five sides and is in the shape of a ring.
FDDI	ANSI and ISO	Fiber-optic cable. The double D is a reminder that it is a double-ring topology.
WIFI	IEEE 802.11	The 11 looks like two antennas.

The Physical Layer of Ethernet

8.7.1: All Ethernet cabling terminates with RJ-45 heads, uses a star/extended star topology, has a range of 100 meters (328 feet) per segment, has four twisted pair of wires (but their usage varies), and all specs are defined by TIA/EIA. Table 20-3 shows the differences in Ethernet cabling.

Table 20-3   Ethernet Cabling Comparison

Cabling	Speed	Cable Category Rating	Wires Used
10BASE-T	10 Mbps	3, 4, or 5 (normally 5)	2 pairs
100BASE-T	100 Mbps	5, 5e, and 6 (normally 5)	2 pairs
1000BASE-T	1000 Mbps	5, 5e, and 6 (normally 5)	All 4 pairs

The Physical Layer of WIFI

8.7.2: The physical layer of WIFI may seem like a contradiction in terms. After all, the whole point of wireless is to avoid the physical connection. Still, WIFI has to move the physical data, in this case in the form of radio signals. All WIFI standards for the A+ exam are defined by IEEE 802.11. The four standards are a, b, g, and n. The a standards are not compatible with any of the others and have a very small range of 150 feet (45.7 meters). It is rare to find it today. The b and g standards are interoperable with each other, and n will work with both b and g. Table 20-4 compares the IEEE 802.11 standards, summarizing their differences.

Table 20-4   Wireless Comparison

802.11	Bandwidth	Frequency	Max Range
a	54 Mbps	5 GHz	150 feet (45.7 m)
b	11 Mbps	2.4 GHz	300 feet (300 m)
g	54 Mbps	2.4 GHz	300 feet (300 m)
n	540 Mbps	2.4 or 5 GHz	984 feet (250 m)

Bluetooth

13.1.1: Bluetooth is generally used to connect one device to another (sort of like a wireless USB cable). It is actually meant to replace infrared (IR), which it does superbly. The protocol supports file transfer and streaming signals. It uses a frequency-hopping technology, so it is harder to hack and it does not interfere with other devices that function in its 2.4-GHz frequency range. Bluetooth is widely available in laptops and cell phones. A MAC address scheme allows one Bluetooth controller to connect with up to eight devices.

Homework

Memorize the OSI chart in Table 20-1. It is not listed in order of importance because *it is all important.*

Review the physical and logical topologies.

Review the various groupings of network devices, both logical and physical.

If you think networking is confusing, have several people explain IP networking to you in their own way. Chances are that you know someone who speaks networking. Buy that person a coffee and ask him or her to explain it to you. You can find dozens of networking introductory tutorials online, too.

Funwork

Google "fiber-optic submarine cable system map" and look at a map of undersea fiber cables.

In a new browser, go to http://science.nasa.gov/Realtime/Jtrack/ (make sure your Java is updated). Click the 3D version. Drag the world around a little and click on several dots. Each one is a satellite in orbit.

Here is the fun part: Display both the ocean map and the satellites and realize that every piece of data, TV broadcast, phone traffic, radio signal, civilian communication, military communication, every channel, and every flood of data traffic uses these routes and only these routes. It isn't some nameless, faceless "cloud" controlled and maintained by someone else. Further, realize that more often than not, there is a piece of Cisco equipment on both ends of each of these lines and the transmitters for each satellite ground station. Seriously. And it is people like you who make these things work.

Anytime you stream audio video, download something from the web, or send an e-mail, you are using these actual satellites, submarine cables, and the myriad microwave and land-based systems.

Right now, you are studying for the end-user devices. But you truly need to understand the bigger picture and your role in it.

Networking: Part 2 of 2

A+ Essentials Exam Objectives

Objective 5.2: Install, configure, optimize and upgrade networks

Objective 5.3: Identify tools, diagnostic procedures and troubleshooting techniques for networks

Key Points

Today continues the networking discussion by comparing the OSI reference model (covered yesterday) with the TCP/IP model. You also review network protocols and the organizations that standardize various aspects of networking so that devices and technologies from different vendors can work together. These topics relate to Chapter 8 of the IT Essentials v4.0 course.

OSI and TCP/IP Models

8.8, 8.8.3: The OSI reference model is the basis for all networking protocol stacks. TCP/IP is used almost universally and is based on the OSI model. It combines several layers. A+ exam questions regarding the OSI model are notoriously convoluted, so read them carefully. This is a perfect opportunity to make a brain dump. At the beginning of the exam, jot down the OSI model and the TCP/IP model right next to it. Annotate each with important concepts and devices. Then begin to answer questions about networking models. The TCP/IP model acronym spelled from bottom up is the name Anita. Table 19-1 compares the OSI and TCP/IP models.

Table 19-1   Comparing the OSI and TCP/IP Models

OSI	TCP/IP	Memorizing Tips
Application Presentation Session	Application	Apps (remember the mnemonic A-P-S from application, presentation, and session) function in the application layer.
Transport	Transport	Same name, same layer.
Network	Internet	The Internet is a large collection of networks.
Data link Physical	Network access	The network access layer has two words in the name and is created by two OSI layers.

Network Protocols

8.3.4: The soup du jour is alphabet with a sprig of layered protocol. Fortunately, in many cases you really need only to focus on the definitions rather than what the abbreviations stand for. For the A+ exam, be sure that you know the abbreviations in Table 19-2 and what they are used for. If you need to know what each abbreviation stands for, refer to the IT Essentials v4.0 course.

Table 19-2   Network Protocols to Know for the A+ Exam

Protocol	TCP/IP Layer	Need to Know (In Order of Importance)
IP	Internet	Specifies source and destination addressing.
ICMP	Internet	Use the **ping** command to verify connectivity.
HTTP	Application	Loads web pages.
HTTPS	Application	Loads secure web pages.
HTML	Application	Determines web page layout and content.
FTP	Application	Downloads files and transfers files.
DNS	Application	Translates IP addresses to www.friendly.name.
SMTP	Application	Sends e-mail.
IMAP	Application	Gets e-mail.
POP	Application	Gets e-mail.
TCP	Transport	Is reliable, slower, and supports HTTP, FTP, and SMTP (anything that really needs to be correct on the other end). Connection orientated.
UDP	Transport	Is unreliable but fast. Used for streaming audio and video and for transmissions that can afford some data loss in lieu of speed. Connectionless.
ARP	Internet	If the IP is known, use this to find the MAC of a nearby network device.
SSH	Application	Is text based and provides secure remote access to a PC.
Telnet	Application	Old text-based system for remote access. Use SSH instead.
RIP	Internet	Is used by routers to choose paths for packets.
IPX/SPX	N/A	Novell's alternative to TCP/IP.
VoIP	N/A	Allows anyone with a microphone, speaker, a PC, and an Internet connection to use those as a phone.
NetBEUI	N/A	Old simple networking protocol with no capability to use the Internet and not good for large networks. Also called NetBIOS.

Standards Organizations

8.6: Standards organizations work behind the scenes and allow for interoperability among similar devices often made by competing companies. This is why we have common interfaces like universal serial bus (USB) and peripheral component interconnect (PCI). Imagine if there were no standards whatsoever. Everything would be proprietary, and nothing would work with anything else. Note that all of these organizations are really quite important. The Internet and computer would be a truly scary place without their standards. The order of importance listed in Table 19-3 has to do with the standards organizations you will most likely see on the A+ exam.

Table 19-3   Standards Organizations

Standards Organization	Need to Know (In Order of Importance)
IEEE	Institute of Electrical and Electronics Engineers Ethernet, Token Ring, WIFI
ISO	International Organization for Standardization OSI layered networking model
ANSI	American National Standards Institute FDDI
FCC	Federal Communications Commission Assigns frequency ranges and amplitude restrictions for WIFI, IR, Bluetooth, and radio signals
UL	Underwriters Laboratories Certifies that electronics meet safety codes
TIA/EIA	Telecommunications Industry Association/Electronic Industries Alliance Category 5 wire arrangements, called pinouts
CCITT	Comité Consultatif International Téléphonique et Télégraphique Modems and faxes
IAB	Internet Architecture Board Makes rules for the Internet
IEC	International Electrotechnical Commission Defines the units we use, such as mega, kilo, hertz, and bits

AT Commands

8.9.3: Once upon a time, long, long ago, we used modems; actually, analog audio tone generators that connected to each other over phone cables, and we manually established connections using commands entered in a command-line interface (CLI). This technology is pre-web, pre-CD, even pre-mouse. Call it job security, but dialup networking is still a part of the material for the A+ exam. Table 19-4 contains the basic AT commands.

Table 19-4   AT Commands

AT Command	Keywords
AT	Attention
AP	Pulse
ATDT	Dial tone
ATA	Answer
ATHO	Hang up
ATZ	Reset
ATF	Factory reset
AT+++	Break

Internet Connections

8.10: Internet service providers (ISP) offer high-speed Internet connections. Table 19-5 lists the most common methods in their order of importance for the A+ exam.

Table 19-5   Internet Connections

Broadband Connection	Need to Know (In Order of Importance)
POTS	Plain old telephone system (or service) uses a modem and is slow (56 kbps).
ADSL	Asymmetric digital subscriber line. 8.10.1 asynchronous is the most common form of DSL. It is slower upstream (toward the ISP) and much faster downstream (toward the client). Common ADSL speeds (downstream/upstream): 768 kbps / 364 kbps 1.5 Mbps / 384 kbps 3 Mbps / 512 kbps 6 Mbps / 768 kbps (Source: AT&T DSL plans) DSL requires the use of filters for the telephones so that the voice traffic and the data traffic do not interfere with each other. Designed for residential clients and small office/home office (SOHO) environments, DSL has a very quick download speed but is not designed to support high traffic in and out as a web server or FTP site.
Cable	Cable TV providers use coaxial cable to provide many services, including Internet access. It is very fast. However, performance varies because it is a shared medium. Everyone in a building, block, street, and so on shares the same connection. If someone is using a lot of bandwidth, others will see a drop in performance.
Satellite	Satellite is 56 kbps up and 500 kbps down. It is slower than cable and ADSL but can provide service almost anywhere, such as on a boat or in a motor home. Leaves and weather may adversely affect satellite Internet performance.

Table 19-5   Internet Connections

Broadband Connection	Need to Know (In Order of Importance)
PRI ISDN	Primary rate ISDN is a T1 line. It has 24 64-kbps B channels, of which 23 are used together to achieve speeds of 1.544 Mbps. The D channel is used for signal timing, starting and stopping the sessions. Europe has 30 B channels and can have speeds up to 2.048 Mbps.
BRI ISDN	The basic rate interface (BRI) has three wires: two B channels that can carry 64 kbps and a D channel that can carry 16 kbps. BRI uses both B channels for data and the D channel for timing, initializing, and ending the call. This use of the B channel is similar to the session layer on the OSI model.
PLC/PLN Mains/PLT	Power line transmissions (PLT) is a technology that uses the power grid to send data from place to place. The power grid is a network of conductive wires that is already in place and well maintained and that connects nearly everyone. It is ideally suited for a communications system, although it is not very fast.

Troubleshooting Networks

8.12: The majority of home networks use an integrated services router (ISR), often just called the router. This device sits in the center of the star/bus topology, shares an ISP connection with the WLAN, provides access and firewall security, and uses networking to share resources, such as files and printers. When troubleshooting a network issue, always start with the physical layer. Network interface cards (NIC) must be connected with a cable from the PC to the switch and from the switch to the router. In a WLAN, the antenna must be in range, and compatible with the router. 802.11a NICs must be with 802.11a routers. All the others (b, g, and n) are backward compatible. In both LAN and WLAN environments, blinking lights both on the NIC and the router indicate network traffic. That is a good sign. If you don't see lights, check the physical layer again.

Exploring ipconfig /all Outputs

Use the command prompt and enter **ipconfig /all**. The output will include the IP address, subnet mask, and gateway. It will also list the MAC address and hostname. Those will be important later.

If the output says "media disconnected," go back to the physical layer and double-check plugs and cables. You might have a bad cable or network device. Check for visible damage to cables, and make sure the router and switches are powered.

If the IP address is 169.254.x.x, you know right away that the NIC is set for DHCP but the PC did not get an address. As a result, the automatic private internet protocol addressing (APIPA) protocol in Windows automatically assigned an IP address to the NIC. This will not work on your network. Issue the command **ipconfig /release** followed by **ipconfig /renew**. This process asks the DHCP server for a new IP address. If you get a new one (normally 192.168.0.x), great. Move on to ping. If you get a 169.254.x.x number again, check the router or DHCP server. It is either not connected to the network or not set to give out IP addresses.

In a WLAN environment, the router might be using a MAC address filter. That security feature prevents unknown MAC addresses from getting IP addresses, and thus prevents the PC from gaining access to the WLAN. Go to the router and confirm that your MAC is included on the "allowed" list of MACs in the MAC filtering page.

If you get no response from **ipconfig /all**, go to the Device Manager (**Start > Run**: **devmgmt.msc**). Make sure the NIC is enabled and has appropriate drivers. If the NIC is not present in the Device Manager, go to the BIOS. Make sure it is enabled. If the NIC is a peripheral component interconnect (PCI) or PCI express (PCIe), open the case (don't forget your antistatic wrist strap) and verify that the NIC is securely in the expansion slot. Go to Network Connections (**Start > Run: ncpa.cpl**) and make sure your NIC is represented by an icon. If it is not there, go back to the Device Manager, BIOS, inside, and so on. There is still something wrong with the physical layer. Note that laptops often have a button on the side that turns on and off the NIC and Bluetooth connections.

Troubleshooting TCP/IP

TCP/IP is not installed by default in Windows 95. For all other Microsoft operating systems, it is the default network protocol. From Network Connections in the Control Panel, right-click the NIC. Trace to Properties and add TCP/IP (you might need the OS CD). After you have installed TCP/IP (actually, "bound" it to the NIC), you can set the IP address manually or let DHCP handle the addressing scheme. Use **ping** to verify the protocol stack is working properly. First ping 127.0.0.1, the loopback address. Then ping your own IP address, your gateway, and then a remote site (for example, **ping www.cisco.com**). If there is a failure somewhere, go to that device and troubleshoot from there. In more complicated LANs or WLANs, use **tracert www.cisco.com**. The trace route command returns all the networking devices that are working properly. Note that some routers and firewalls drop **tracert** requests in an effort to fend off denial-of-service (DoS) attacks. A failed **tracert** does not necessarily mean a network problem.

Other Network Troubleshooting Techniques

ipconfig /? shows all the arguments of the command. A particularly useful one is **ipconfig /flushdns**. This forces the resolution of Domain Name System (DNS) entries. Other less-used commands are **NSLOOKUP**, which asks a DNS server what IP address is mapped to a specific friendly name, and **NETVIEW**, which shows other PCs in your workgroup.

Homework

Today offered lots of charts to memorize. Take a break and explore your network. From the command prompt, find the IP address of your PC, the hostname, and the gateway. What is the subnet mask? What class is the address?

Go down the many paths and keep a flowchart of the built-in XP Home and Small Office Network Troubleshooter. To start it, go to **Help and Support** in the Start menu. Click the **Networking and the Web** tab. Click **Fixing Networking or Web Problems**, and then **Home and Small Office**. Right before your exam, review the paths.

Next, memorize the networking charts. You have the A+ exam in five days! You have entered the complaint-free zone. No complaining allowed for the next five days. Besides, it's all easy sailing from here.

Funwork

If you have access to wireless devices, set up a WIFI spot.

Use Bluetooth on a laptop to transfer pictures to and from a cell phone.

Use a Bluetooth connection to a cell phone to send and receive faxes.

Download and try the free versions of VoIP (Skype, for instance). Lots of fun.

Security

A+ Essentials Exam Objectives

Objective 6.1: Identify the fundamental principles of security

Objective 6.2: Install, configure, upgrade and optimize security

Objective 6.3: Identify tool, diagnostic procedures and troubleshooting techniques for security

Objective 6.4: Perform preventive maintenance for computer security

Key Points

Security is an entire domain on the CompTIA A+ exam. Today is an easy day (and a little bit fun), but not any less important. Today you will spend time in Chapter 9 and Chapter 16 of the IT Essentials v4.0 course.

Security Threats

9.1: Not to sound like a conspiracy theorist, but yes, threats really do exist (threats that you as a technician cannot ignore). Some very smart and motivated people, often called hackers, want to know what you know. They want your company's payroll information. They want to know your customers' credit card numbers. Competitors may want to see you spend some quality downtime rebuilding databases and servers, or a neighbor might have a gripe about limited parking and start sending threatening e-mails from your account, launching denial-of-service (DoS) attacks with your name on them, or stealing your customer records. The problem is, hackers get to attack over and over again until they finally find the weak spot. You have to defend and defend and keep defending because hackers have all the time in the world.

9.2: Hackers work like this: They send out lots of feelers, spyware, port scanners, or whatever their preference. They are like wolves lunching on a pack of caribou. No wolf will take on a full-grown buck with a rack of antlers, 1200 pounds of hooves' pressure, and a really bitter attitude. They look for the sick, old, weak, injured, or, as in the case of a network hacker, clueless targets. The attack is quick. The hacker uses the information or more often sells it to the highest bidder. If hackers score big, they may blackmail the company and threaten media exposure. Imagine how much a bank would pay to "buy back" the financial records of its customers. Imagine how short your career would be if that bank were your computer client. Point: Taking security seriously is a career-enhancing move. Table 18-1 lists the basic kinds of attacks and their characteristics.

Table 18-1   Security Threats

Attack	Characteristics (In Order of Importance)
Theft	Theft is a major problem because of the cost and portability of the equipment and software.
DoS	Denial of service attacks a PC by flooding it with useless requests.
DDoS	Distributed denial of service is a DoS attack run by zombie machines to maximize the effect and make the attack difficult to trace.
Physical damage	Nothing takes down a website quicker than unplugging the server, or worse.
Trojan horse	Posing as harmless or even helpful software, a Trojan horse is really doing nasty things behind the scenes, like remotely controlling the target's PC or reading, modifying, or deleting files. These often come in the form of e-mail attachments or ActiveX, Java, or Javascript programs.
Worm	Worms are self-replicating software that fill hard drives and modify and spread to others. It is the most "virus"-like attack.
Phishing	This attack gains information from the target by pretending to be a technician or account representative or other trusted person.
Replay attacks	Replay attacks use packet sniffers to find a packet and gather usernames and passwords to be used later. Packet sniffers are a really cool tool for useful information, such as finding out who on your network is doing exactly what.
Spoofing	Spoofing changes the IP address, MAC, or any other identifying marker on a PC to pretend it is someone else.
DNS poisoning	DNS poisoning changes the entries in a Domain Name System (DNS) so that traffic is routed to a malicious site rather than to the legit target. This is especially bad if the malicious site looks and feels like the real target. If it looks like online banking, it must be legit, right?
Brute force	An example of brute force is password cracking by trial and error. Programs run millions of combinations and will happen upon the right combination eventually. The more complicated the password, the longer this process takes. Before they run a proper brute-force attack, password crackers will run a dictionary attack. All normal words are compared to the password file, and it takes a matter of seconds to discover an unhardened password this way.
Man-in-the-middle	Taken from a real espionage technique, this type of attack involves a sender, a receiver, and a secret man-in-the-middle. The sender sends a message to the receiver, and the man-in-the-middle intercepts the message along the way. He can then keep the message, or worse yet, forward false or misleading information to the receiver. Suppose you enter a username and password for a website. You get denied. Hmm. You try a different one that you use for other accounts. It doesn't work, either. You try again with a third password. Perhaps it was the other username. You try all the different usernames you use. The man-in-the-middle now has not just one, but many (perhaps all) of your usernames and passwords.
SYN flood	A SYN flood opens ports and requests attention just like a DoS.

WIFI Security

9.3.4: One of the toughest networks to secure is a WIFI connection. Everyone can hear everything being said. It is like yelling across a room full of people. Even if the message is not intended for everyone, and even if those who can probably won't pay attention to your conversation, you don't need to use this medium to explain personal problems or share credit card information. On the other hand, it is hard to downplay the convenience and ease of use of a WIFI connection. Table 18-2 lists the best WIFI security practices, which you will likely find on the A+ exam.

Table 18-2   WIFI Security

Security Technique	Characteristics (In Order of Importance)
Use antivirus (AV) software	This is a must. It allows the computer to have a fighting chance (a bit like white blood cells).
Use an adware-removal application	Ad-Aware is one of the most common applications, and a free version is available.
Update the OS and applications	Service packs and updates are often issued to address holes in security. Use them!
Install a firewall	Hardware firewalls have one in and one out. Traffic entering a network is analyzed by the firewall, which determines whether the traffic is legit. Software firewalls shut down ports except for the ones normally used and assigned to useful applications such as e-mail, web, and FTP.
Change the default password on the router	Username: Admin Password: Admin Admin is the standard and really needs to be changed on your router.
Use WEP encryption	Wired Equivalency Protocol (WEP) offers simple encryption and requires a key to be entered when initially connecting to a network. 64 bit is good, but 128 bit is better.
Harden passwords	Harden passwords by using many characters, uppercase and lowercase letters, symbols, and numbers, and by requiring new passwords frequently.
Don't broadcast your SSID	Not broadcasting the SSID means you will have to manually tell the devices on your WLAN the name of the network (the SSID). Others looking for networks will not see your network at all.
Use WPA and WPA2 encryption	Wi-Fi Protected Access (WPA) offers better encryption than WEP, and WPA2 is the current standard.
Use MAC filtering	The router issues IP addresses only to recognized MAC addresses. Good, but can be spoofed, and it is difficult to add new users. Not good for dynamic hot spots.
Update the router's firmware	Vulnerabilities are always being discovered, even in the firmware. Flash the router like you would a BIOS. (Read and follow the manufactures directions.)
Use LEAP or EAP-Cisco	Lightweight Extensible Authentication Protocol (LEAP), also called EAP-Cisco, is especially good when using Cisco routers and equipment.
Use WTLS and WAP	Wireless Transport Layer Security (WTLS) and Wireless Applications Protocol (WAP) are used on portable devices and are good for narrow-bandwidth conditions.

AV, Spyware Removal, and Definitions Updates

9.4: Don't run two AV applications simultaneously on the same PC. They attack each other's virus definition files. Do run one AV application, a good one. This is your second line of defense. The first is to keep malware from entering by using firewalls and security-awareness training for users. If a virus gets onto the PCs, a good AV will analyze the behavior of every file and watch for anything suspicious. This is called heuristics. The AV software should be set to automatically update its virus definitions and scan the PC at regular intervals. Sophisticated programs run when the system is busy or unattended so that the user is unaware of the reduced performance. Third-party spyware-removal software, like Ad-Aware, works with the AV like a second pair of eyes. Good AV programs from Norton, McAfee, and Microsoft include integrated spyware-removal tools.

Firewalls

16.2.3: Hardware firewalls act like a gate sentry that analyzes packets as they enter and exit a network. It works alongside the routers and switching equipment. Software firewalls close all network ports on a PC and allow only specific kinds of connections. Those are typically web, downloading, e-mail, and other common connection types.

User Training and Password Policies

9.3.3: Passwords are cracked all the time. If you haven't learned this skill, you will pick it up sooner or later. A client comes to you with a forgotten password. Is it hacking to break in and recover that data for the customer? Bad guys do this using three methods: by installing a Trojan keystroke monitor, brute force, or social engineering. The best thing we can do is harden passwords with numbers, symbols, and capital letters and make them expire so that new ones need to be used.

Troubleshooting Security

9.5: In IT and networking, you need to keep complete and detailed records. Security is no exception. Document what threats exist for your company, and audit the performance and security of your network periodically. Make a use policy and enforce it. If an event occurs, such as a theft or compromised data, document every aspect, even if it makes you look bad. Locking up laptops and other important devices is a good idea. Using biometric devices helps verify exactly who was where and had access to what. Radio frequency identification (RFID) tags can help track devices. Securing the equipment out of reach in server rooms and tamper-resistant screws help thwart unwanted access to the hardware. The BIOS password can be set to prevent changes to the BIOS or access to the computer. This is easily countered by the reset jumper on the motherboard.

Homework

Check your security center applet in the Control Panel. If it is all good (firewall: on, auto updates: enabled, AV: present and updated), pat yourself on the back and review the attacks and characteristics table. If not, get busy and download, install, and update an AV application and a spyware remover. Check out Download.com for these utilities.

Afterward, check out Days 25 to 23. Skim the reading and the curriculum to see whether there is anything that doesn't quite make sense. If so, write it down and research it on the web. Learn it, own it. Knowing the OS is a cornerstone of the A+ exam.

Funwork

In the way that bad guys want to know what you know, you need to know what they know. Go read some bad-guy blogs. Don't post anything there. They use newbies as target practice. Have some fun sleuthing around the dark underbelly of the web. Start with search queries of the different kinds of attacks.

Find a trial download keystroke monitor from a reputable site. Download.com is a good place to start. Monitor your own PC. Be legal about this. Some states and provinces have strict guidelines about espionage. Make sure it is you that you are spying on. If you have never seen this kind of stuff before, it will prove to be a real eye-opening experience. Google the phrases *password harvesting* or *forgotten passwords XP*. Could you recover files for a customer using an XP Pro CD?

Environmental Issues

A+ Essentials Exam Objectives

Objective 7.1: Describe the aspects and importance of safety and environmental issues

Objective 7.2: Identify potential hazards and implement proper safety procedures including ESD precautions and procedures, safe work environment and equipment handling

Objective 7.3: Identify proper disposal procedures for batteries, display devices and chemical solvents and cans

Objective 8.1: Use good communication skills including listening and tact/discretion, when communicating with customers and colleagues

Objective 8.2: Use job-related professional behavior including notation of privacy, confidentiality and respect for the customer and customers' property

Key Points

Today you review on-the-job hazards and safety tools all techs need to be aware of. Working in a customer environment also requires you to act professionally and responsibly. These topics relate to Chapter 2 and Chapter 10 of the IT Essentials v4.0 course.

Hazards

2.1: What are the safety hazards in your work area? Dangling cords, live electricity, exposed electronics, sharp edges on the cases, and lifting heavy boxes, to name a few. It isn't coal mining, but it is still plenty dangerous. Your clothing is a good place to start. Most uniforms for computer repair are polo shirts and khakis and rubber-soled (nonconductive) shoes. This is not just for comfort. Notice there is no conductive silk tie or long sleeves. The clothes are relatively inexpensive, so snags and toner spills are not financially catastrophic. Keep jewelry to a minimum if not absent. Picture yourself trying to retrieve an earring that has become wedged between the rollers of a laser printer. Name tags can even be a problem. More than one techie has had the horrific experience of a tie or lanyard dragged inside a copier machine. Funny, yes, but also dangerous.

Fire Safety

2.1.1: When using a fire extinguisher, remember: PASS. **P**ull the pin. (It takes more force than people realize). **A**im (A rookie mistake is to aim the spray at the flames, which are above the actual fire. Aim low.) **S**queeze the trigger. (Take and hold a big breath first because white powder, soot, ash, and hot cinders will go everywhere. Be ready for that.) **S**weep back and forth. Ideally, start the stream between you and the fire. That way, the propellant will push the fire away from you.

Fire extinguishers are rated by how well they put out different kinds of fires. Because yours is likely to be an electrical fire, the extinguisher should have a high C rating. Table 17-1 describes extinguisher ratings. CO_2 extinguishers are ideal for computers. Proper use of the different kinds of fire extinguishers might be worth another trip to YouTube.

Table 17-1   Fire Extinguisher Ratings

Rating	Use	Memorization Tips
A	Ordinary combustibles	A as in *all*, everything, ordinary stuff, paper, wood, carpet, and more.
B	Flammable liquids	B as in *bottle*. Every technician has a bottle of >70% isopropyl rubbing alcohol for cleaning.
C	Electrical equipment	C as in *computers*.
D	Combustible metals	D as in *degrees*. If you have a metal fire, use the extinguisher and then get out immediately. Metal fires rage at thousands of degrees.

Material Safety and Data Sheets (MSDS)

2.1.3: Material safety data sheets (MSDS) are found online. Inventory your work area and print out the pertinent MSDSs from the Internet. You need an MSDS for every hazardous material on the premises, including seemingly ordinary items, such as cleaners, solvents, and fuels (propane cylinders, heating oil, natural gas). Have them available for inspections, and if an emergency of some kind occurs, hand them to the incident commander. (That is, hand them to the firefighter who stands near the engine with a radio and a bad attitude, not the guys going in wearing a breathing apparatus. He could care less about paperwork.)

If something really bad does happen, write down everything, every detail, every person who was there, the time, date, weather, what you had for lunch that day, literally everything, and call your lawyer. Newbies make easy scapegoats. Don't be one.

Blocking door access, covering the fire extinguisher, disabling smoke alarms, and bypassing electricity shutoff are big no-nos. The Occupational Safety and Health Association (OSHA) specifically looks for those sorts of things. They also look for cords along the floor that could create tripping hazards. OSHA inspectors also look for daisy-chaining power strips. This is particularly dangerous because you can connect too many devices that draw too much power for the gauge (thickness) of the wire. Too small a wire and or too much current creates resistance and heat—lots of it. This can melt the PVC insulation, which not only creates a poisonous gas, but can cause a short between the wires and start a fire. Do not daisy chain power strips of surge protectors.

Tools

2.2: It is tempting and sometimes wise to limit the number of tools you lug around. After all, you don't need much, really. A Leatherman tool has most of the screwdrivers and pliers you will need. In addition, you should have a multimeter, compressed air, window-cleaning wipes, 70% isopropyl rubbing alcohol and cotton swabs, an antistatic wrist strap and mat, and a CD wallet with a legit copy of all the operating systems that you support. On those OS CDs, you can find utilities and disk management software such as Format, Fdisk, Scandisk or System File Checker, Defrag, and Disk Cleanup. Other tools you should have are antivirus protection, an adware and spyware remover, drivers, service packs, a USB network interface card (NIC) with drivers, a notebook, flashlight, and maybe some specialized test equipment or tools for cable making. It seems like a lot, but you should be able to fit everything in one bag. If you have the luxury of a bench and shop, the sky is the limit for tools. Table 17-2 lists other tools that you might see on the A+ exam.

Table 17-2   Less-Common Tools Found on the A+ Exam

Tool	Description
Torx	A star-shaped driver for specialized nuts and bolts.
Hex	A six-sided driver often referred to as an Allen wrench.
Part retriever	Long extension tool used to reach inside of deep narrow places to retrieve lost parts. Use the finger type (nonmagnetic) around (and especially inside) a PC.
Paint brush	A 1-inch paintbrush is useful for cleaning vents and removing dust from hard-to-reach places.
Flash drive	Useful for transferring files and performing quick backups.
Loopback tester (port tester)	These test ports by wiring the output back to the input. Send a signal, and it will test the port.

Electrostatic Discharge

2.2.1: Electrostatic discharge (ESD) is a vicious killer of electronics. It can strike silently, and you won't even know how or when it happened. It is caused when you and the equipment have different voltages, which is almost always. We pick up and lose electrons as we walk around and touch things. Cool and dry environments like those found in repair shops make ESD more prone to occur. Always, always touch the metal chassis before you touch anything else inside the PC. Making an connection with the electrical ground neutralizes static electricity. An antistatic wrist strap maintains that connection for the duration of your work. Antistatic mats create a static-free work area ideal for repairing electronics.

Disposing of Computer Components

2.1.3: Batteries must be taken to a collection center for recycling; you cannot legally just throw them away. Check your local government guidelines for specific locations. And because computers contain all kinds of potentially hazardous chemicals and metals, they, too, need to be disposed of properly or recycled. If your company is fined for failing to properly dispose of waste, your boss will want to know what steps you have taken to educate the employees about this. You need to have a good answer. Further, this is another great reason to keep detailed notes.

Customer Support

10.2: Think about the times you've called a customer support number. How long were you kept waiting to speak to someone? When you finally did reach a human, was it easy to speak with the person, or did that person have difficulty communicating with you? Regardless of accent or language barriers, did he or she use terms you didn't understand? Did the customer service personnel take the time to explain those terms? Did they interrupt you to finish your sentence, or hurriedly arrive at a conclusion, disregarding your input? Did they ever use your name, besides perhaps just the one time at the beginning of the conversation?

Now you are providing customer support. If your loved one called you for technical help, you wouldn't make those kinds of mistakes. In fact, those kinds of mistakes would be disrespectful. Remember that the person who calls you for help is somebody's loved one. They are your boss. They are your colleagues. They are your family, friends, and your neighbors. If they called you from somewhere foreign to you, from a place you perhaps can't even pronounce, they are still all of these things. Treat them as such. If language or accents prevent effective communication, consider online live chats.

Customers do not speak geek. You do. Sometimes other techies call tech support and you can speak in your shared language, but that is not usually the case. Generally, it is a perfectly intelligent person who is unfamiliar with a new thing. What if you were to trade places with a auto mechanic or a cosmetologist for a day. Would you have a bunch of "dumb" questions? Imagine how lost you would if those around you in your new field communicated only in jargon and acronyms and referred to "common knowledge" (uncommon to you).

Realize the role you have. You have the answers, they have questions and the money. Further, they know other people with both questions and money. Work together, clarify, simplify, and be professional. If you do so, you will soon be known as the computer go-to person. And for heaven's sakes, don't lose or break customers' property or data.

Service Level Agreements

10.2.6: It is hard to quantify exactly what good customer service is. One technique is a service level agreement (SLA). It is a description of exactly what the customer can expect from you, which specific equipment you will support and for how long, costs, diagnostics, preventive maintenance, and penalties for failing to adhere to these descriptions.

Homework

Walk through your place of business or home and make a list of hazardous materials. Download the MSDSs from the web and impress your employer. Establish a specific place where batteries can be stored until properly disposed of. Many can be recycled; none can legally be thrown away with the "regular" trash.

Check the blogs and forums to determine which tools you need, and don't be shy about asking what utilities other people use. Those are the *real* tools.

Funwork

Macintosh computers are notoriously easy to fix, so Mac technicians can focus their efforts and training on customer service. Go to a local Apple store and hang out by the Genius Bar. Quite frankly, Apple has the best customer service technicians anywhere. Just listen to the interactions while pretending to ogle the newest addition to the iEverything world. Hear how they use both open- and closed-ended questions. Pay attention to how the technicians listen to their customers. They are experts at listening. They always repeat the customer's question back to the customer so that the customer knows that the technician heard correctly. Seldom do you hear them use jargon, other than marketing terms such as IEEE 1394, SMS, and so on. Never do they talk down to their customers. It really is an outstanding example of how technicians can and should interact with customers.

In the unlikely case the technician isn't following these practices, stick around anyway to see how the customer reacts. Then, seek out another technician who is providing good customer service to compare how that technician's client responds differently to the better treatment.

Essentials Review Day

You made it! The major work is over. Today you will put the finishing touches on your exam preparation. You will make a "cheat sheet" and take some practice tests.

The Cheat Sheet Study Technique

Make a cheat sheet. *This is not an actual cheat sheet.* Use both sides of one piece of paper to write down everything you might forget while taking your A+ exam. It is a way of practicing your brain dumps, mnemonics, and memorized charts. Write down any statements that will help you.

Now do the same thing over again, and again. Eventually, you will be able to do this from memory. When you can do it for memory, you *know* the material.

Review this sheet one last time right before your test, but don't actually bring it into the testing center with you. Your intentions could be misinterpreted by the staff.

For the record, cheating on any certification exam is a horrible idea. It is also expensive considering the price of these exams. The proctors are smart people; they look for cheating. You will be on camera, and most of all… you don't need to cheat.

Homework

Take some free online practice exams. (Make sure they are 2006 objectives.) This is a great opportunity to expand your "cheat sheet" if necessary. A great place to practice is http://www.proprofs.com.

Funwork

Go do something different today. Seriously, you have spent a great deal of time preparing for this exam. Reward yourself with a meal out, a walk in the park, a concert, a dance club, or whatever you call fun. Everyone needs recess.

Most important, though, get a good night's sleep!

Essentials Exam Day

The Perfect Score

The perfect score is the one that passes. 900 out of 900 on the A+ is like a 2400 on the SAT: very, very rare. Don't let mean techies who suffer from IT bravado tell you otherwise. Ask them to show you their perfect score report.

Keep it in perspective. Unlike a perfect SAT that provides unparalleled academic opportunities, a perfect A+ score will never hold the same clout. Point: Don't stress over it. A simple passing score on the A+ is just as good as a great score. This is what you need to focus on. Here are some exam details and reminders:

- 90 minutes.

- 100 questions.

- 75% to pass.

- Don't forget two forms of picture ID.

- Bring a method of payment (for example, a voucher or credit card).

- Get there early.

- Don't bring any electronic devices, water bottles, paper, or writing utensils. (Pen and scratch paper are provided.)

- Use the bathroom before the test (seriously).

Before the Exam

Review your "cheat sheet" right before the exam. Do not cheat. Remember, cheating is for stupid people, not for you. As soon as they hand you scratch paper and a pen, write down all your brain dumps, tables, mnemonics, charts, diagrams, religious prayers, whatever you like. Be sure to give this back to them at the end of the exam.

During the Exam

Keep in mind the following few tips while taking the exam.

RTDQ

Read the doggone question (RTDQ). It might seem like common sense, but you didn't just spend two weeks and a couple hundred dollars to miss questions because you were stressed and in a hurry. Slow down and read every word in every question, twice. Think about what the question is asking. But do not think so much that you read things into the question. Treat this process like customer service. Repeat the question to the "customer" for clarification.

Then, and only then, read the possible answers. On a standard multiple choice question, 75% of the answers are there to trick you. They are not your friends. Do not give them time to insert doubt and fear. Just eliminate the obvious distracters and make an informed decision.

The Most Important Test-Taking Tip

When you get a question to which you do not know the answer, take a breath and call that one a loss. Eliminate the obvious incorrect answers (the distracters) and make an educated guess from the remaining options. Remember it only takes 75% (675 points out of 900) to pass. It is better to take a small loss on a few questions so that you can instead focus on the overall win.

After the Exam

This is the fork in the road. Immediately following your exam, your Exam Score Report will include a breakdown of how you did in each domain. Analyze your scores by domain to determine which test to take next.

Here are the next exams explained by domain percentages. Their content and focus vary. You need take only one of these to finish your A+ Certification. Find the one that most resembles your score report and choose that section of the book to continue on your path to A+ Certification. In addition to the score analysis, you might take some 602, 603, and 604 practice exams to get a feel for the material.

220-602 Field Technician

Field technician is the jack-of-all-trades path. This person is hired by an IT department in a company to be the tech guru. If you can't pinpoint any specific area that you excelled in, this might be your next exam. If you have no particular desire to be a reclusive bench tech or customer-service-oriented remote tech, consider this exam. Table 15-1 outlines the domain percentages for the 220-602 exam.

Table 15-1   220-602 Field Technician Exam Domain Percentages

Domain	%
Personal Computer Components	18%
Laptop and Portable Devices	9%
Operating Systems	20%
Printers and Scanners	14%
Networks	11%
Security	8%
Safety and Environmental Issues	5%
Communication and Professionalism	15%

220-603 Remote Technician

A remote technician goes out and fixes the problem at the customer's site. If you are a people person and can live with operating systems, this is your next test. This exam contains no laptop or safety and environmental issues. Table 15-2 shows the domain percentages.

Table 15-2   Remote Technician Exam Domain Percentages

Domain	%
Personal Computer Components	15%
Operating Systems	29%
Printers and Scanners	10%
Networks	11%
Security	15%
Communication and Professionalism	20%

220-604 Bench Technician

Bench technicians do not typically interact with customers. As the name suggests, they stand at a bench and computers come to them. If you are good with hardware and good at memorizing all the little details that accompany hardware, this is for you. Gone are the Operating Systems, Networks, and Communication and Professionalism sections, as you can see in Table 15-3. If those areas gave you trouble, you might consider this test. It is a narrow and focused exam.

Table 15-3   Bench Technician Exam Domain Percentages

Domain	%
Personal Computer Components	45%
Laptop and Portable Devices	20%
Printers and Scanners	20%
Security	5%
Safety and Environmental Issues	10%

Choosing your next exam is a big decision. Sleep on it.

Part II

Taking the Field Technician Exam 220-602

Hardware: A Closer Look

A+ 220-602 Exam Objective

Objective 1.1: Install, configure, optimize and upgrade personal computer components

Key Points

Field technicians go to the end-user site to install, troubleshoot, and repair things. While on site, they are often peppered with questions ranging from their opinions about Vista to workplace politics. It requires people skills, a level head, and good troubleshooting skills (a Jack-of-all-trades). Today you will focus on topics related to Chapter 11 of the IT Essentials v4.0 course.

Seriously SCSI

11.3.6: It is time to learn all the gritty details about small computer system interface (SCSI). Far too many people believe that *SCSI* is synonymous with *server*. The fact is that after 20 years of development and countless versions, SCSI is still half as fast and twice the price of serial advanced technology attachment (SATA), not to mention the fact that SATA drives are so easy to install an end user could do it. (But don't tell your customers that.) Because some customers demand SCSI and some servers still use it, we must still support it.

The three most common problems found in SCSI arrays are

- Wrong family (type)
- Wrong device number (ID)
- No termination

Every device in a SCSI array must be the same SCSI type. A 68-bit-wide cable will not connect to an 80-pin drive, a narrow 8-bit interface will not play with a 16-bit-wide one. Rule of thumb: Just as you do for processors and motherboards, confirm the compatibility before you buy.

Wide means it is 16 bits of parallel data, and *narrow* is 8 bits and newer. SCSI is similar to SATA in that it is serial. Unless otherwise specified, it is an 8-bit-wide (narrow) bus.

The 80-pin cables include power in the cable, just like SATA drives. The 50- and 68-pin interfaces require a Molex power cable. Something to seriously consider when building a SCSI system is the wattage of the power supply and the number of Molex plugs. Fifty-pin cables use Centronics plugs, like the printer end of a parallel cable.

Single-ended (SE) cable lengths are 1.5 (5 feet) to 6 meters (roughly 20 feet). These lengths are not a problem for internal devices, but these distances can be limiting for external printers, scanners, and other bulky external devices that probably ought not take up premium desk space.

High-voltage differential (HVD) cables can go up to 70 m but have speed limitations. At that length, it is time to look at networking options.

The happy compromise is low-voltage differential (LVD). For most applications, 12 m is just fine. Notice that the cables with 80 pins support 15 devices. Table 14-1 lists SCSI types and their details. Note that the oldest SCSI technologies are listed first.

Table 14-1   SCSI Comparison Chart

SCSI Type	Speed	Pins	Number of Devices
SCSI-1	5 MBps	50 or 68	7
Fast SCSI (SCSI-2)	10 MBps	50 or 68	7
Fast Wide SCSI (SCSI-2)	20 MBps	68 or 80	15
Ultra SCSI (SCSI-3)	20 MBps	50 or 68	7
Wide Ultra SCSI (SCSI-3)	40 MBps	68 or 80	7 or 15
Ultra 2 SCSI (SCSI-4)	40 MBps	50 or 68	7
Wide Ultra 2 SCSI (SCSI-4)	80 MBps	68 or 80	15
Ultra 3 SCSI (Ultra160/m)	80 MBps	50 or 68	15
Wide Ultra 3 SCSI (Ultra160/m)	160 MBps	68 or 80	15
Wide Ultra 320 SCSI	320 MBps	68 or 80	15

Legacy Expansion Slots

11.4: Table 14-2 lists older expansion slots. They are often not tested on the A+ exam, but are sometimes used as distracters.

Table 14-2   Legacy Expansion Slots

Expansion Slot	Need to Know (In Order of Importance)
ISA (industry standard architecture)	16 bit, 8.3 MHz, supports Plug-and-Play and is usually colored black.
PCIX (PCI extended)	64-bit version of peripheral component interconnect (PCI). Currently, much less common than peripheral component interconnect express (PCIe).
MCA	Micro Channel Architecture, manufactured by IBM.
EISA	Extended ISA wider bus (32-bit), longer slot.
VESA (Video Electronics Standards Association)	(VL-Bus, VESA Local Bus) If accelerated graphics port (AGP) is the father of a PCIe video card, its grandfather is VESA.

Old-School D Plugs

1.5: Serial and parallel ports use D plugs. The *D* refers to the trapezoid shape of the grounded housing that surrounds the pins. The number of pins ranges from 9 pins, as in DE9, to 50 pins of the DD specification. The three that are likely to be on the Field Technician exam are DA15 (a.k.a. joystick port), DB25 (parallel if female, serial if male), and the DE9 standard serial port. These ports are found when a computer is connected to cash registers, robots, chip programming consoles, exotic or old printers, and other far-from-typical, end-user devices (such as Cisco networking devices). Note that the VGA port and joystick port are both 15-pin D plugs. The difference (besides usage) is that the joystick has two rows and the VGA has three rows of five pins.

The name DB9, sometimes with an *M* at the end to designate male, has given way to the name RS232 or just serial.

IEEE 1284 vintage parallel ports come in three flavors: standard parallel port (SPP), enhanced parallel port (EPP), and extended capabilities port (ECP). SPP is unidirectional (one way) and slower. EPP is bidirectional and uses a direct memory access (DMA) to increase speed. ECP is faster still, bidirectional (two way), and the current standard parallel port. A standard parallel printer cord has a Centronics port on the printer end and a DB25 on the other.

Game controllers today are almost always USB. This was not always the case. Older sound cards often have a 15-pin female port (DA15) designed for game controllers, lovingly referred to as joysticks. VGA ports are also 15-pin female ports, but they are arranged in 3 rows of 5, whereas the DA15 has 2 rows and looks like a shorter parallel port.

D plugs and the VGA port have threaded screws that can secure the plug to the port. Good news: They won't fall out. Bad news: If the computer is shoved against a wall, the secured port will snap and break the actual motherboard inside. If they are plugged in but not tightened, they will simply become unplugged if force is applied to them (in which case, you just have to reconnect it). A broken motherboard is often the economic death of a PC. It is a shame to see a serial port cause the death of an otherwise good machine.

Absolute Power Supplies

11.3.1: Occasionally, you will find an oddly shaped PC, such as a really small shoebox-shaped PC or flat U1 or U2 rack-mounted server. These devices don't fit a regular advanced technology extended (ATX) power supply or motherboard. In addition to the wattage and number of DC plugs on the power supply, several unique form factors provide power to these exotic case configurations. Table 14-3 lists these.

Table 14-3   Oddly Shaped Power Supplies

Power Supply	Supports
TFX12V	Low-profile ATX
LFX12V	Low-profile BTX (balanced technology extended)
SFX12V	FlexATX
CFX12V	Micro BTX (L shaped)

Homework

Review SCSI. It is a source of tricky exam questions and a topic with which many new technicians have not had much experience.

Memorize the legacy expansion slots.

Definitely be able to identify and know the differences between DB9, DB15, DB25, and VGA ports.

Download a copy of all the acronyms used on the A+ exams from the CompTIA website (http://certification.comptia.org/a/). It is a part of the objectives downloads.

Funwork

Walk up to an IT old-timer and say, "I remember a time people used floppy disks and a 10/100 NIC was awesome." Bring a comfy chair because the old-timer will likely counter, "Oh yeah, I remember a time when…." These legacy guys love to sit around, perform backups, watch status bars, and reminisce about the good old days. Ask them about old printers, coaxial network cables, 3-n-300 NICs, D plugs. Let them spend half an hour telling you how it once was.

Yes, it is as painful as you imagine, but also enlightening and useful, too. Consider who writes the questions for the A+ exam. It is important to hear the old pro's perspective on things because that is the angle from which the test is written.

Listen to the vocabulary, diction, acronyms, and verbs. Match what you know with what they know. That overlap is where the test focuses. Question them and find out what is important in their opinion. Find out why "this or that" outdated concept or technology is still *so* crucial to understand. These guys really are a font of knowledge. Be respectful, and remember many of them saw the dawn of our field. They get lots of cool points for being there. When you have had your fill of Leave It to Geezer, have someone text you with something really important to do. Otherwise, you might be stuck there until you, too, are an IT old-timer.

Hardware Troubleshooting

A+ 220-602 Exam Objective

Objective 1.2: Identify tools, diagnostic procedures and troubleshooting techniques for personal computer components

Key Points

Today you will cover troubleshooting monitor and audio issues, which is an important concept in the real world and one that may appear on the A+ exam. From Chapter 11 of the IT Essentials v4.0 course, you will explore keyboard problems. Troubleshooting hardware is really a critical part of your job. It is also one of the most fun parts.

Troubleshooting Monitor Issues

Sometimes, you will find multiple video ports on a computer:

- Dual-, triple-, quad-monitor video cards (one card that supports multiple monitors).

- Multiple video cards each support a monitor.

- One card that supports different video modes. It will use any combination of digital visual interface (DVI), video graphics array (VGA) component video, and high definition media interface (HDMI). These cards usually send the same signal out all ports.

- An integrated video card with an additional video card installed in an expansion slot. In this case, always plug the monitor into the standalone video card, not the integrated one. Often, it is disabled automatically when a video card is present in an expansion slot.

Be able to identify the monitor LED colors. An amber (or yellow) color means that the monitor is on but not receiving a signal from the PC; that is, the monitor is expecting but not getting information to display. The monitor could be unplugged, turned off, or in sleep/power-saving mode. Make sure the monitor has power. A green light means the monitor is on and receiving a signal. You should see stuff on the screen. If not, explore settings on the monitor (such as contrast and brightness). If still nothing, recycle or dispose of the monitor according to local government codes.

Modern display devices are usually quite good at recognizing the resolution and automatically adjusting. Sometimes that is not the case. Restart the PC and press F5 during startup. In 9x, enter safe mode and reduce the resolution in the Display Properties in the Control Panel. In NT/XP/Vista, choose last known good configuration.

Video driver issues are easy to spot: wrong colors, too few colors, black borders around the screen (unused screen). In XP, use the Driver Rollback feature in the Device Manager. In all operating systems, go online and download the latest drivers for your video card and install them. If the problem prevents you from seeing well enough, use a different computer and burn the drivers to CD.

Before writing off a monitor, plug it into a known-good PC and see whether the problem still exists. If doing this resolves the symptoms, look at the RAM and video RAM. Not enough of either will wreak havoc on the video quality. (Imagine playing a high-graphics video on an older business-class PC, for example.) You can lower the refresh rate in the Display Properties or in the application. Another source of video problems is the cable. Look for sharp bends, abrasions, and bent or missing pins.

Can You Hear Me Now?

For some reason, "no sound" is among the most common end-user complaints. The fact is that there are volume controls all throughout the layered PC model. At the physical layer, the speakers need power and a connection to the sound card. Speakers often have their own volume control. The connection uses a mini stereo jack formally known as 3.5 mm TRS (tip, ring, sleeve). The standard card has pink, blue, and green sound ports. Pink and blue are audio in. Microphones (as in headsets and speech-to-text or teleconferencing scenarios) should use the microphone (mic) input. The main speaker out is green. It is usually a stereo port, to support a left and right signal. Better sound cards have many kinds of ports, including for Dolby 5.1 and for subwoofers and all kinds of shapes and arrangements of speakers. Plugging the audio devices into the wrong ports makes for a very quiet multimedia experience.

Digital audio signals, such as Sony/Phillip Digital Interconnect Format (S/PDIF), must be connected to speakers that can decode binary signals and turn them into analog sound. This process is called digital to audio conversion (DAC). Modems and microphones use this technology and the reverse, aptly named audio to digital conversion (ADC).

At the OS layer, there are more volume controls in the Control Panel and via the system tray icons on the taskbar. Even the applications themselves usually have a volume control.

At every layer, these volume controls need to be set for midrange. In addition, make sure that volume is not muted at any of these sources of volume control. Also, consider that the speakers might be broken. Use known-good speakers to test this possibility.

Beyond that, the sound needs to be enabled in the BIOS and the correct driver must be installed. To test the sound, make sure you test it from a CD, a file, or video, and from the Sounds applet in the Control Panel. Further, every conceivable event in the OS can be assigned a sound. That is also handled in the Sounds applet in the Control Panel. If the Sounds applet does not recognize the audio device, go back to the BIOS, drivers, and physical installation. Something went wrong.

Quirky Qwerty

11.4.6: A user complains of a keyboard malfunction. You might be tempted to label it a PEBCAK error (problem exists between customer and keyboard). Often it is. However, if the keyboard types incorrect characters, it could be one of several issues. Laptops typically overlay a 10-key keypad over the QWERTY keyboard. The Num Lock key toggles between normal keyboard and the 10-key keypad. When entering passwords, this and Caps Lock can be most frustrating.

The Keyboard option in the Control Panel allows for exotic keyboard support. Dvorak is another way to arrange the keys on a keyboard in a way that is more ergonomically correct. You can change this in Regional and Language Options in the Control Panel.

Language packs and special characters are also another source of strange keyboard issues. Languages are handled in the Control Panel. New language packs are found on the OS CD and are available from MS online, too. Word and other word processors have autocorrect features that automatically respell commonly misspelled words. Occasionally, the programming makes unwanted changes. Although that is beyond the scope of the A+ exam, it is a common customer question.

If the keyboard does not type anything, check the physical layer first. Older systems that use PS/2 ports for the keyboard and mouse are easy to switch accidentally. They are usually color coded or otherwise indicated by icon (so that you can determine which is for the keyboard and which is for the mouse). In the absence of any indication of which is for the mouse and which is for the keyboard, know that the keyboard is the one closest to the motherboard. PS/2 input devices are not hot swappable. You will need to restart the PC for them to work.

Wireless keyboards are nice but pose another layer of problems. If they use infrared (IR), the keyboard and receiver need to be lined up like a remote control and TV. The range of radio frequency (RF) coverage varies by make and model. When working with wireless devices, consider the needs of the presenter in an auditorium versus the needs of an office worker. Wireless keyboards can also interfere with each other. If someone can move your arrow and his own, too, use the dip switches or jumpers inside to change the frequency to avoid that kind of interference. Some wireless keyboard/mice systems use a button to activate. Look for this when troubleshooting such systems. A final note about wireless devices: They eat batteries. Check there first when troubleshooting. Also consider rechargeable batteries (Earth first and all).

Homework

Use the Help feature built in to Windows to troubleshoot the following problems. Run the tool multiple times and explore the many divergent paths in this troubleshooting tree:

- The mouse does not move the arrow.

- The keyboard types the wrong characters.

- The speakers do not make sound.

- The monitor does not display anything.

Funwork

Find another computer person (yes, it certainly could be the IT old-timer from yesterday), buy him a coffee, and spend some time role playing. He calls you for PC help. It starts with you saying, "Hi, my name is… How may I help you?" He replies by describing the symptoms, but seems to have a bad attitude. Your job is to balance troubleshooting with customer service. Although you may be facing one another in this exercise, on the phone you cannot see the person or the computer. The caller is your eyes, ears, and hands, and you are the brains of the operation.

It might seem silly at first, but role playing is truly one of the most important activities you can do to prepare you for help desk work and the A+ exam. This exercise can be done via texting or instant messaging (IM), too.

Do the preceding activity but add different kinds of customers, such as the mean manager in a hurry, the 8-year-old whose report won't print, another tech person like yourself, and the teenager who can't connect his laptop to his phone via Bluetooth and uses the words *like* and *dude* way too much. Scale your interaction and vocabulary to each of these situations. Mix it up and be creative.

Hardware Preventive Maintenance

A+ 220-602 Exam Objective

Objective 1.3: Perform preventive maintenance of personal computer components

Key Points

Today is the last general PC hardware day. You will cover more specialized hardware, such as laptops, printers, and so on in the coming days. Today you will cover safety and tools from Chapter 11 and cleaning from Chapter 2 of the IT Essentials v4.0 course.

Maintenance Toolkit

11.2.2: The A+ Field Technician exam (220-602) covers the basic toolkit. It contains Phillips and flat-head screwdrivers and hex and torx drivers. A basic five-in-one screwdriver has most of what you need.

The basic kit also includes some seldom, if ever, used tools like a three-prong reach tool to grab fallen screws or jumpers. A hemostat is a fancy name for long tweezers that close and lock. Typically, these are used in surgery, not computer repair. The integrated circuit (IC) puller removes old BIOS chips. Modern ones are EEPROM (erasable programmable read-only memory), nonremovable chips. The fix is a flash update rather than an IC puller. In the unlikely event you need to use the IC puller, be sure that the new BIOS chip is oriented correctly. Unlike the CPU that has a missing pin or some other keyed method, BIOS chips have a half circle on one end that needs to correspond with a similar shape printed on the motherboard.

Your toolkit will grow and change as your needs change. If you need much more than a few tools and a CD wallet full of operating systems and utilities, you really ought to consider taking the PC to a shop. The bench tech has every tool under the halogen lamp. Day 12, "The Right Tool for the Right Job," of Part IV covers those tools.

Safety First

11.2.1: You will be in unfamiliar environments every day. These are some safety basics likely to appear on the A+ Field Technician exam. They are also generally good ideas:

- *Do not* eat or drink or make a mess in your work area.

- *Do not* wear jewelry or watches.

- *Do not* look at lasers in printers or scanners or fiber-optic cables.

- *Do not* wear an antistatic wrist strap when working with high-voltage stuff like wall testing power, laser printer, CRT monitors, or power supplies.

- *Do* use an antistatic wrist strap when inside the PC.

- *Do* turn off the power and unplug the power cord.

- *Do* cover the sharp edges inside the PC with tape.

- *Do* have a fire extinguisher and first-aid kit near by.

Cleaning Solutions

2.3.4: The A+ Field Technician exam will likely ask you about when to use what cleaning product. The following is a list of cleaning best practices:

- Make sure the PC is off (remove any batteries from laptops).

- Remove any peripherals; they might have their own power supply.

- Spray mild detergent onto the lint-free cloth, not onto the PC directly.

- Never use abrasive or lint-laden materials, such as paper towels on soft LCD screens, lenses, CDs, scanners, print or optical readers, anything that could get scratched or is sensitive to dust from the rag.

- Monitors and most PC components are best served with antistatic materials. Use them if it is an option.

- A solution of >70% isopropyl alcohol is used for cleaning electrical contacts.

- Never use solvents or glass cleaner (which often include ammonia) on an LCD screen.

Homework

Make your toolkit. Collect all the utilities, disk managers, antivirus software, emergency boot disks, and so on and burn them to brand new CDs and store the originals in a safe. Put all this in a backpack or case.

Review the charts from Days 31 and 30, especially the interrupt request (IRQ), direct memory access (DMA), and I/O addresses.

Funwork

"Make" a point-of-sale (POS) computer system. Of course, it is just a pretend one, but you will see a great example of how all your hardware knowledge is applied in the real world. Price out the pieces and make sure the components are compatible. It needs a thermal printer for receipts and a laser scanner that reads barcodes. Make sure it includes an application that can understand bar-codes. If you want a challenge, find a scale that communicates with your PC for weighing pro-duce. Don't forget that many products use radio frequency identification (RFID) in addition to bar-codes. Redundancy and reliability is important here because this is a mission-critical computer. Can you make a cheaper system than commercially produced POSs? Don't forget the credit card reader and software to run all the devices. There is an entire industry within the computer repair world dedicated to creating and supporting POSs. Compare your POS system to that of the pros. There are all-in-one portable (handheld) POS systems.

Laptops and Peripherals

A+ 220-602 Exam Objectives

Objective 2.1: Identify fundamental principles of using laptops and portable devices

Objective 2.2: Install, configure, optimize and upgrade laptops and portable devices

Objective 2.3: Use tools, diagnostic procedures and troubleshooting techniques for laptops and portable devices

Key Points

Truly, laptops and cell phones are the future of PCs. This is a little scary for us in the repair business because both laptops and cell phones are rarely fixable considering the cost of replacement and rapid price depreciation. Entire offices are converting to laptops because they are often as cheap as their desktop counterparts. They use less electricity. And we can't forget the coolness factor. Today you will focus on topics from Chapter 6 and Chapter 13 of the IT Essentials v4.0 course.

Networking for Laptops

13.1: There are five main methods to connect a portable device wirelessly to a network or to the Internet: Bluetooth, infrared (IR), cellular WAN, local WIFI, and worldwide satellite.

Because laptops, personal digital assistants (PDA), and other portable devices scream "steal me," it is never a good idea to store anything you can't afford to lose. Network drives or their more formal parent network file servers enable you to set up a share point to save your work there, either as a backup or exclusively if security is an issue. The data capacity of a proper file server can be mindboggling. Consider the database servers that run Amazon.com. Network file servers allow for multiple users to modify a common file. This central point is both good and bad for reliability. It greatly simplifies backups, but it is a central point of failure, too.

Networked projectors are a great networking device for several reasons:

- The presentation files are sent like transferring a file to a network file server, complete with permissions and security.

- Because the files live directly on the projector, this eliminates the need for expensive, fragile, extremely long video cables.

- It frees up the presenter to carry around a simple remote instead of being tied to a podium with a PC. It is also possible to stream the presentation across the network, but you run the risk of glitchy performance in a high-network-traffic environment.

Video RAM

13.3.4: Remember the drawback to integrated video cards? They use the system memory and the southbridge, tying up critical resources that should be used for other things, such as the CPU. If your customer (or you) is price shopping for a bargain-basement laptop, make sure that it has good graphics. It should have its own video random access memory (VRAM) and preferably have a brand name like NVIDIA or ATI. You will pay more at the outset, but your eyes will not tire as quickly and you will get better overall performance from your laptop.

Hot Swappable and Not Swappable

6.4.2: Mistaking a device that is not hot swappable for one that is can let out the magic blue smoke that makes it work. It is really important to know which devices are hot swappable and which are not so that you do not destroy both the device and the motherboard. Table 11-1 reviews what is and what isn't hot swappable for all PCs, not just for laptops.

Table 11-1   Drive-Swapability Comparison

Hot Swappable	Not Swappable
SATA drives	PATA drives
Modern SCSI array drives	RAM
FireWire	PCI, PCIe, PCIX, AGP, ISA
USB	PS/2
PCMCIA	Serial
HDMI, DVI, VGA	Parallel

Measuring Memory and Speed: When Size Matters

6.3.4: When customers ask, "How big is this memory card?" they are not concerned about the physical dimensions or even bytes. We computer geeks know that "memory" is RAM, dynamic and volatile. Customers purchasing a camera know memory as flash, static, like USB or solid-state drives that we call storage. Marketing people take the blame for this confusion. Still, we do not want to parse words with customers, especially when commissions and repeat business are on the line. Customers expect an answer in terms they understand.

Digital cameras are rated in megapixels. Flash storage is measured in bytes. The resolution (number of megapixels) and the size of the field of view determine the size of the JPG file. These are approximate values, but they should give you some ballpark answer either for a customer or on the A+ exam. Of course, the short answer is the more storage, the more megapixels, the better. Music and video take up considerable room. A typical popular music MP3 song is roughly four minutes and takes about 4.3 MB of space at a standard 128-kbps compression. Video MPG4 using the standard H.264 compression is measured in minutes. The quality and resolution of photos and video greatly affect the size of the files. These file sizes and limitations hold true for any storage device, iPods, cell phones, cameras, even HDDs. Table 11-2 gives you and your customers a feel for file size and capacity.

Table 11-2   Flash Memory in Real-World Terms

File Type and Quality	512-MB Memory Card	1-GB Memory Card	2-GB Memory Card
3-megapixel JPG	500	1000	2000
6-megapixel JGP	180	320	640
12-megapixel JPG	80	160	320
128-kbps compressed MP3	120	240	480
H.264 compressed MPEG4	70 min	140 min	280 min

Storage cards are measured in access speed, just like optical drives: n x 1.5 MBps = access speed. "N" is the rating. For example, 40X means 40 x 1,500,000 bytes per second = 6 MBps access speed. Why is this important? Speed and quality go hand in hand with multimedia. How often have we opted not to watch a video online because it was loading too slowly, or was too poor a quality to see what was going on? Table 11-3 lists common speeds of flash storage.

Table 11-3   Flash Memory Access Speed

Rating	Speed
40X	6 MBps
66X	10 MBps
80X	12 MBps
133X	20 MBps
266X	40 MBps

Bluetooth Classes

13.1.1: Normally, as the version or class number increases, so does performance. This is not the case in Bluetooth. Class 1 is the longest range, with the most power (and also the most hearable by others). An earpiece for a cell phone does not need a Class 1. On the other hand, that might be exactly what is required at a sporting event or auditorium. Table 11-4 lists the three Bluetooth classes, power ratings, and distances.

Table 11-4   Bluetooth Class Comparison

Class	Max Watts	Max Distance
Class 1	100 mW	100 m
Class 2	2.5 mW	10 m
Class 3	1 mW	1 m

Homework

Memorize the swappable and not swappable devices in Table 11-1.

Review the flash memory information in Tables 11-2 and 11-3.

Memorize the Bluetooth information in Table 11-4.

Funwork

Your company just got a new e-mail system and wants to streamline training by offering it in the form of a downloadable video. Price out a video camera with external microphone inputs for better sound quality. Make sure it is a good one because you are going to be in charge of this project. More, you are going to be *in* these videos teaching your friends and colleagues. They wouldn't dare tease you about your Emmy-quality performance, would they? This is a surprisingly realistic scenario and another good reason to practice and improve your people and presentation skills.

Operating Systems: A Closer Look

A+ 220-602 Exam Objective

Objective 3.1: Identify the fundamental principles of operating systems

Objective 3.2: Install, configure, optimize and upgrade operating systems

Key Points

Today you review the command switches, shared folders, languages, and accessibility options. You can find these topics in Chapters 5 and 15 of the IT Essentials v4.0 course.

Command-Line Switches

5.1.2: The A+ Field Technician exam (220-602) is notorious for asking about the command-line switches. The next few tables are commands and the switches you should know. Also know that in Vista, you either need to be logged on as an administrator or run the command prompt (CMD) as an administrator to give you access to all of these commands. Right-click the icon and select **Run as Administrator**.

dir

The **dir** command shows the contents of the directory. Table 10-1 lists the **DIR** switches.

Table 10-1   dir Switches

Switch	Explanation
/o	Sort files by order.
/oe	Order by extension.
/on	Order by name (alphabetically). (This is the same as **/o**.)
/og	Order by group (directories first).
/od	Order by date (most recent at the end).
/os	Order by size.
/p	Display the output page by page (nice feature when working with very long directories).
/w	Display the output wide, across the screen.
/a	Display the files and their attributes.
/s	Show all the files in the current directory and the files in subdirectories. Note: This could take a while. Ctrl-C will break it so that you can do something else besides watch thousands of files scroll past.

xcopy

xcopy syntax is a little trickier because you need to specify the source and destination and then any switches:

```
xcopy [source] [destination] [switch]
```

By default, **xcopy** removes any read-only attributes unless you use the **/k** switch. Table 10-2 lists the **xcopy** switches.

Table 10-2   xcopy Switches

Switch	Explanation
/h	Copy hidden and system and regular files.
/k	Copy all the file attributes.
/o	Copy the ownership and access control list (ACL) information with the files. This requires new technology file system (NTFS).
/e	Copy everything, including subdirectories, and empty directories.
/s	Copy everything, including subdirectories, except empty directories.
/f	Show full source and destination filenames during the copy.
/a	Make quick backup by copying only files with archive set in **ATTRIB**. Does not reset or interfere with the regular backup schedules.
/g	Copy encrypted files to destinations that do not support encryption, like CD, jump drives, and the like. Note: This is used for data recovery (or hacking) when the key is lost. But bring a lunch if you are going to wait for the data to be unencrypted.
/r	Overwrite any read-only files in the destination directory.
/u	Copy and overwrite only files that already exist in the destination.
/v	Verify each new file in the destination.

attrib

5.4.9: Unfortunately, you need to memorize more than the RASH mnemonic. We already know the *R* means read-only, *A* includes an archive bit used during backups, *S* identifies a system file so we leave it alone, and *H* is to hide a file from end users so that they leave it alone. For the Field Technician exam, you need to know how to use **attrib** to modify file attributes. The graphical user interface (GUI) does not provide all the attributes. Knowing the command-line interface (CLI) gives you more control. Table 10-3 shows the attrib switches.

Table 10-3   attrib Switches

Switch	Explanation
+	"Add" or set the attribute.
-	"Subtract" or clear the attribute.
/s	Apply the attribute changes to all the files with the same attributes in that directory and all subdirectories. (Be careful with this one.) Don't confuse this switch with *S* for system.
/d	Change the attributes of the actual directory (folder).

format

5.4.1: Manual CLI formats from the command line are rare today. Nonetheless, you need to be familiar with **format** switches in Table 10-4 for the A+ exam.

Table 10-4   format Switches

Switch	Explanation
/fs	Followed by **fat32** or **ntfs**, manually chooses which file system to use.
/v	Followed by what you want to name the volume (drive).
/q	Uses a quick format.

ipconfig

8.9.2: ipconfig shows the network information of the PC. Note that the command is **ifconfig** in Linux and Mac OS X. Table 10-5 shows the **ipconfig** switches.

Table 10-5   ipconfig Switches

Switch	Explanation
/all	Show MAC address, IPv6 address, hostname, and other detailed information and the basic IP address.
/release	Release the IP address back to the DHCP server for use somewhere else. This command assumes that the PC runs on a network and is assigned an IP address dynamically via a DHCP server.
/renew	Ask the DHCP server for a new IP address.
/flushdns	Clear the Domain Name System (DNS) server cache. When "friendly" names like http://www.cisco.com get mapped to some other IP address, it might be time to issue this command.

The ping Command

8.3.5: The **ping** command requires a hyphen before its switches and prefers lowercase letters. Table 10-6 shows **ping** switches.

Table 10-6   ping Switches

Switch	Explanation
-t	Keep pinging until told not to with a Ctrl-C.
-w	Change the wait time (in milliseconds) for each reply.

System Folders and Users

5.4: The arrangement of folders in XP is organized around a multiuser environment. In that environment, users are organized into standard or restricted users. This allows users access to only their files and folders. In 9x, everyone has access to all folders and system files. In addition, 9x uses FAT32, which is hardly a secure file system. In the NT/2000/XP/Vista environment, administrators can access everything. NT and XP have hybrid users (for example, power users, who have some admin privileges, and guests, who essentially have none). Guests are disabled by default for security reasons. Vista takes it a step further and recommends that all users be standard, and the administrator account is disabled by default. This has been met with some grumbling from techs, all of whom need to enable the account to do anything. However, once you enable the admin account, the user access control (UAC) haunts your every move.

Shared Folders and Naming Conventions

15.4.2: In 9x, NT, and 2000, sharing needs to be enabled in the Network Settings in the Control Panel. Right-click the network connection, and select **Properties > Install > Service > Add**. Right-click **Services > Add**. In XP and Vista, sharing is enabled by default.

Mapping a Network Drive

5.5.1: A mapped drive is a convenient way to use a network drive. From My Computer, choose **Tools > Map a Network Drive**. Enter the location either by IP address or by the universal naming convention (UNC). The UNC is a way of using friendly names for network locations. Two backslashes (\\) precede the hostname of the PC. Then use single backslashes for specific shared folders or resources such as printers (for example, \\PC_*hostname**specific_folder*). Every time the OS loads, it will reconnect to that drive, and it will show up as another drive in My Computer. (Reconnect at Logon must be checked for this to work correctly.) This gives applications easy access to load and save work to that network drive. On the other side of that connection, make sure the user has the correct permissions to access that drive. It is not uncommon to have a read-only mapped drive for reference material, and another drive with full permission to save work. Further, in some security-conscious environments, it may be wise to prevent saving any work locally, even on jump drives. This also greatly simplifies backups when everyone's work is on one server. Of course, it also means there is a single point of failure.

Frequently, you will see a path that says %SYSTEM ROOT% at the beginning. Because the system files are stored in slightly different places, a general term called *system root* or just *root* in the Linux world is shorthand for "wherever you keep your OS files." Usually, for us, it is a primary active partition in the HDD named C: in a folder called Windows or WINNT, and more specifically, Windows\SYSTEM32 or WINNT\SYSTEM32. In the computer world, you will come across some very different system roots, including network drives, live CDs, and embedded systems, where the OS kernel files are stored in unusual locations.

Language Packs

12.2.1: Installing a new language on a PC is tricky. The best way to add languages is during the installation. If you are running Vista Home, you are out of luck. Look for third-party vendors or upgrade to Ultimate or Enterprise for language packs. Microsoft did not score many foreign relations points on this one. Nonetheless, Ultimate, or Enterprise edition, and any XP edition have a Control Panel applet called Keyboard and Languages. There you will need to enable right-to-left or Asian language support if you are installing such a language. The actual installation likely will require the OS CD/DVD.

Accessibility Options

5.5.2: The Control Panel also has an Accessibility Options applet that enables you to customize the OS to better accommodate people with special needs. This is a great place to use your people skills. For example, for those who have a difficult time pressing two keys simultaneously (such as Ctrl-C), set the StickyKeys function. For people with no sight, consider Narrator (**Start > All Programs > Accessories > Narrator**). Couple that with speech recognition and you've created a powerful combination. For people with limited sight, check out high contrast in the Display Properties, large fonts in browsers, and Magnifier. Another option is an onscreen keyboard. It is slow and tedious, but slow is much faster than not accessible. Also, keep in mind that these features are helpful for anyone with compromised dexterity, such as SCUBA divers, hazmat crews, and astronauts.

Homework

Fun with switches: Google the phrase *free bandwidth test* and take a benchmark measurement. Make the traditional ping bomb. Use your switches to create a ping that mimics a denial-of-service (DoS) attack on your own PC. Use the loopback 127.0.0.1 as the destination. Alter the number and duration until your computer is constantly answering itself to the point that the bandwidth is significantly reduced. Consider what would happen if the target were attacked by multiple PCs. That is the premise of a distributed DoS (DDoS) attack.

Funwork

Visit My Home 2.0 at http://www.2pointhome.com. Watch several episodes. It is a home makeover show, but is all about listening to customer's needs and finding exactly the right equipment and software to fit their needs.

Operating Systems Troubleshooting

A+ 220-602 Exam Objective

Objective 3.3: Identify tools, diagnostic procedures and troubleshooting techniques for operating systems

Key Points

Troubleshooting operating systems is a challenge. Often, a backup and reinstall is quicker, but that takes all the fun out of it. Today you will spend time in Chapter 5 and Chapter 16 of the IT Essentials v4.0 course. You will learn about permissions, administrative tools, and remote connections.

Raising the Dead: Operating System Recovery

5.6: Successfully using safe mode, automatic system recovery (ASR), emergency repair disks (ERD), System Restore, and Recovery Console will make you a hero to customers with crashed operating systems. You don't need to tell them how you were magically able to raise their PC from the dead.

Windows 9x systems have traditional F5 safe mode or F8 for safe mode with options. ERDs boot the computer when the master boot record (MBR) is corrupt. ERDs are made with the SYS.EXE command or from the Add/Remove icon in the Control Panel.

Windows XP took the ERD a step further with ASR. For ASR or ERD to work, the emergency CD or DVD must first be made when the system is working well. Get the system to a "perfect state" (that is, cleaned up, defragged, restore points, the works), and then run NTBACKUP.EXE. Follow the wizard. Note: Use a new 2 GB+ partition or DVD as the destination for the ASR file. You will need a floppy disk, CD, DVD, Network boot or some other media to tell the ASR process where the ASR file is located.

When you need to use it, boot with the XP CD and press F2 to start the ASR. It will delete everything on your PC and take it back to the point when the ASR was made. This is essentially a DIY system restore CD like those that come with brand-name computers.

System Restore takes snapshots of your computer, and you can go back to that point after a problem occurs. Make a restore point right before you make any big change, install or uninstall a program or device, download an update, or anything that you might want to undo. Going back to a restore point does not remove the file that caused the problem, but it does uninstall the offending software. Real computer geeks know how to use the system restore from the command prompt during a partial boot even if an ARD was not made. Restore points are automatically made during most basic events. You can use this to your advantage. From a command prompt, run **C:\Windows\system32\restore\rstrui.exe** in XP or **C:\Windows\System32\rstrui.exe** in Vista.

Recovery Console is accessed by inserting a boot CD and running **D:\i386\winnt32.exe /cmdcons** in the Run window. This gives you many commands and command-line access with full administrator privileges. Ever wonder how to recover data from a password-protected PC? Know the commands and pick the lock.

Administrative Tools

5.5.3: The power tools of the Microsoft world are found in the Administrative Tools icon in the XP and 2000 Control Panels. Windows 98 has these tools scattered around the Control Panel. The following is a list of commonly used power tools:

- Services MMC (Microsoft Management Console) displays all the services currently installed on your PC. Right-click a service to stop, start, pause, or resume. To enable or disable the service, trace to Properties. In that menu, you can also choose whether the service starts automatically or manually.

- The Computer Management MMC allows the administrator to create, format, defrag, and delete HDD partitions and removable storage media.

- The Event Viewer lists all the errors that have been generated. This is a good place to find trouble spots.

- Performance Monitor measures CPU performance, RAM usage, HDD usage, and many other things. If you are going to enhance the performance of a PC by adding or replacing something, use this tool to take a before and after picture. Customers love that sort of thing.

Problems with Permissions

16.3.1: By now, most programs automatically install with the permissions and shortcuts ready to go. In some situations, however, you might want to select which user has access to which programs. For a user with restricted permissions to use a program, you must place a shortcut in the user's Start menu or desktop. For everyone to have access, even users not yet created, you must place the shortcut in the All Users Start menu or desktop.

If the user needs access to the entire folder or the program is not multiuser friendly, you need to go to that folder and manually assign the user to have Full Control, List the Contents, Read and Execute, and Read or Write permissions. This can get very tricky and tedious. A solution to this is share-level control. It allows a password to protect areas of the HDD to avoid the hassle of tracking down shortcuts and individual permissions (as is the case in user-level control). To make it even more complicated, each file can be assigned its own set of permissions for each user. They are the same permissions as folders, but instead of choosing to list the contents, you can grant Full Control. Full control allows the user to take ownership, which is important if you are going to open the file from a different user.

Remote Desktop Connection and Remote Assistance

5.5.3: Remote Desktop Connection and Remote Assistance are helpful utilities that allow you to be somewhere else and connect to a computer to configure it. They prove especially useful when the PC is in another city or country. Of course, these utilities are also a hacker's dream. You can find these services in the Accessories part of the Start menu. The target computer needs to be set to allow remote control. (Note that XP Home edition can serve only as a destination of a remote connection. It does not have the ability to establish this connection without using third-party software.) Right-click **My Computer > Properties**, and then click the **Remote** tab. From there, you can allow or disallow Remote Assistance and Remote Desktop Connection. The only difference between these technologies is that Remote Assistance asks the person seated at the target PC to accept the connection. Remote Assistance should not be confused with Remote Access. Remote Access assumes that no one is sitting at the target PC and is used for long distance maintenance.

If you haven't experimented with these utilities yet, do so. It will change your perspectives on networking, operating systems, security, and airfares.

Homework

Make a flowchart for troubleshooting an OS that won't boot. This is going to be a big chart and should assume there are no physical layer (hardware) problems. What errors could be displayed? What do they tell you?

If you don't have a set of A+ exam flash cards yet, it is time to get some. Ask your friends, search online (make sure the cards test 2006 objectives), or ask current or former computer teachers. Pearson Education offers a truly great flash card product called CompTIA A+ Cert Flash Cards Online, available at InformIT (http://www.informit.com/).

Funwork

Explore 3D desktops for XP and Vista.

If possible, explore Remote Desktop Connection and Remote Assistance.

Visit labrats.tv and enjoy the shows.

Operating Systems Preventive Maintenance

A+ 220-602 Exam Objective

Objective 3.4: Perform preventive maintenance for operating systems

Key Points

Proper maintenance of an OS is critical to its health. Updates, Scandisk, defrags, and disk cleanup all contribute to a clean, efficient OS. Today you will cover topics in Chapters 5, 12, and 16 of the IT Essentials v4.0 course.

What Really Happens at Startup?

5.4.7: You need to know what happens at startup because the three most common customer words are, "It won't start." After ruling out obvious issues, like the computer is not plugged in, monitor brightness, and so on, we are faced with the daunting task of troubleshooting the actual startup sequence. If it truly is a startup problem, start by pressing F5 at the splash screen, and then select the last known good configuration. Once booted, check out the Event Viewer in Administrative Tools to see what happened and which file failed. And as the final step, edit the MSCONFIG to prevent the bad startup file from launching again. If you can't solve the problem with these, it is time to reinstall the OS. Also, if you are able to boot, that is a great time to make a quick backup of the customer's files; after all, you might not have another chance.

In Windows 9x/Me, the boot sequence went like this:

1. After power-on self test (POST), BIOS looks for MSDOS.SYS and IO.SYS and copies them into RAM.

2. IO.SYS loads SYSINIT.

3. SYSINIT locates and finds the DOS kernel and CONFIG.SYS.

4. CONFIG.SYS manages the memory and fundamental devices.

5. SYSINIT loads COMMAND.COM, which contains basic or native DOS commands.

6. The COMMAND.COM runs AUTOEXEC.BAT, which is a boot honey-do list for device drivers and applications to run at startup. On that list is Start Windows.

That was back when the world was simple. In Windows NT/XP/Vista, it is a little more complex:

1. After POST, which now checks all the embedded and integrated devices, BIOS looks for the master boot record (MBR). It is found on the first active partition. The MBR figures out which kind of file system is running, and then loads NTLDR.

2. NTLDR protects the system by switching to protected mode and starts the file system.

3. NTLDR reads BOOT.INI. This is particularly important for dual-boot PCs. Dual-boot PCs use BOOT.INI or BOOTSECT.DOS to manage which OS to boot.

4. NTLDR runs NTDETECT, which installs device drivers. NTLDR then runs NTOSKRNL.EXE and HAL.EXE. These files begin services and further separate the hardware from software, with the hardware abstraction layer (HAL).

5. NTLDR loads the HKEY_LOCAL_MACHINE\SYSTEM Registry hive that loads the device drivers.

6. Finally, NTLDR passes the torch to NTOSKRNL.EXE, which loads WINLOGON, and the user is prompted for logon credentials.

For better or worse, you really ought to spend the time and commit the NT/XP/Vista boot sequence to memory.

Custom OS Installations

12.2.2: After experiencing a few installations, you probably realize you have better things to do than babysit status bars and click Next. There are actually four ways to speed up this process.

Unattended Installation

An unattended installation uses an answer file that automates the questions it would normally ask you. This system works fine until some little thing changes, such as a new HDD or a new expansion card. Every little thing needs to be accounted for and correctly answered in the file. Tweaking these answer files is often as time-consuming as a regular install.

Local Image

Imaging an HDD is a great way to bypass the quirky answer file. Get a perfectly configured, defragged, secured, and updated OS installation. Run a third-party imaging application, such as Norton Ghost, and then you can at any time restore your computer back to its original state, including removing any programs and files that were downloaded. Remember that restore points only alter what has changed since that point. Using restore points does not "undownload" software. Imaging reformats the partition and recopies the image so that the PC is exactly the way it once was.

Network Deployed Image

Imaging works beautifully when you have many identically configured PCs, especially when you use a deployment server. Be sure to run Sysprep to make the OS transportable to other computers. Network image server software is made by third-party vendors. Deployment servers can send the OS through the network to a PC.

Automatic Network Deployed Image

ImageYou can take imaging a step further by setting the network interface card (NIC) to work with a preboot execution environment (PXE), or "Pixie," and running a remote installation service (RIS). You can have a fresh installation ready for you every morning (that is, no spyware, no temp files, no half-baked end-user modifications, just a clean slate).

Updating the Operating System

16.4.1: Be sure you know when you would *not* enable automatic updates. Consider the length of time a dialup would take to download a proper service pack. You wouldn't want the PC to be installing the service pack while giving a presentation. Best to burn a copy of the service pack to CD from a PC with a high-speed connection or schedule it at night.

Homework

Restore points (discussed yesterday in Part II, Day 9, "Operating Systems Troubleshooting"), backups, disk cleanup (Part I, Day 23, "Operating Systems Troubleshooting"), and Scandisk and defrag (Part I, Day 29, "Hardware Installation") should be well ingrained by now. You will likely be asked the same basic questions about these topics as you were on the Essentials exam, so definitely review these topics.

Funwork

Download and burn live CDs of Ubuntu or Knoppix and explore the Linux environment. Run them from the CD. Do not install them on your machine unless you are serious about using Linux.

Printers and Scanners: A Closer Look

A+ 220-602 Exam Objectives

Objective 4.1: Identify the fundamental principles of using printers and scanners

Objective 4.2: Install, configure, optimize and upgrade printers and scanners

Key Points

Today is an in-depth look at printers and scanners. These topics relate to Chapter 14 of the IT Essentials v4.0 course.

Printer RAM and Firmware

14.3.1: If the users on a network complain that only half of their document printed, it might be that the shared printer does not have enough memory and it is relying on the PCs to hold the document in their queue. The RAM on a network printer should more than exceed the size of the documents it receives. Keep in mind peak printing times will require even more RAM. Basically like any computer, the more RAM, the better.

Firmware updates for printers are rare, but they do exist, and they can greatly improve performance. Like any firmware upgrade, check the manufacturer's website, and then double-check that it is the correct file before downloading. You wouldn't want your color laser printer to think it is suddenly a desktop inkjet. Download the file and follow the directions from the manufacturer.

Scanner Software

14.4.2: Many applications work with scanners. Once an image is scanned, it is usually modified or at the very least saved as a JPG or GIF by an application. The application can do several common tasks, which you need to be familiar with for the A+ exam. Scanners can resize the picture, for example. Going smaller is easy, but bigger tends to get grainy. Keeping the aspect ratio (usually by holding the Shift while dragging the edge of the picture) will prevent distortion. Scanners love dark, solid, high-contrasting colors like text on white paper. Most scanners have difficulty with handwriting, pencil, and colored or lined paper. Just like a photocopier, lightening and darkening the image can help. Another cool trick that scanner software can do is sharpen an image. It increases the contrast among subtle colors and lines. Taken to extreme, it looks like CD art.

Advanced graphics programs can convert the image from a raster (lots of dots) to a vector image (lines and points). Raster images do not size-up well, but vector images can be whatever size you need. A drawback of vector is it is not subtle. To get a complicated picture, you need a great many points and lines, which requires a tremendous amount of graphics processing called *rendering*.

Consider how many lines and points are processed in the rendering of a Pixar movie. They use true supercomputers to get the job done. Remember, someone has to fix those ultrafast PCs and workstations, someone just like you.

WYSIWYG

14.2.2: What you see is what you get (WYSIWYG or sometimes WYSIWUG) is not a stage name; it is an actual computer industry acronym. It originally applied to print preview features of early applications that did a better than average job of displaying what the printed paper would look like. Later, the same problems occurred in website development applications. Different browsers interpret the codes differently. At some level, the computer needs to tell the printer what the page looks like. This is called Page Description Language (PDL). It has three flavors: Printer Command Language (PCL), PostScript (PS), and graphics device interface (GDI). You will see these as options in printer drivers. If given the choice, go with PS. It is cross-platform and does a great job of displaying images and text accurately. GDI treats everything as a picture, and the computer tells the printer exactly where to put each dot. PCL is the printer language from HP and is the standard among printers today.

The Clean and Happy Printer

14.5.3: It is not uncommon to find an old workhorse laser printer somewhere in an office full of brand new PCs. If maintained, the printers will often live through several generations of PCs. The first step to a long, happy printer life is to keep it away from ammonia. The ammonia can, over time, damage the plastic case, rubber belts and rollers, and the delicate PVC-coated wires inside. Heat and sunlight are not friends of printers either.

Turn off and unplug the printer. Use a vacuum on loose toner and dust, a damp cloth for general cleaning, and periodically follow the manufacturer's recommendation for cleaning the rollers and other parts. That usually involves special cleaners and cotton swabs. A 1-inch-wide paintbrush is a life saver when working in small areas that the lint-free cloth cannot reach.

Homework

Memorize the six steps of the laser printing process outlined in Day 22.

Most of what you need to know about printers for the Field Technician exam was covered in the Essentials exam. Take this easy day and review Days 22 and 21 in the Essentials section.

Funwork

Everyone needs a good workhorse laser printer. Go find a good deal on 1200 dpi Duplex Network monochrome printer. Even if it isn't for you, your customers will likely need something like that.

At the website https://renderman.pixar.com/, you will find that Pixar is actually a computer company that happens to make great films. Who said nerds weren't cool? Find out the hardware and software requirements for RenderMan. You might be surprised.

Troubleshooting Printers

A+ 220-602 Exam Objectives

Objective 4.3: Identify tools and diagnostic procedures to troubleshoot printers and scanners

Objective 4.4: Perform preventative maintenance of printers and scanners

Key Points

As a field tech, you will likely troubleshoot printers as a part of your job. Today you will cover topics from Chapter 2 and Chapter 14 of the IT Essentials v4.0 course.

Paper Sizes: Letter, Legal, and A4

14.6: Paper size is a constant issue when printing cards, notes, signs, and other oddly shaped documents. Even when printing normal documents, the printer needs to be told what size paper to use. Letter is used in the United States to print 8.5 by 11 inch documents. The European A4 paper size is 8.25 by 11.75 inches (actually 210 mm by 297 mm), close but more than enough to seriously change the format on the print job. Legal paper is several inches longer than letter and A4 and can cause problems when accidentally printing legal-length documents on standard-sized paper.

Reduce, Reuse, Recycle

2.1.3: Being able to print has advantages. On the flip side, printing is expensive both in terms of money and the environment. The ugly reality is that unless it is special photograph or a life-insurance policy, everything that a printer prints will at some point be disposed of, often in less than a month. The ink is quite toxic, laser printers in particular use a tremendous amount of electricity; and next time you heave a box of paper around, just imagine the logistics of its manufacture, storage, and transportation. That is a lot of energy, resources, and cost for a very temporary thing.

Your clients are almost always ready to save money if not the good Earth. Reusing paper as scrap is an easy cost-saving method. Just make sure the printed stuff on the other side is not sensitive or libelous. From a troubleshooting perspective, know that some printers don't like to use leftover paper. Double-sided printers are expensive initially but greatly reduce paper consumption. The easiest option is to develop a "think before you print" awareness among your customers and employees.

Refilling inkjet cartridges looks good in concept, but the application is less than ideal. The Field Technician exam is all about onsite work. Do not refill ink at a customer's site. It is a Murphy's law magnet. If all goes well, it can be a way to save some money. However, any savings will be quickly negated if you need to replace a customer's carpet or office furniture because of spilled ink. Take the cartridges and refill them somewhere else. Note that because ink is no friend of the environment, don't do this in a sink.

Toner: The Good, the Bad, and the Messy

14.5.3: Most toner cartridges can be sent back to the manufacturer for refurbishing and refilling. Purchasing these used cartridges is a way to save money. The number one rule about cleaning up toner is don't spill it in the first place. It is affected by static electricity. It is powder, the consistency of baking soda. Do not mop it up. Do not sweep it unless it is on a nonporous surface like a linoleum floor. Do use a vacuum cleaner with a HEPA filter. Do test the vacuum on regular dust before vacuuming up the toner, lest the toner get wafted into the air to form an ink-infested storm in your customer's office (not a career-enhancing move).

Common Printer Problems

14.6.2: Printers tend to have a few basic problems. They are not like operating systems with countless possible issues. Here are three common problems, symptoms, and solutions.

Paper Pickup Problems

The printer's rubber wheels, called "paper tires," get tired and brittle. They are not as "grabby." Professional rubber restorer is a common solution that all techs can use to breathe new life into lackluster paper tires. Also check the spring tension that holds the paper up to the rubber rollers. The paper itself can be a problem. Some printers are very picky about paper. If you suspect this, some experimentation is in order. For the A+ exam, remember that *cool*, *dry*, and *dust-free* are keywords associated with paper and ideal paper storage. In the real world, printers and paper do not typically live in such luxury.

Tick, Tick, Tick

Repetitive lines or tick marks or any repeated pattern on the printed document means that something is on the rollers. In the best-case scenario, it can be fixed by replacing the toner cartridge. If not, seek your manufacturer's advice on how to clean or fix this problem. Be really sure you follow their directions exactly, because the laser has capacitors that can electrocute you, even while unplugged from the wall. It might be time to relegate the printer to in-house, non-presentation-quality printing.

Fog of Pages

If the pages look like there are patches of fog where the words drift off into whiteness, the toner is running low. Take out the cartridge. Carefully and slowly shake it from side to side to move the toner inside around to evenly distribute it, and then place it back in the printer. Go buy a replacement cartridge. Soon it will be light text, then no text.

Homework

Right-click an installed printer icon in the Printers applet in the Control Panel. Print a test page, and then click **No** to indicate that it didn't print. Doing so launches the Printer Troubleshooting Wizard. Answer the questions and follow the troubleshooting flowchart. Map it out as you go along. Go back through the wizard and answer the question differently each time. You will do this to fill in more of the flowchart. Take that flowchart with you and review it before your Field Tech exam.

Pick an exam topic that still scares you a little, tear it in small pieces, and learn each piece. Divide and conquer. Ask your forums and friends. Go own that knowledge. You have a test in less than a week.

Funwork

Do some research at HP.com and HP.lexmark.com on problems, drivers, and applications. You will most likely be supporting these printers, and these resources will help you troubleshoot printers and scanners and other devices.

Google the phrases *digital printing press*, *astronomy imagining*, *MRI and x-ray images*, or *underground imagining*. Scanners and printers go far beyond the all-in-one. These big-ticket items are serviced by people like you.

Networking: A Closer Look

A+ 220-602 Exam Objectives

Objective 5.1: Identify the fundamental principles or networks

Objective 5.2: Install, configure, optimize and upgrade networks

Key Points

In our increasingly connected world, networking is a fundamental skill for all techs. Today you will cover topics in Chapter 15 of the IT Essentials v4.0 course and learn more about ports, cables, and file sharing.

Ports of Call

15.2.2: For the A+ exam, you are expected to know which ports common protocols use. Table 5-1 lists the most common networking protocols, their ports, and a brief description. When manually configuring firewalls, you need to know these.

Table 5-1   Ports and Protocols

Protocol	Port	Description
HTTP	80	Basic web surfing
HTTPS	443	Secure web pages
POP	110	Web-based e-mail
IMAP	143	Transfer e-mail from a server to a client
SMTP	25	E-mail outgoing to a server or between e-mail servers not from server to client
Telnet and SSH	22 or 23	Command-line interface (CLI) remote access
FTP and TFPT	20 or 21	Downloading files
DNS	53	Friendly URL names
DHCP	67	Autoconfigure network settings

Wire Drill

15.3.1: Unshielded twisted pair (UTP) has the basic categories of Category 3 for phones and Category 5 for computer networks. UTP has a catchment area of 100 meters (328 feet), meaning the cables should not exceed this length. TIA/EIA standards allow for 90 m of horizontal run (in the walls and ceilings). This leaves 10 m for patch cables (outside the walls). Patch cables are use to connect devices in a room to the wall jack. There are physical limitations in the walls, access holes, HVAC (heating, venting, and air conditioning), pipes, ducts, lights, fans, and so on. Physical networking is not an easy task. If you need more distance than 100 m, consider connecting a fiber-optic cable to an intermediate distribution facility (IDF). An IDF has its own 50 m Category 5 area it can cover. Fiber-optic cables can be as long as several kilometers.

So why not just use fiber optic to the desktop? You can, but Category 5 is cheap, easy to install, and can easily support 10BASE-T and 100BASE-T wiring configurations. As users' network demands increase (for, among other things, streaming video, gaming, and videoconferencing), we need to support increasing speeds. 1000BASE-T uses all eight wires, and it is advisable to step up the cable to Cat5e, Cat6, or even Cat6A. Cat 6 and 6A have more twists to improve protection from crosstalk and line noise.

File Sharing

15.4.2: File sharing uses network file system (NFS) or server message block (SMB) protocols. SMB is used when sharing files among Windows, Mac, and Linux. The service needs to be first installed, then running, then the folder must be shared and files must be present. This assumes the network is correctly set up. If not, file sharing is a moot point.

Homework

Reread the networking section (Day 19 and Day 20) in the Essentials section and ask network people questions. If you ask a network person about these basic things, that person might look at you in a strange way. Remember, what we learn in networking early on is quite different from the reality. Networking pros live in that reality. It is like asking Stephen Hawking to help you with your physics homework. If they start using terms such as *cloud computing, variable length, classless, IPv6...* thank them for their time and find a lesser networking person (maybe someone who installs cabling). PC techs who do this stuff every day are another good resource; networking folks see a much bigger picture and would expect you to understand some things that are not really part of the PC tech's domain.

Funwork

Caution: This is seriously geeky stuff worthy of tape-repaired glasses and vinyl pocket protectors. Google the phrase *DIY WIFI antennas*. Explore the myriad antenna designs. Some range from small curved paper and wire, to coffee cans, all the way to satellite dishes. If you dare, build one of these antennas (directional ones are really interesting) and measure the signal strength compared to the professional ones. See how many service set identifiers (SSID) you can pick up from your neighbors. (Don't go snooping around on people's unsecured networks. Just because you might leave the windows open does not give strangers the right to explore your house.)

Network Troubleshooting

A+ 220-602 Exam Objectives

Objective 5.3: Use tools and diagnostic procedures to troubleshoot network problems

Objective 5.4: Perform preventive maintenance of networks including securing and protecting network cabling

Key Points

Today you will play "follow the packet," and briefly review fiber-optic cabling, all from Chapter 15 of the IT Essentials v4.0 course. "Follow the packet" and the homework (and funwork) will help put networking concepts into context (and action) for you.

Follow the Packet

15.8: One way to look at a network is to follow the packet. This is an important skill in troubleshooting because at any point along the way, something can go wrong. Table 4-1 follows a file download step by step.

Table 4-1   Follow the Packet

Event	Potential Problems
The user navigates to the URL and clicks Download.	If the Domain Name System (DNS) is corrupt or not up-to-date, the server's IP address may not be mapped to the user-friendly URL.
The file on the server is divided into several pieces called *packets*.	The protocol stack (usually TCP/IP) could not be installed or properly bound to the network interface card (NIC).
Source and destination IP addresses are assigned to each packet.	Network Address Translation (NAT) and Port Address Translation (PAT) issues on the user's end could mislead the server, in which case the packet is sent to a phantom destination.
Source and destination MAC addresses are assigned to each packet.	If Address Resolution Protocol (ARP) tables are not built yet, the server will not know who its neighbors are. The **arp -a** command displays a list of known IPs and MACs of local PCs.
Each packet is sent to the NIC.	The NIC could have wrong or missing drivers or theoretically could have any number of resource conflicts (interrupt request [IRQ], direct memory access [DMA], I/O), although today it is highly unlikely. Hooray for Plug-and-Play! The NIC Properties Advanced tab is where you resolve these issues (if you ever need to).

continues

Table 4-1   Follow the Packet   *continued*

Event	Potential Problems
The NIC translates the packet into signals (wired, wireless, fiber, audio).	This is generally not a point of failure.
At each hop along the LAN, new source and destination MAC addresses are applied, but the source and destination IPs never change.	The number one troubleshooting technique is a visual inspection of the cable. Pinched, frayed, knotted, or otherwise abused cables should be highly suspect. Use a cable tester or known working PC to ping through the cable to verify its effectiveness. Better yet, replace the cable.
	In a wireless network, you have signal strength and access filters such as wireless protected access (WPA) and MAC filtering to worry about.
	Intermediate switches and hubs could not be powered, or the network cables are not connected. Blinking lights indicate network traffic (a good sign). Switches take some time after they turn on to listen to traffic and learn the location and names of the nearby devices. Don't expect a switch to begin working immediately when turned on.
The packets pass through the gateway, and the router chooses the best path to the destination.	The router might not be configured correctly. The gateway IP address on the PC and the LAN interface IP address must be identical, as must the subnet masks. (Note that the identical subnet mask thing isn't really true. But at this level, on the A+ exam, it is.) There are countless other configuration issues at this point, including NAT and PAT, hardware firewalls, and more.
After leaving the web server, traveling through countless routers and switches, the packets arrive at the user's PC.	This is the proverbial "cloud." It is a collection of Internet service providers (ISP), long-distance communications, switching stations, satellites, and so on (the same cloud from the funwork in Day 20). We don't really need to understand every device through which the packet travels so long as the packet gets there.
The packet flows through the user's LAN as it did on the server's LAN.	The same potential problems exist on any LAN.
The packets are reassembled and checked for accuracy.	In a User Datagram Protocol (UDP) environment, like streaming video, lost packets are ignored. This makes online videos quick to load but glitchy. In a TCP environment, like downloading a file, lost pieces are unacceptable. A resend is coordinated with the source PC, until all the packets are accounted for.
The OS searches for an appropriate application to read the file's extension, making the download ready to be opened or run by the user.	You can't view the site correctly because of a missing plug-in or can't launch the program because of an unassociated extension. The file could be compressed (zipped) or could be encrypted.

Seeing the Light

15.1.1: This is what you really need to know about fiber optics as a PC repair technician: Don't bend the cable too much. It is a glass rod and can break. Also, the inside walls of the cable are shiny, to reflect any stray light back into the fiber. The problem is too much bend can cause the light to shine back at itself. In some situations, this can prevent the light from getting to the end of the wire. The light or laser inside the cable doesn't look nearly as cool as you might think, and depending on the mode it can be very harmful to your eyes. Even technicians with cabling certifications sometimes inadvertently bend the cable. When that happens, we just go buy a new cable.

Homework

If you have the opportunity, connect a few computers and switches and cables. Ping everything, and then share files using server message block (SMB) (Samba is an open source version) or network file system (NFS). In the real world, this is called network-attached storage (NAS) This is also the basis of home theater servers and web servers, and even game servers. Next, have someone (a fellow computer person) "break" your network in three ways. Do this by inserting faults: unplug something, change NIC settings, mess with the firewalls, and so on. (No peeking.)

Set a timer and see how long it takes for you to find and fix all three faults. Ask your friend for three more (and different) faults and try to beat your time. This lab really does give you firsthand experience applying the networking concepts. If you don't have access to PCs, switches, and cables, with your Cisco Networking Academy login credentials, you can download Packet Tracer from http://cisco.netacad.net. Hint: Go through the tutorials first.

Funwork

Google the phrase *Peter Packet*. Follow the links to the games on the Cisco website. Yes, the very serious Cisco Systems, Inc., has a fun side, too. These games greatly simplify networking concepts and are highly entertaining.

Another great resource is a video at http://www.warriorsofthe.net.

Security, Environment, and Customer Service

A+ 220-602 Exam Objectives

Objective 6.1: Identify the fundamentals and principles of security

Objective 6.2: Install, configure, upgrade and optimize security

Objective 6.3: Identify tool, diagnostic procedures and troubleshooting techniques for security

Objective 6.4: Perform preventive maintenance for security

Objective 7.1: Identify potential hazards and proper safety procedures, including power supply, display devices and environment (that is, trip, liquid, situational, atmospheric hazards and high-voltage and moving equipment)

Objective 8.1: Use good communication skills, including listening and tact/discretion, when communicating with customers and colleagues

Objective 8.2: Use job-related professional behavior, including notation of privacy, confidentiality and respect for the customer and customers' property

Key Points

Today you will cover topics from Chapters 2, 9, and 16 of the IT Essentials v4.0 course. Topics range from encryption to the environment. You are a few short days away from being A+ certified. Excited? You should be. You've earned it.

Firewalls

16.2.3: A good security plan uses layered defenses, including hardware and software firewalls. Firewalls work in three ways:

- **Packer filtering:** Packet filtering is the most common and straightforward. Firewalls that use packet filtering either block or allow packets by using basic criteria, source or destination IP address, ports, or protocols. The disadvantage of packet filtering is it is not subtle. It is a reliable but inflexible gate guard. Sometimes legitimate packets get filtered because they are different.

- **Proxy filters:** Advocates for a kinder, gentler network community allow packets of all persuasions to enter or leave and use more-sophisticated rules. These proxy filters are really more concerned about network intrusion than about internal issues.

- **Stateful packet inspection:** Stateful packet inspection looks for unfamiliar packets and hides the bodies. Once a rogue packet enters the target network, the hacker will never hear from it again.

Hardware firewalls are expensive and difficult to set up and configure, but they don't impact the individual PC's performance. Plus, the hardware firewall can support an entire network.

Hash

16.2: Secure Hash Algorithm (SHA) and (message digest algorithm 5) MD5 are like checksums in that a number is generated by the actual message. A checksum counts the number of bits in a packet and inserts that number in the packet as a reference. The receiving PC reads the checksum number and counts the bits in the packet. If the number of bits and the checksum number are not equal, something has been lost or changed. SHA and MD5 work the same way, but the algorithms are much more complicated. They verify that nothing was lost or altered in the transmission.

Encryption

9.3.3: Symmetric encryption is like two people having identical keys to a house. In fact, the term key is used to refer to the password. It would be foolish to give the key to your house to anyone who wants to deliver a package. Keep in mind that the point of encryption is to prevent those not involved in the transaction from seeing what is in the box. So what do you do with the box? You can't leave it out side. You can't give away your key to strangers. Enter asymmetric encryption. Let's build a foyer that is locked both at the front door and internally to the rest of the house. The public key gets the package into the house and away from prying eyes. The private key that only you hold gets the box into your house. To put this analogy back in technical terms, a message is encrypted in such a way that you need both keys to open it: one for the sender (private) and the other for the receiver (public). This system authenticates both parties and requires both parties to participate in the encryption process. It is not a perfect system, but it is much better than nothing.

Virtual Private Networking

16.2.1: Virtual private networking (VPN) uses a token (not to be confused with Token Ring network topology) to encrypt a message. That message is sent through secure tunnels to the receiver, who uses the token to unencrypt the message.

A Geekspeak Translation Guide

10.2.1: The field technician interacts with the public. Often customers attempt to do something, fail, call you, and then want to stand around and learn. This is an opportunity to be annoyed or to make a friend, your choice. When talking to curious spectators, be sure to use their language, not ours. Remember that you need to tailor your language to match their level of understanding. If the customer took Geekspeak 101 but didn't major in it, you can use that to your advantage. It is a huge compliment to the DIY-ers when you use some technical terms, but not so many that it overwhelms them. Here is an example of how to speak customer.

Geekspeak:

> The unknowledgeable customer put an HDD in the computer and could not find it in the BIOS. The jumper on the new drive was not set correctly on the PATA HDD. The old one is still master, and the new one is set for CS. I needed to change them both to CS and plug the new HDD in the end to make it master. Now you are able to see both in the BIOS.

Translation for the customer:

> Whoever put this hard drive in the PC did a good job. However, it was not quite configured properly. A small matter of jumpers and cables fixed the problem, and now you can see it in the BIOS. Do you have any questions?

Notice the use of positives and minimizing the problem. A quick explanation of the solution proves to the customer two things. One, he almost had it right. Two, it was worth calling you for help. Both of these are huge customer service bonuses in your favor.

Environment

2.1.3: Just a quick review from the Essentials exam: You should know about material safety data sheets (MSDS) and local government procedures for proper disposal of batteries and electronic equipment. Remember that ink and toner are bad for the environment and remember to use proper cleaning techniques. Also, laptops are better than PCs for the environment because they draw less power and have less physical material. See Day 17, "Environmental Issues," if you need further review.

Homework

Reread Days 17 and 18 because questions about security, customer service, and environmental issues on the Field Technician exam (220-602) are similar to those on the Essentials exam.

Funwork

The following is an "action-packed" techno thriller, so to speak. As the story unfolds, you will be asked, "How did you do that?" Your job is to use your knowledge of PCs and operating systems to fill in the commands, techniques, and procedures to complete the story. Good luck!

A mean-spirited computer technician has been fired, and he maliciously encrypted his most valuable work on his Windows XP Professional desktop PC. He corrupted the boot files so that the computer simply will not boot. He planned to negotiate with his former employer by holding the data and the entire contents of the HDD "hostage." He didn't actually "steal" anything; his work is still physically on the computer at the office.

In his ranting, he let his IT bravado get the best of him. He unwisely alluded to a backup plan. There is, evidently, some sort of virus named killer.bat ready to deploy in the scheduled tasks on boot that only he can stop. He is demanding $10,000 in exchange for the encryption key and XP password necessary to get into his PC, stop the virus, and recover and decrypt his data. (This might seem farfetched, but the scenario is more real than you might think!)

This is where you come in. The employer would rather pay you $5000 instead of bowing to this manipulative ex-employee. This is your chance to prove your worth. You are able to boot to a command prompt (How did you do that?) and can see all the files regardless of that fact that some were marked hidden and system (How did you do that?).

The CD burner requires Windows apps, which requires a full boot, and a jump drive is not recognized in the command-line interface (CLI). However, after installing an identical SATA drive (How did you do that?), you are ready to copy everything over to the new drive minus the read-only and encrypted key support. You enter the command, and the data is now on a new drive without killer.bat. (How did you do that? See Part II, Day 10, "Operating Systems: A Closer Look.")

You took that drive to another PC that had proper antivirus software and data forensics. You were able to isolate the encrypted files and some e-mails that will likely be used as evidence against the ex-employee in court. (Go online and find out how you did that.) Then, because those e-mails were discovered, this is now a criminal investigation, so you hand the whole thing over to the police.

You can go ahead and run decryption software on the files, but it might take you a while (because you are not a law-enforcement agency, and so have to start with dictionary and brute-force attacks). Contrary to popular belief, law-enforcement agencies have "backdoor" keys to most encryption software. After all, it is in the encryption manufacturer's best interest to work with law enforcement lest they be charged as an accessory to a crime. It usually takes law enforcement, using super computers, just a few short minutes to crack a key. If this sounds like the kind of work you would be interested in, these jobs really are out there.

220-602 Review Day

This is a light day in preparation for your test tomorrow. Enjoy it and relax.

By Any Other Name

The computer industry is full of different names for the same thing. These synonyms are cumbersome and challenging for the new techie. The following is list of some of the synonyms found in the IT industry and on the A+ exams. People will argue that there are subtle differences among these terms and phrases, but it is a good place to start:

- Fault isolation = troubleshooting.

- Load = copy to RAM = run = execute = launch = double-click.

- Mini stereo plug = headphone jack = 3.5TSR.

- PC = IBM clone = computer = system = machine.

- Component = device = part = field replaceable unit (FRU).

- RS232 = DB9 = DE9 = serial port.

- Documentation = release notes = ReadMe files.

- Card = I/O card = adapter card = expansion card = PC card.

- Control Panel icon = applet = configuration application = configuration utility.

- 9x = 95a, 95b, 98a, 98b, Millennium Edition (Me).

- 2K = 2000.

- Pins = contacts = channels = width = conductors.

- Bits per second = bps = b/s.

- Throughput = transfer rate = network speed. (Bandwidth is a measure of ideal speed, not the throughput actually realized.)

- Mini ATX = micro ATX = flex ATX.

- S/PDIF = SPDIF = digital audio interface.

- PCIX (peripheral component interconnect extended) is **not** PCIExpress (PCIe).

Brain Dumps

Practice the following brain dumps:

- PC layered model

- Motherboard map

- OSI and TCP/IP models

- TIA/EIA 568 A and B (wire color arrangements)

- XP boot sequence

- Laser-printer process

- General troubleshooting process

Write Your Own Practice Questions

One of the best kept secrets of academic success is to outthink the teacher. After a few tests, you should know what kinds of questions that teacher, or CompTIA in this case, asks. You have seen a real test and probably several practice tests. Write down the questions as you think they will appear on your exam. This is a skill that is honed and refined over the years. Once you master this, schooling of any kind gets much, much easier. With a little practice, you can do this, too. Answer your own questions and review them right before you enter the room for your exam tomorrow.

Homework

It's time to make your "cheat sheet" study sheet and remake it a dozen times or until you can do it all from memory. The following is a start:

- A good fuse has 0 ohms of resistance, and a blown fuse has an infinite amount of resistance.

- Customers might not always be right, but you must always treat them with respect.

- The manufacturer's website is the best place to find the most up-to-date drivers, software, and documentation.

- Gather information from the customer first, then the PC.

Funwork

Do *something* away from the computer that is fun and a little different from your usual routine: Go out with an old friend you haven't seen in a while. Or take in a movie you wouldn't normally see. Or perhaps visit a museum that you have never been to. Maybe go to a concert featuring music that's not your usual taste. Go to dinner somewhere exotic.

Go to bed early.

220-602 Exam Day

It is easy to see yourself as 90 minutes away from the end. This is a tempting but dangerous trap. Remember, you are a professional. A professional finishes what was begun. A professional puts forth the same effort at the end as the beginning. A professional gets it done correctly, every time.

Before the Exam

Before the exam, sleep well and eat well. Do not eat sugary or starchy foods the morning of the exam. Review your "cheat sheet." As soon as they hand you scratch paper and a pen, write down all your brain dumps, tables, mnemonics, charts, diagrams, religious prayers, whatever you like. Be sure to give your notes back to them at the end of the exam.

During the Exam

During the exam, remember: One question at a time; that is, read the darn question (RTDQ). Don't let distracters do their job. Don't read too much into the questions. Always eliminate obviously wrong answers when stuck on a difficult question. This ups your odds if you have to guess. Do not hurry toward the end. You will have plenty of time to be excited afterward. Focus on each question, one at a time. Remember how much effort you put into preparing for this exam and the money you invested in your education and the test! You want it to be money and time well spent.

After the Exam

After the exam, write down the questions (someplace away from the exam center) that you remember stumped you. Look up the answers right away. You'll feel better knowing the answers. Go enjoy the rest of your day. You deserve it.

You will get your test scores as soon as you finish, but it will take few weeks to a month to get the actual certificate. Be sure and frame that certificate and hang it on the I-Love-Me wall behind your desk. For good measure, tuck the score sheets behind the certificate in the frame just in case you need to prove something later. Along with the certificate, you will receive a plastic card for your wallet.

The computer industry is constantly growing and changing. There is a never-ending supply of new and interesting technologies. Keep learning. Get on a tech RSS feed, subscribe to a periodic e-mail newsletter, join a Linux or Mac users group, participate in forums, and attend a conference. CompTIA conferences are really quite good. Remember, you are an IT professional. It is your responsibility to maintain your knowledge and skills. It is a big and fast-moving field. Enjoy the ride. Good luck!

Part III

Taking the Remote Technician Exam 220-603

Remote Hardware Troubleshooting

A+ 220-603 Exam Objectives

Objective 1.1: Install, configure, optimize and upgrade personal computer components

Objective 1.2: Identify tools, diagnostic procedures, and troubleshooting techniques for personal computer components

Objective 1.3: Perform preventive maintenance on personal computer components

Key Points

Today you will cover how to talk to customers, troubleshooting PCs remotely, and a little more SCSI. Topics are from Chapters 3, 10, and 11 of the IT Essentials v4.0 course.

Remote Technician

A remote tech solves problems remotely via phone, e-mail, or chat. The focus is people skills, and troubleshooting printers, scanners, and operating systems. Hardware is not a big focus. Safety, environmental issues, and laptops are absent altogether. It is time to schedule the 220-603 exam for two weeks from now. It is tempting to postpone and make it a month or more from now. This is a dangerous trap because prolonging the inevitable only increases stress and anxiety.

Connecting over the Phone

10.2.1: Physical connectivity accounts for the majority of hardware issues you will troubleshoot from a standard help desk. A difficult part of your job is asking people to do basic tasks without sounding condescending. Don't ask, "Is everything plugged in?" This translates into, "Listen dumb-dumb, are you smart enough to figure out how to plug in a cable?" Further, what do you suppose the answer is going to be? Besides, how would they know? They called you.

Let's revisit this with big, broad, divergent questions first. "So, tell me what happened," or simply, "How may I help you?," "What have you already checked?," or "Walk me though your previous troubleshooting," are great places to start. Follow up with nonaccusatory "why's" and "then what's" and "for how long's?" Gradually narrow the questions to specifics like "What color?," "What kind of noise?," "What did the error say?," "Every time it boots?" This makes your customer into a colleague with whom you are working to fix something.

Getting a Clue

10.4.2: When faced with vague troubleshooting scenarios, you can sometimes use keyword clues to narrow the possibilities. For example, a customer reports, "It won't start." When you ask the customer if he hears any sounds coming from the hard drive, the caller reports a clicking noise. This noise is a good indication to you that the HDD has crashed and might need to be replaced. Table 14-1 lists and translates some of the most common clue words that you might hear from customers and find on the A+ exam.

Table 14-1   Getting a Clue

Keywords	Probable Cause
Clicking noise	HDD crash.
Vibrating or "lawnmower" noise	An internal cable is touching a fan.
Automatically shuts down after a short time	The cooling fan is not plugged in or some other cooling issue.
"Missing OS" error message	Incorrect boot sequence or HDD crash.
Dual boot	Check BOOT.INI (GRUB if Linux).
Amber light (on monitor)	Monitor not receiving signal; check physical connections or the PC.
Green light (on monitor)	Monitor receiving signal, check contrast, brightness, and so on.
No light (on monitor)	Plug in the monitor power cord and turn it on. (No joke, you might see this on the exam.)

Beep-Beep

3.9.1: PCs used to use a speaker to beep out a code that you then could look up in the documentation to decipher. Today, a more standardized set of codes exists. A successful power-on self test (POST) gives one or two short beeps right before it turns control over to the OS. This should not be confused with long beeps. Table 14-2 maps the number of beeps to the meaning and cause. It is rare today to find a motherboard with a built-in speaker. The only clue we get today is that it will not POST.

Table 14-2   BIOS Beep Codes

No. of Beeps	What Is Wrong?	What to Replace
1	Refresh timer error	RAM.
2	Parity error	RAM.
3	Failed the read/write test	RAM.
4	Timer not operating	Motherboard.
5	Processor error	CPU.
6	8042 gate A20 test error	CPU or motherboard.
7	Processor exception interrupt error	CPU.
8	VRAM error	Video card (or motherboard if integrated video adapter).
9	ROM checksum error	BIOS chip (or flash the BIOS).
10	CMOS checksum error	Motherboard. Checksum errors can sometime mean a dead BIOS battery. Check and see whether the BIOS will remember a date and time. If not, the battery needs to be replaced.
11	Failed the cache memory test	CPU or motherboard.

Just a Little SCSI

11.3.6: It is rare that you will troubleshoot small computer system interface (SCSI) remotely. If you do, there are some common problems and solutions you need to know. SCSI is shaped like a bus topology, with daisy-chained drives and devices and physical terminators or a device at each end. The boot drive is numbered 0 (or lowest available), the controller is the highest number available, and the other devices are manually numbered by jumper and connected sequentially to the cable. Cables range in size from 50 pins to 80 pins, and the number of devices ranges from as few a 1 drive to 15 drives. SCSI is typically used in groups of three to six in server redundant array of independent (or inexpensive) discs (RAID) arrays because they are hot swappable.

Homework

It is possible that you chose this path because you don't like hardware. If that is you, reread Days 31–28. This might sound counterintuitive, but the fact is that hardware is 15% of this test. There is a catch. This time, read it through the eyes of a remote technician. Consider how you would explain or troubleshoot these concepts to a remote customer.

Funwork

Listen to podcasts of Car Talk at http://www.cartalk.com. These guys troubleshoot car problems during a call-in radio show. Know that they have a reputation for being wise guys. People who call them for help know they will be teased. (That kind of behavior while working at a help desk is considered... not career enhancing.) Don't focus on their humorous antics. Instead, listen to how they troubleshoot using the wide-to-narrow approach. They often find the problem is a "user error." Listen to how they handle it with humor but respectfully. Their opinions are often sought to support arguments among "end users." Make sure you are well versed in the current IT debates. People make big-ticket purchases based on your opinion, so make certain that your judgments are factually based and not based on ad campaigns and PR. Notice how they always close with the customer.

Troubleshooting from a Distance

A+ 220-603 Exam Objectives

Objective 2.1: Identify the fundamental principles of using operating systems

Objective 2.2: Install, configure, optimize and upgrade operating systems

Objective 2.3: Identify tools, diagnostic procedures and troubleshooting techniques for operating systems

Objective 2.4: Perform preventive maintenance for operating systems

Key Points

Today is all about connecting to computers remotely. These are wonderful tools for the remote technician. Topics covered today come from Chapters 5, 10, 15, and 16 of the IT Essentials v4.0 course.

Remote Assistance

5.5.3: Remote Assistance provides you with a picture of what the user sees, and you can control that computer remotely. This is a powerful tool. You and the customer can talk or text in real time while looking at the customer's computer.

To enable Remote Assistance on the target computer in Windows XP and Vista, go to **Start > Control Panel > System > Remote Settings**. Check boxes and settings enable or limit the kinds and durations of connections. If you have no intention of ever using Remote Assistance, disable this service for security reasons.

To respond to Remote Assistance in Vista, click **System > Advanced System Settings > Remote**. In XP, click **Start > Control Panel > Help and Support**. You will need to enter the password the customer has provided you. Note: Do not include the password in the text or document that requests the help. It is like leaving the keys hanging from the sun visor of an expensive car.

Remote Assistance Assistance

10.4.3: It might seem strange to troubleshoot a troubleshooting tool, but Remote Assistance requires the following to work:

- To offer assistance, you need XP Pro or Server 2003 or 2008 or Vista. XP Home can accept but not offer help.

- You need a password. This is a great opportunity to use a hardened password.

- Port 3389 must be open on the computer and any intermediary firewalls.

- Terminal Service must be running for any remote access to work: **Control Panel > Administrative Tools > Services**. The string value of HKEY_LOCAL_MACHINE\SOFT- WARE\Microsoft\Ole EnableDCOM = Y must be enabled in the Registry (REGEDIT.EXE).

- Both you and the customer need to run Windows Messenger (or other Messaging Application Programming Interface [MAPI] compatible service), e-mail, Outlook, or Outlook Express.

- Make sure the group policy on the customer's computer is set to allow remote assistance. The command to run Group Policy Editor in XP is GPEDIT.MSC.

Some of this is pretty obscure stuff, and most of it is set up by default. Usually, a mere check box enables or disables these settings. However, this is the kind of information that remote techs need to know for the A+ exam.

Remote Desktop

10.2.2: Remote Desktop Connection (RDC) is subtly different from Remote Assistance. In a Remote Assistance environment, the customer asks for help. In an RDC environment, the remote computer or device is under your authority. Consider a server or router that resides hundreds of miles away that needs a service turned on. After the plane trip, hotel, meals, and ground transportation, that would be a very expensive few mouse clicks. So why not have someone there who can do it? Customer-based equipment is often not administered by them, but rather by you. They typically don't care about making it work; they pay you to deal with it.

To initiate an RDC, click **Start > All Programs > Accessories > Remote Desktop**. Enter the name or IP address of the target computer. Remote access needs to be enabled on the target (or destination) computer. Right-click **My Computer> Properties**, and then select the **Remote** tab. From there, you can allow or disallow Remote Assistance and Remote Desktop Connection.

If you using an Integrated Services Router (ISR) as in a home network, you will need to allow for port 3389 to be open. Most ISRs use a check box (for example, Allow Applications and Gaming or Allow Virtual Servers) as a user-friendly way to open that port.

There are dozens of remote desktop programs with varying capabilities. RealVNC, I'm In Touch, NetSupport Manager, and Symantec's pcAnywhere are good remote control programs that also work with Linux and Mac, and many provide monitoring from cell phones.

Remote Access

5.5.1: *Remote access* is a general term that describes accessing a PC or server and even modifying files but not remotely controlling the PC or server. The best example of this is simple file sharing or web servers. A piece of the computer is dedicated for remote access, but the rest of the PC is off limits.

Shared Folders

15.4.2: In Windows 9x, NT, and 2K, enable sharing in the Network Settings in the Control Panel. Right-click the network connection and choose **Properties**. Click **Install > Service > Add**. Right-click **Services > Add**. In XP and Vista, sharing is enabled by default.

Mapping a Network Drive

5.5.1: A mapped drive is a convenient way to use a network drive. From My Computer, choose **Tools > Map a Network Drive**. Enter the location either by IP address or by the Universal Naming Convention (UNC). The UNC is a way of using friendly names for network locations. Two backslashes (\\) precede the hostname of the PC, and a single backslash (\) precedes specific shared folders or resources like printers. The format looks like this: \\PC_HOSTNAME\SPECIF-IC_FOLDER. Every time the OS loads, it reconnects to that drive and it shows up as another drive in My Computer. (For this to work correctly, Reconnect at Logon must be checked.) This gives applications easy access to load and save work to that network drive. On the other side of that connection, make sure the user has the correct permissions to access that drive. It is not uncommon to have a read-only mapped drive for reference material and another drive with full permission to save work. Further, in some security-conscious environments, it may be wise to prevent saving any work locally (even on jump drives). When everyone's work is on one server, the backup process is greatly simplified. Of course, it also means there is a single point of failure. Do not confuse "mapping a drive" with "drive mapping," which assigns a letter to an HDD partition.

Telnet and SSH

15.2.2: The parents of Remote Assistance and RDC are Telnet and Secure Shell (SSH). These are CLI-driven connections between computers. For these to work, Terminal Service must be running. Telnet and SSH sessions are initiated from the command prompt. Just enter **TELNET** followed by the target name or IP address. You then log in as a local user with a local password. Once in, you have the access of that user on the remote machine. Telnet is less secure because it uses plain-text passwords. SSH is third-party software that runs in much the same way as Telnet, but with more capabilities and security than Telnet.

VPN

16.2.1: You know that encryption uses keys and algorithms to scramble data. That scrambled file is sent through unsecure networks and then unencrypted at the other end. What if you set up a device or software that can do this so quickly that you can have RDC-like connections to other trusted networks. A packet that contains nothing more than a mouse movement or real-time screen shots is encrypted and unencrypted through a "tunnel." It virtually appears like a private network.

To set up a virtual private network (VPN) in XP, go to **Network Connections > Add New Connection**. In Vista, go to **Network and Sharing Center > Set Up Connection or Network > Connect to Workplace**. Enter the computer name or IP address. You will need some form of authentication, or you can set it up so that any user can use it. Once you are authenticated on the remote computer, you are a trusted member of that network.

Big Brother

16.1.3: Spyware, monitoring software, remote assistance… It's all semantics. Really, it is the same basic tool used for different jobs. There are many legit reasons to spy on or monitor a computer user's activities. Often, the reckless user unnecessarily exposes the company to liability. Sending a threatening e-mail, revealing company or trade secrets, misusing bandwidth with file sharing, and the list goes on.

If you are the one responsible for this monitoring, be absolutely certain of the legality. Many states are very serious about protecting the individual's right to privacy. It is a good idea to make sure you are on the right side of the law. Also, you should know where you, your employer, and the law stand if you learn about genuine unlawful behavior of your target. What responsibilities do you have if while exploring an excessive use of bandwidth you discover stolen credit card numbers, the sale of state secrets, or evidence of drug use? These are unfortunately very real scenarios. What is your responsibility at that point? Don't guess; know ahead of time.

Homework

Make a remote assistance request and answer it. Do this with a friend over the Internet or between two local computers. Afterward, use Remote Desktop to control another PC. Can you terminate your own session from the other PC? Can you transfer documents via a remote session? Find out.

Funwork

Review the "Remote Desktop" section of this chapter. In a lab or home with many computers, RDC to a computer, and then through that one RDC to another, and then another. Map it out on paper. It might resemble a cheesy hacker movie, but it still pretty fun.

Command Prompt: That Old Time Religion

A+ 220-603 Exam Objective

Objective 2.1: Identify the fundamental principles of using operating systems

Key Points

Today is all about using the command-line interface (CLI) to make remote support more effective. Chapters 5 and 8 of the IT Essentials v4.0 course contain the topics for today.

CLI on the Phone

5.5.1: It might seem counterintuitive to use CLI while remotely troubleshooting. We generally keep the user out of the CLI. The reality is that the command prompt greatly increases the accuracy of your communications and lets you focus on the troubleshooting and customer service part of the call. In the following scenarios, you, as tech support, need to know the IP address on the customer's wireless network interface card (NIC).

Scenario 1: Using CLI

You: Click **Start**. Click **Run**. Enter **CMD**. Enter **ipconfig**.

Customer: Okay.

You: Can you read to me what it says next to "IP address?"

Customer: 192.168.100.4.

You: That's, 192.168.100.4 (while writing it down)?

Customer: Yep.

You: Great, thanks!

Customer: No problem.

Scenario 2: Using GUI

You: Do you see the wireless network icon in the system tray? (Note: Don't use terms like *system tray*.)

Customer: No.

You: It's in the lower-right corner.

Customer: No.

You: It looks like a tiny computer that has two parenthesis-like semicircles on the right side, as if it were making a sound.

Customer: I see the speaker thingy. Is that it?

You: No, the computer with the half-circles.

Customer: Do you want me to click on the speaker thingy?

How frustrating! You haven't even navigated to Network Properties yet. For the record, you could ask the customer to hover the arrow over these icons, and the help bubbles would indicate their use.

Command-Line Switches

5.1.2: For the A+ Remote Technician exam (and for the real world), you need to know about the switches on common CLI commands. The next sections describe the commands and switches you should know. Also know that in Windows Vista, you need to either be logged on as administrator or run the CMD as administrator to give you full access to all these commands. To run any application as administrator, right-click the icon and select **Run as Administrator**.

dir

dir shows the contents of the directory. Table 12-1 shows the **dir** switches.

Table 12-1   dir Switches

Switch	Explanation
/o	Sorts files by order.
/oe	Orders by extension.
/on	Orders by name (alphabetically. This is the same as /o.)
/og	Orders by group (directories first).
/od	Orders by date (most recent at the end).
/os	Orders by size.
/p	Displays the output page by page (nice feature when working with very long directories).
/w	Displays the output wide, across the screen.
/a	Displays the files and their attributes.
/s	Shows all the files in the current directory and the files in subdirectories. Note: This could take a while. Ctrl-C will break it so that you can do something else besides watch thousands of files scroll past.

xcopy

The **xcopy** syntax is a little trickier because you need to specify the source and destination and then any switches, as follows:

```
xcopy [source] [destination] [switch]
```

By default, **xcopy** removes any read-only attributes unless you use the **/k** switch. Table 12-2 shows the **xcopy** switches.

Table 12-2   xcopy Switches

Switch	Explanation
/h	Copies hidden and system and regular files.
/k	Copies all the file attributes.
/o	Copies the ownership and access control list (ACL) information with the files. This requires new technology file system (NTFS).
/e	Copies everything, including subdirectories, and empty directories.
/s	Copies everything, including subdirectories, except empty directories.
/f	Shows full source and destination filenames during the copy.
/a	Makes quick backup by copying only files with the archive set in attrib. Does not reset or interfere with the regular backup schedules.
/g	Copies encrypted files to destinations that do not support encryption, like CD, jump drives, and the like. Note: This is used for data recovery (or hacking) when the key is lost. But bring a lunch if you are going to wait for the data to be unencrypted.
/r	Overwrites any read-only files in the destination directory.
/u	Copies and overwrites only files that already exist in the destination.
/v	Verifies each new file in the destination.

attrib

5.4.9: Unfortunately, you need to memorize more than the RASH mnemonic. You already know the *R* means read-only, *A* includes an archive bit used during backups, *S* identifies a system file (so we leave it alone), and *H* is to hide a file from end users so they leave it alone. For the Remote Technician exam, you need to know how to use **attrib** to modify file attributes. The GUI does not provide all the attributes. Knowing the CLI gives you more control. Table 12-3 shows the **attrib** switches.

Table 12-3   attrib Switches

Switch	Explanation
+	"Adds" or sets the attribute.
-	"Subtracts" or clears the attribute.
/s	Applies the attribute changes to all the file with the same attributes in that directory and all subdirectories. (Be careful with this one. Don't confuse this switch with *S* (for system).)
/d	Changes the attributes of the actual directory (folder).

format

5.4.1: Manual CLI formats from the command line are rare today; nonetheless, you need to be familiar with **format** switches in Table 12-4 for the A+ exam.

Table 12-4   format Switches

Switch	Explanation
/fs	Followed by **fat32** or **ntfs**, manually chooses which file system to use
/v	Followed by what you want to name the volume (drive)
/q	Uses a quick format

ipconfig

8.9.2: ipconfig shows the network information of the PC. These switches are particularly important to know for your exam. Note: It is **ifconfig** in Linux and Mac OS X. Table 12-5 shows the **ipconfig** switches.

Table 12-5   ipconfig Switches

Switch	Explanation
/all	Shows MAC address, IPv6 address, hostname, and other detailed information and the basic IP address.
/release	Releases the IP address back to the DHCP server for use somewhere else. This command assumes that the PC runs on a network and is assigned an IP address dynamically via a DHCP server.
/renew	Asks the DHCP server for a new IP address.
/flushdns	Clears the Domain Name System (DNS) server cache. When the "friendly" names like www.cisco.com get mapped to some other IP address, it might be time to issue this command.

ping

8.3.5: ping requires a hyphen before its switches and prefers lowercase letters. Table 12-6 shows the **ping** switches.

Table 12-6   ping Switches

Switch	Explanation
-t	Keeps pinging until told not to with a Ctrl-C
-w	Changes the wait time (in milliseconds) for each reply

Homework

Schedule a task from the CLI using the **AT** command. In a command prompt, enter **AT/?** and explore the variables and switches. The syntax is essentially this: At this computer, at this time/date, do this thing. Schedule a backup or a defrag for late tonight. Check in the morning to make sure it ran. Can you schedule tasks and utilities to run on other computers? That's definitely a useful (and powerful) tool. Caution: The **/delete** switch can negate useful scheduled tasks, such as scheduled antivirus and OS updates. Take care when using this command.

Funwork

Visit My Home 2.0 at http://www.2pointhome.com. Watch several episodes. It is a home makeover show, but is all about listening to customers' needs and finding exactly the right equipment and software to fit their needs.

Microsoft and Me

A+ 220-603 Exam Objective

Objective 2.1: Identify the fundamental principles of using operating systems

Key Points

Today you will take a closer look at the operating system. You will cover licensing, cabinet (CAB) files, play "identify that file," and then learn multiple methods to accomplish the same task. Topics from Chapter 5 and Chapter 12 of the IT Essentials v4.0 course are covered today.

License and Registration, Please

5.5.5: A common call to tech centers is this: "What is a product key and why won't my computer work?" Windows XP works with no key for 30 days. After that, the user must contact Microsoft and pay for a product key.

A related call is this: "I added a new computer on the network, but it cannot connect to the server." In the Windows server world, administrators purchase a finite number of Client Access Licenses (CAL) from Microsoft. This should reflect the size and usage of the server and network it supports. CALs are categorized as per seat, per server, per processor, or per user. Remember that a physical server may run dozens of services, each of which requires a CAL. Likewise, one physical server can span many boxes. Plan ahead and purchase more than you need. CALs do apply to the Internet Information Server, Microsoft's web server, thank goodness.

Hailing a CAB

A CAB file is almost exactly like a Linux tarball. It is a collection of files and folders archived (grouped) and then compressed. Think of it like a hiker's frame pack. Gear, clothing, food, water, fuel, maps, and espresso maker are gathered and then compressed to make the pack one easy-to-carry unit. CAB files contain drivers, services, and protocols that were not important in the initial installation but might be later. To take the analogy a step further, some things like text documents compress well, like a down sleeping bag. Others, like photos, hardly change shape when compressed, like a water bottle. And just like that pack, to get something out of a CAB file, it needs to be extracted (that is, uncompressed and ungrouped). The aptly named EXTRACT.EXE performs this trick.

Windows XP has built-in support to explore CAB files. You can simply view them like you can any zipped file. However, in Windows 9x, NT, and 2K, you need an archive manager. EXTRACT.EXE will do this, and third-party software such as WinRAR, PKZip, WinZip, and countless other graphically based utilities work well, too.

Never Forget a Face

12.2.8: Can you identify the name of the file from what it looks like? What is this file called, and what does it do? Hint: Look at the OS names in the last two lines, for example:

```
[boot loader]
timeout=30
default=multi(0)disk(0)rdisk(0)partition(1)\WINDOWS
[operating systems]
multi(0)disk(0)rdisk(0)partition(1)\WINDOWS="Windows XP Professional" /fastde
   tect
multi(0)disk(0)rdisk(0)partition(2)\WINNT="Windows 2000 Professional" /fastde
   tect
```

Anytime you see a file with several lines of multi(0)disk(0)... you know it is BOOT.INI.

How about this blast from the past:

```
DEVICE=C:\WINDOWS\HIMEM.SYS
DEVICE=C:\WINDOWS\EMM386.EXE RAM HIGHSCAN I=B700-B7FF D=64 H=255
DOS=HIGH,UMB
FILES=100
BUFFERS=20
LASTDRIVE=E
SHELL=C:\WINDOWS\COMMAND.COM C:\WINDOWS /E:1024 DEVICEHIGH=C:\CDROM\CDDRV.SYS
   /E: DEVICEHIGH=C:\WINDOWS\SETVER.EXE DEVICEHIGH=C:\WINDOWS\IFSHLP.SYS
DEVICEHIGH=C:\WINDOWS\COMMAND\ANSI.SYS
```

This is CONFIG.SYS. An easy way to remember this is that our job is to "config" a "device" (notice that the first two lines begin with *device*). We know CONFIG.SYS as a graphical user interface (GUI) utility with check boxes, but for every check, you add, delete, or edit a line in this text file.

Here is another oldie but goodie:

```
@ECHO OFF
PROMPT $p$g
SET PATH=C:\WINDOWS;C:\WINDOWS\COMMAND
LH C:\WINDOWS\COMMAND\MSCDEX.EXE /D:
REM LH C:\WINDOWS\SMARTDRV.EXE /X
LH C:\MOUSE\MOUSE.COM or EXE
```

This is AUTOEXE.BAT. ECHO and PROMPT are dead giveaways. Note the SET PATH line that tells where to find the OS.

Know All Roads

For the A+ exam, be prepared to describe multiple ways to accomplish tasks. This is exactly why it is advisable to spend time with many different techies and learn their tricks. Here are some examples of multiple paths to the same ends.

Check the version of the OS:

- CLI: **ver**.

- **Control Panel > System Properties**.

- Right-click **My Computer** and click **Properties**.

See which files are shared on your PC:

- Navigate to Shared Docs, Videos, Pictures, and so on.

- Look for files with the hand under them.

- Look at yourself in Network Places.

Move a file:

- Right-click, drag the icon, and then select **Move Here**.

- CLI: **copy** [*source path*] [*destination path*].

- Select the file. In the File menu, click **Edit > Cut** and navigate to new location. Then from the File menu, choose **Edit > Paste**.

Show your IP address:

- Click **Control Panel > Network Connections**. Right-click the **Network Connection** icon, click **Properties**, choose **TCP/IP**, and click **Properties**.

- Click the **Network** icon in the system tray. Click **Properties > TCP/IP > Properties**.

- CLI: **ipconfig**.

Determine the name of your PC:

- CLI: **hostname**.

- CLI: **ipconfig /all**.

- CLI: **net config workstation**.

- Click **Control Panel > Network Connections**. Click **Advanced** in the menu bar, trace to Network Identification, and click **Computer Name**.

- Click **Control Panel > System > *Computer Name***.

Navigate to the Device Manager:

- CLI: **devmgmt.msc**.

- Choose **Control Panel > Administrative Tools > Computer Management**. Follow the shortcut to the **System Tools > Device Manager**.

- Choose **Control Panel > System > Device Manager**.

- Right-click **My Computer** (on the desktop or Start menu), and then click **Properties > Device Manager**.

Homework

Google the phrase *XP shortcuts*. Learn and practice multiple ways to do tasks. This knowledge is excellent for the A+ exam, but it also helps your "street cred" among techies.

Also visit Software Tips and Tricks (http://www.softwaretipsandtricks.com) to find out how others have solved the same problems you're troubleshooting.

Funwork

Try these steps, but remember to just look at the files:

Step 1   Run **Notepad.exe**.

Step 2   Click **File > Open**.

Step 3   Select **All Files** (not just .txt).

Step 4   Navigate to **C:\Windows\System32 directory**.

Step 5   Open some recognizable files and programs.

CAUTION: Do not make any changes, just look. Seriously, even one altered digit or character can totally mess up an OS.

You will see a lot of programming gibberish, very *Matrix*-like, but most have some text that configure running environments, dependencies, processing, and security. After a while, you will begin to see commonalities and patterns. Executables have certain variables that supporting files do not. This is a quick peek at the behind-the-scenes world of Windows. Like exploring the HKEYs in the Registry, it cannot be stressed enough the awful ramifications of making unknowledgeable changes to these documents.

If you want a closer look, download a hex editor and view the same files. This decodes some of the gibberish into English. The significance of looking at these files is a little like metacognition (thinking about thinking). In these very files exist the actual codes that program the CPU, RAM, and HDD that make the collection of lifeless devices into a PC.

Comparing Operating Systems

A+ 220-603 Exam Objectives

Objective 2.1: Identify the fundamental principles of using operating systems

Objective 2.2: Install, configure, optimize and upgrade operating systems

Key Points

Today's topics relate to Chapter 5 and Chapter 12 in the IT Essentials v4.0 course. It is important to learn some basics about other operating systems and to be able to look at Windows through the eyes of Linux and Mac users. Learning a little about other operating systems helps reinforce what you already know about Windows, in much the same way studying a foreign language improves your primary one.

Comparing Windows XP, Macintosh OS X, and Linux

5.4.9: The next few sections are a comparative look at the three operating systems found on the A+ exam. Without a doubt, the exam focuses on Windows. These are topics you really ought to know about the other operating systems for the A+ exam and to make you a more useful person in an increasingly cross-platform world.

A Different Look at Windows

It is time for a mindbender. On your desktop, there is an icon called My Computer. Nearby are other icons. Below is a taskbar and Start menu. Are these other desktop items not on My Computer? Perhaps on someone else's computer? Let's not start with the idea of My Network Places. Imagine the whole Internet inside of one program called Internet Explorer. No? It gets worse. Inside My Computer is an icon called C: that contains, among many things, the path Windows\Documents and Settings. In that directory you find… yourself (your user). How can you be out here and in there? Is there another desktop inside your user with its own My Computer? How far does this go?

The answer is: nowhere. It is a hall of mirrors. These directories really do live inside of one another, but the user interface maps back to the actual location instead of endlessly down the C: rabbit hole.

The logic behind the real versus perceived directory structures lay in permissions. We want users to have an intuitive interface and the flexibility to store, modify files, and even install devices. As administrators, we want the ability to lock them out of sensitive places. Think of end users exploring like you did in yesterday's funwork. Imagine the fun they might have in the command prompt exploring new friends like FORMAT and DEL.

You will spend some time during the homework familiarizing yourself with the Windows directory structure, but first we will look at the Mac and Linux directory trees and installation procedures to compare and contrast these three families of operating systems.

A Look at Macintosh OS X

The core of Mac OS X is called Darwin, a UNIX version. Apple customized a layer called Aqua that provides a very Macish, user-friendly graphical user interface (GUI), like a pretty skin pulled tight over the geeky but sleek UNIX.

The directory structure has many main folders at the root level:

- A System folder holds system files unchangeable by users other than root.

- A Library folder holds user-controllable settings like fonts, support files (Microsoft calls these dynamic link libraries, or DLLs).

- An Applications folder contains… you guessed it: applications.

- A Users folder has a folder for every user, has a home directory, and contains settings particular to that user.

- There is a Network folder for networking

- A Volumes folder contains the drives just like My Computer.

Does all this sound familiar? The command-line interface (CLI) called Terminal in Mac OS X is found in the Control Panel or **Finder > Applications > Utilities**.

A Look at Linux

Linux is open source, which means anyone can do what they want with it. This leads to huge number of versions and offshoots of Linux. We will focus on the commonalities found in major distros like RedHat, SuSE, and Ubuntu.

The end-user interface works like any point-and-click, drag-and-drop GUI. Linux is a text-based OS with a GUI overlay. Linux has many tiny specialized programs rather than fewer all-in-one programs like Microsoft's Add/Remove Programs, Network Connections, and Device Manager. Each program, network setting, and driver is copied into the correct directory and manually configured. The following is a list of facts that every self-respecting Windows person should know about Linux:

- Linux boots by copying the master boot record (MBR) to RAM.

- LILO or GRUB is the boot file that controls the rest of startup.

- .confs are configuration files (which are like text-based Control Panel applets).

- The system kernel is called kernel /bzImage-2.6.14.2. Note that the version number 2.6.14.2 is just an example.

- The system kernel is loaded along with initrd /initrd-2.6.14.2.img. Initrd (or Initial Ram Disk) is similar to config.sys. It contains instructions on how to access drives and file systems.

- /dev/hda is essentially the C: drive.

- ext2 and ext3 are file-allocation types, like FAT and NTFS are to Windows.

- The command **MAN** after any command is like the switch **/?** in the command prompt. It will describe usage and syntax of the command it follows.

- Root is the administrator account.

- Terminal is the CLI.

- The command **su** lets you execute a command as root while logged in as a restricted user.

- **ifconfig** displays network interface card (NIC) configuration, and you can change the settings using this command. However, if you want the changes to last longer than the current session, you must edit the network config file at /usr/sbin/system-config-network-tui.

All this emphasis on text-driven interfaces is daunting at first. Really, it is a blessing in disguise. Because it is designed to be a server platform, you can actually boot Linux without KDE or GNOME, and go straight to text. This prevents the PC from spending tremendous amounts of processing and energy redrawing the screen. Further, the CLI-driven interface is the perfect environment for scripting. Be sure to have a good reference book, and a very patient Linux-speaking friend or Linux User's Group (LUG) nearby when you get serious about learning Linux.

Installing Applications on Operating Systems

5.4.9: This section describes installing operating systems in Windows, Mac, and Linux.

Installing an Application in Windows

When installing an application in Windows, typically you download the application and unzip it. You then double-click the icon that closest resembles setup.exe.

In the case of a CD, the autorun starts the process. You answer questions, and the code and shortcuts are copied. Remember, in Windows 9x and Me, you need to restart the OS before many programs and settings will take effect.

Installing an Application in Mac OS X

When installing an application in Mac OS X, whether downloaded or from CD, make sure the disk image (.dmg) is unpacked (unzipped). Mount the program installer with a double-click. If the package is the actual application, just drag it to the Applications folder. Like Windows Explorer, the left side of the window has a list of commonly used shortcuts. If the application is still a package (.pkg), double-click and follow the directions (just as you do for a Windows installation). The last step is to unmount the installer by dragging it to the trash. To keep a shortcut in the Dock (the all-in-one system tray/taskbar), launch the program and **Ctrl-click** the icon in the Dock. Select **Keep in Dock**. Mac is all about the user experience, the path of least resistance. Hardened Windows fans have difficulty letting go of complicated tasks and procedures. If that is you, go check out Linux.

Installing an Application in Linux

Linux is not designed to be user friendly. It is designed to be fast, stable, and skinny. Many efforts have recently made Linux much more consumer oriented. Arguably, Ubuntu is the most user friendly. For some reason, Linux developers actually think that end users love to memorize and issue commands in a CLI. This is why Linux is made by and for computer people.

When installing applications in Linux, first you need root (administrator) permission. This is done by logging in as root or by using the **su** command. Programs often come as tarballs (.tar.gz). These are compressed and packaged files to make it easier and quicker to download. The command **tar - x** extracts the tarball. Now look at the extensions. If it is .bin, look in the ReadMe files (typically, install.sh) to find out where to copy the files. If it is source code, it must first be compiled (turned into a .bin) before being installed. Ask a Linux person about that process.

Thankfully, most distros today use RedHat Package Manager (RPM) or Debian Installer (.deb) files, which are similar to Windows installers, to launch the setup and answer the questions. Developers still can't seem to divorce themselves from the CLI. If it is a Debian distro like Ubuntu, the command is **apt-get install**, followed by the .deb name. RedHat uses **yum install**, followed by the RPM name. With such an easy-to-use, consumer-driver interface, it is a wonder why there is essentially no home-market penetration. Still, it is an outstanding server platform.

Homework

You need to become intimately familiar with the Windows directory structure. The Windows file structure shown in Figure 10-1 is the beginning of your homework. Using Windows Explorer on your computer and really big paper, create a more comprehensive map of your computer. Make the initial boxes really big because there is a lot in each directory.

How detailed? As much as reasonable. Basically, if you have heard of it, draw it. If it is an .exe .bat .com, draw it. If it is a cloud of .dlls and .tmps, abbreviate these by drawing a small cloud of .dlls and .tmps. In System32, just hit the familiar files and leave the rest.

It is a little tedious to draw it out, but it really helps solidify in your mind where things are actually located. It is a little shocking how this big piece of paper will pop back into your mind when the A+ exam asks you a question about the location of a file. You will know exactly where it is.

Take this one step further and draw lines that represent permission shortcuts from some key applications (such as IE, Office applications) to the users' desktops.

Pin this on your wall where you can't help but see it for the next 10 days.

Figure 10-1   Windows File Structure

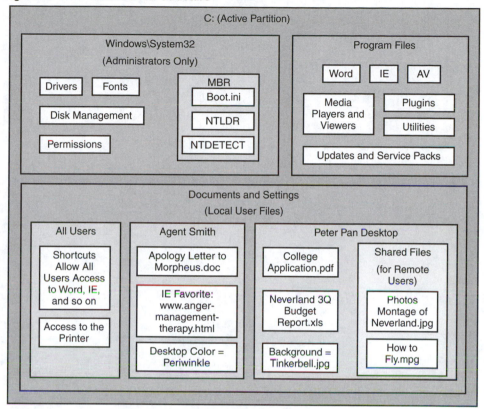

Funwork

Go get a breath of fresh air, see a movie, go out to eat, do something somewhere else. After that homework, you deserve a break.

Opening Windows

A+ 220-603 Exam Objectives

Objective 2.2: Install, configure, optimize and upgrade operating systems

Objective 2.3: Identify tools, diagnostic procedures and troubleshooting techniques for operating systems

Key Points

Today relates to topics in Chapter 5 and Chapter 12 of the IT Essentials v4.0 course. You will cover upgrades to Windows, policies, the Registry, and backward compatibility.

Upgrading Windows

12.3: Many customers think that a new OS is like a new car. A more correct analogy is a new OS is like building an SUV on a scooter: lots of great features, but no go. In most cases, the user experiences a decrease in overall performance because of all the extra features and supporting files. There is a commonly held belief among techies that upgrading is never a good idea. If given the option, you should always back up the data and perform a clean install. Regardless of an OS upgrade, it is a great idea to do this periodically. It cleans out all the clutter, dead downloads, lurking viruses, and weird HDD sector issues. It's like a PC day at the spa. It noticeably improves performance. Here are some upgrading rules:

- You should have a really good reason to upgrade the OS. Newer ones are larger and tax the system more than the leaner, older ones.

- Windows 3.1/95(a) cannot be upgraded to XP (picture the SUV built on the scooter analogy).

- Windows 9x should not be upgraded to any NT-based OS, NT, 2K, XP, servers, and so on because 9x uses only FAT32, and the NT really should use NTFS; however, it is possible. Make sure your customer knows this.

- Windows NT 4 with Service Pack 6 and Windows 2000 can upgrade to XP Professional only.

Cisco, Dell, Microsoft, and Apple are all older than most of their customers. This is a novel thought for people over 35 who are often the decision makers. There was a time when Microsoft was a scrappy young company fueled by new technologies and bristling with pride. Today, the matured (and wiser) Microsoft is more about market share and risk exposure than lunchtime volleyball games. Figure 9-1 is a big-picture view of the Microsoft family tree. For the newbies, it is a history lesson. For the oldbies, it is memory lane road trip. This diagram is greatly oversimplified because the actual family tree with every edition, version, and service pack would fill this book many times over.

Figure 9-1   Microsoft OS Family Tree

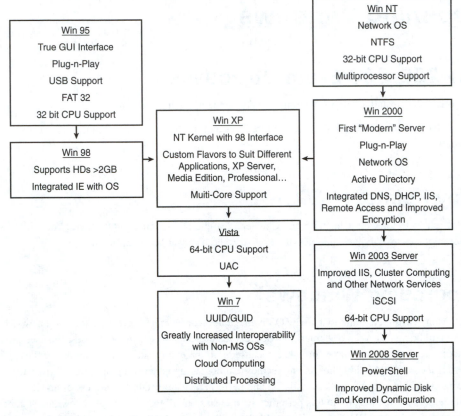

Distributions of Windows XP

12.1: Besides the basic XP versions Professional, Home Edition, Media Center, Tablet PC Edition, and 64-bit Edition, there are other distribution issues to consider. When reinstalling, troubleshooting, or adding a new service from the OS CD, use the discs that came with the computer. Many original equipment manufacturer (OEM) CDs contain device drivers customized to suit that device, or more often a family or product line. This really cuts down on the network interface card (NIC) driver game (when you need the NIC driver to use the NIC to get the driver for the NIC). OEM versions are particularly important when you're dealing with exotic hardware, touch screens, fingerprint readers, or smart card readers.

It is not uncommon that a company purchases computers from only one vendor. It might be limiting from a purchasing perspective, but this really does work in your favor. If you tend to service the same set of computers, you should have in your toolkit the OEM CDs for those models. Your customers sometimes do not have the foresight to keep these CDs. You can save them $50 or a $100 and a few days shipping. (Make sure they realize how your preparedness saved them time and money, but don't rub it in.)

Microsoft also has "thin" versions of XP sold at a lower price and aimed at specific foreign markets or to comply with fair trade agreements. Be sure you know what you are buying. Some of them are very limited. Lastly, because of trade embargos and other politics, you cannot legally ship, sell, or otherwise transfer some software to certain countries. These restrictions are akin to enforcing prohibition, but it is still your responsibility to know the laws. Technology has a long history of outgrowing the sluggish legal system. Even some "friendly" states have protectionist laws aimed at protecting their own home-grown products and services. If you are do business with foreign clients, a quick trip to the Department of Justice and Homeland Security websites is time well spent.

Backward Compatibility

5.1.2: You can run programs as though they were in a previous OS environment. In XP and Vista, right-click the program icon. Select **Properties > Compatibility > Run In > Compatibility Mode**. You can run the program as though it were in any Windows OS all the way back to Windows 95. Honestly, how cool is that? That means that real backward compatibility is a mere check box away.

Here is an all too common scenario. Your customer bought an $11,000 program to run an assembly line in 1996. She wants to upgrade the PC (currently Windows 95) to Vista (perhaps so that it can support a network-monitoring tool she can monitor from her office). The drivers that came with the machinery are clearly not designed for Vista. Before you roll your eyes, realize that the solution is shockingly simple. Just run that program as in its own 32-bit, real mode, "privileges be darned" environment. Sorry for sounding like an infomercial, but just ask anyone over 30 about backward-compatibility issues. The backward-compatibility menu also allows for specific run environments, such as 640 x 480 screen resolutions and 256 colors, which some games require. The run as administrator can also be "permanently" set in this menu. Many pre-XP programs require this to run at all. This is a major troubleshooting magic bullet.

The Devil in the Details

5.4.7: Regedit.exe is a powerful tool and needs to be wielded with care. One misstep, such as the wrong string, the wrong value, or any little thing, can have catastrophic consequences. It is akin to reprogramming your DNA.

HKEY_USERS contains subkeys for each user. This gives you considerable control of the user accounts. KEY_CURRENT_USER governs the currently logged-in user. It is actually a link or shortcut to the HKEY_USERS hive subkey specific to the current user. These settings are stored on two files that you need to know for the A+ exam: NTUSER.DAT and USRCLASS.DAT. Know that they contain Registry information pertaining to the users.

HKEY_LOCAL_MACHINE has four parts: Security Accounts Manager (SAM), Security, Software, and System. The files are conveniently named SAM.LOG, Security.LOG, Software.LOG, and System.LOG (with backups that use a .sav extension).

A little about Security: Syskey.exe unlocks the Account Database. Unlocking the Account Database is one common method of forced entry into a Windows OS for data recovery (or hacking). The administrator will copy the SAM and Security files to a network drive or some removable media so they can be viewed via a hexadecimal editor and cracked by encryption software. Another method of attack is to simply replace these files with your own. This method of attack is like stealing a car by replacing the steering wheel. The point: In a secure environment, do not grant end users access to the command prompt.

HKEY_CURRENT_CONFIG is made during each boot and contains the current devices. HKEY_CLASSES_ROOT, actually a subkey of HKEY_LOCAL_MACHINE/Software, contains application information (for example, file associations). If you want to manually change the program that opens an extension, you can do that here. However, it is better to do so by right-clicking **File > Open With > Choose Program**. Then check the box next to **Always Use**. It is a much safer (and easier) way to go.

Policies

5.4.7: The Policy Editor is in the Administrator Tools section of the Control Panel. If it is not there, you could be running Home editions of either XP or Vista. You can download GPEDIT.EXE from many sources and trick the Home editions to follow a policy. This exemplifies the difference between a Home edition designed for cameras, games, music, screen savers, and P2P file sharing versus the security-conscious, no-nonsense work environment of the professional versions. You can also add Group Policy Editor as a snap-in to a Microsoft Management Console (MMC).

When playing with policies, you first need to require hardened passwords. Just make sure your paper recycling bin is big enough to hold all the nasty notes your end users will send you. Next, explore the other sections. Some sections affect the entire OS, some are customized per user, and some are specific to applications. If you haven't seen Policy Editor, it is well worth the experience. Feel the power in each click, and hear end users scream and curse their denied rights. Contain your maniacal laughter while on the phone with a weeping customer. Before you spiral into an Orwellian fantasy, remember that you are responsible for troubleshooting that same PC. Make sure what you are doing is helpful and not just plain mean.

Homework

Explore your Registry, policies, and user privileges. If you are feeling brave, back up your PC and experiment. Create a new user (so that you can delete it later) and restrict or permit access to specific files and applications of your choosing. Test your settings by attempting to access the blocked resources. Can you make a custom group for a printer technician? You don't want him to have access to user files, but he does need to be able to install and run programs and hardware.

Funwork

Entire careers are built around customizing the Registry, refining policies, assigning permissions to users, and creating custom groups. These career builders tend to be very smart but very serious, detail-oriented network administrators. Go find one and ask about his job. Search online for tools and tips on creating XP access control lists (not the router-based ACLs) and group policies. It is definitely a different view of the computer world.

Speaking Fluent XP

A+ 220-603 Exam Objectives

Objective 2.2: Install, configure, optimize and upgrade operating systems

Objective 2.3: Identify tools, diagnostic procedures and troubleshooting techniques for operating systems

Objective 2.4: Perform preventive maintenance for operating systems

Key Points

Today's topics relate to Chapter 5 and Chapter 12 of the IT Essentials v4.0 course. Today you cover keyboard shortcuts, the Windows boot sequence, custom OS installations, and some preventive maintenance.

Keyboard Shortcuts

Nothing says computer expert quite like using keyboard shortcuts rather than the mouse. When on the phone, this is even more critical. How much RAM does the customer's computer have? What service pack is installed? It takes a long time to walk a clueless end user to System Properties. The Windows key and the Pause/Break key will take the user immediately there. Not only does it look cool, it instills confidence in the customer and saves precious troubleshooting time. Table 8-1 contains commonly used keyboard shortcuts in Windows operating systems. For the A+ exam, make sure you know these shortcuts and can distinguish the real ones from distracters.

Table 8-1   Windows Keyboard Shortcuts

Key Strokes	Action
Ctrl-Print Screen	Copies the current monitor view to the clipboard. This can be pasted into Paint to save a screen shot.
Ctrl-Esc	Opens the Start menu.
Windows key	Opens the Start menu.
Windows key-M and Windows key-D	Minimize all open windows.
Shift-Windows key-M	Maximizes all open windows.
Ctrl-X	Cuts.
Ctrl-C	Copies.
Ctrl-V	Pastes.

Table 8-1 **Windows Keyboard Shortcuts** *continued*

Key Strokes	Action
Shift-F10	Right-clicks.
Esc	Closes a menu.
Tab	Scrolls along focus points or window panes. Shift-Tab navigates backward.
Spacebar	Checks boxes and radio buttons to enable or disable options after the focus has been moved there by Tab.
Ctrl-mouse drag	Copies the file.
Ctrl-Shift-mouse drag	Makes a shortcut of the file.
Ctrl-F	Opens a find (search) box in IE, Adobe Reader, MS Office, and most other apps.
F2	Renames files by highlighting the file and pressing F2. Also used in Linux.
F3	Opens to search for files and folders in Windows Explorer.
F5	Refreshes. Also used in Firefox, IE, and Linux.
Alt-Enter and Alt-double-click	Highlight a file in Windows Explorer and press Alt-Enter or Alt-double-click to view the file properties.
Windows key-Pause/Break	Opens System Properties.
Ctrl-Windows key-Tab	In Vista with Aero, it launches Flip 3D; continuing to press Tab scrolls through the open windows.
Alt-Spacebar	Opens up the active window's system menu.
Alt-F4	Closes the current window or application.
Alt-F6	Press F6 to switch between windows of the same program.
Shift and CD insert	Autorun will not start if Shift is pressed while inserting CD/DVD.

What Really Happens at Startup?

5.4.7: You need to know what happens at startup because the three most common customer words are, "It won't start." After ruling out obvious issues like the computer is not plugged in, monitor brightness, and so on, we are faced with the daunting task of troubleshooting the actual startup sequence. If it truly is a startup problem, start by pressing F5 at the splash screen, and then select the last known good configuration. Once booted, check out the Event Viewer in Administrative Tools to see what happened and which file failed. And as the final step, edit the MSCONFIG to prevent the bad startup file from launching again. If you can't solve the problem with these, it is time to reinstall the OS. Also, if you are able to boot, that is a great time to make a quick backup of the customer's files; after all, you might not have another chance.

Another good technique in this case is to use Recovery Console. To set up Recovery Console (before it crashes), put the XP CD in the drive, enter the following at the command prompt or Open menu: **d:\i386\winnt32.exe /cmdcons** (assuming the D: is the CD drive). Having Recovery Console in place before it crashes provides you with myriad troubleshooting tools, including a command prompt and the ability to manage services, read and write data, and format drives. These useful tools make data and even OS recovery much more fun.

In Windows 9x/Me, the boot sequence went like this:

1. After power-on self test (POST), BIOS looks for MSDOS.SYS and IO.SYS and copies them into RAM.

2. IO.SYS loads SYSINIT.

3. SYSINIT locates and finds the DOS kernel and CONFIG.SYS.

4. CONFIG.SYS manages the memory and fundamental devices.

5. SYSINIT loads COMMAND.COM, which contains basic or native DOS commands.

6. The COMMAND.COM runs AUTOEXEC.BAT, which is a boot honey-do list for device drivers and applications to run at startup. On that list is Start Windows.

That was back when the world was simple. In Windows NT/XP/Vista, it is more complex:

1. After POST, which now checks all the embedded and integrated devices, BIOS looks for the master boot record (MBR). It is found on the first active partition. The MBR figures out which kind of file system is running and then loads NTLDR.

2. NTLDR protects the system by switching to protected mode and then starts the file system.

3. NTLDR reads BOOT.INI. This is particularly important for dual-boot PCs. Dual-boot PCs use BOOT.INI or BOOTSECT.DOS to manage which OS to boot.

4. NTLDR runs NTDETECT, which installs device drivers. NTLDR then runs NTOSKRNL.EXE and HAL.EXE. These files begin services and further separate the hardware from software, with the hardware abstraction layer (HAL).

5. NTLDR loads the HKEY_LOCAL_MACHINE\SYSTEM Registry hive that loads the device drivers.

6. Finally, NTLDR passes the torch to the NTOSKRNL.EXE, which loads WINLOGON, and the user is asked for logon credentials.

For better or worse, you really ought to spend the time and commit the NT/XP/Vista boot sequence to memory.

Custom OS Installations

12.2.2: After experiencing a few installations, you probably realize you have better things to do than babysit status bars and click Next. There are actually four ways to speed up this process.

Unattended Installation

An unattended installation uses an answer file that automates the questions it would normally ask you. This system works fine until some little thing changes, such as a new HDD or a new expansion card. Every little thing needs to be accounted for and correctly answered in the file. Tweaking these answer files is often as time-consuming as a regular install.

Local Image

Imaging an HDD is a great way to bypass the quirky answer file. Get a perfectly configured, defragged, secured, and updated OS installation. Run a third-party imaging application, such as Norton Ghost, and then you can restore your computer back to its original state at any time, including removing any programs and files that were downloaded. Remember that restore points only alter what has changed since that point. Using restore points does not "undownload" software. Imaging reformats the partition and recopies the image so that the PC is exactly the way it once was.

Network Deployed Image

Imaging works beautifully when you have many identically configured PCs, especially when you use a deployment server. Be sure to run Sysprep to make the OS transportable to other computers. Network image server software is made by third-party vendors. Deployment servers can send the OS through the network to a PC.

Automatic Network Deployed Image

ImageYou can take imaging a step further by setting the network interface card (NIC) to work with a preboot execution environment (PXE), or "Pixie," and running a remote installation service (RIS). You can have a fresh installation ready for you every morning (that is, no spyware, no temp files, no half-baked end-user modifications, just a clean slate every morning).

Updating the Operating System

16.4.1: Be sure you know when you would *not* enable automatic updates. Consider the length of time a dialup would take to download a proper service pack. You wouldn't want the PC to be installing the service pack while giving a presentation. Best to burn a copy of the service pack to CD from a PC with a high-speed connection or schedule it at night.

Homework

Restore points (discussed yesterday in Day 9, "Opening Windows"), backups, disk cleanup (discussed in Day 23, "Operating Systems Troubleshooting"), and Scandisk and Defrag (discussed in Day 29, "Hardware Installation") should be well ingrained by now. You will likely be asked the same basic questions about these topics as you were on the Essentials exam, so definitely review these topics.

If you don't have a set of A+ exam flash cards yet, it is time to get some. Ask your friends, search online (make sure the cards test the 2006 objectives), or ask current or former computer teachers whether they have some. Pearson offers a truly great flash card product called *CompTIA A+ Cert Flash Cards Online*, available at InformIT (http://www.informit.com/).

Funwork

Visit labrats.tv and enjoy the shows.

A Long-Distance Look at Printers and Scanners

A+ 220-603 Exam Objectives

Objective 3.1: Identify the fundamental principles of using printers and scanners

Objective 3.2: Install, configure, optimize and upgrade printers and scanners

Objective 3.3: Identify tools, diagnostic procedures and troubleshooting techniques for printers and scanners

Key Points

Printers are notoriously difficult to troubleshoot over the phone. They often have limited output displays, and they are dark and dirty inside. Customers really don't want to fix them. What customers really want is for you to tell them where the hidden fix-me button is so that they can print their document and get on with life. These are not easy phone calls. Today's topics relate to Chapter 2 and Chapter 14 of the IT Essentials v4.0 course.

Printer RAM and Firmware

14.3.1: If users on a network complain that only half of their document printed, it might be that the shared printer does not have enough memory and it is relying on the PCs to hold the document in their queue. The RAM on a network printer should more than exceed the size of the documents it receives. Keep in mind peak printing times will require even more RAM. Basically like any computer, the more RAM the better.

Firmware updates for printers are rare, but they do exist, and they can greatly improve performance. Like any firmware upgrade, check the manufacturer's website, and then double-check that it is the correct file before downloading. You wouldn't you're your color laser printer to think it is suddenly a desktop inkjet. Download the file and follow the directions from the manufacturer.

Scanner Software

14.4.2: Many applications work with scanners. Once an image is scanned, it is usually modified or at the very least saved as a JPG or GIF by an application. The application can do several common tasks, which you need to be familiar with for the A+ exam. Scanners can resize the picture, for example. Going smaller is easy, but bigger tends to get grainy. Keeping the aspect ratio (usually by holding the Shift while dragging the edge of the picture) will prevent distortion. Scanners love dark, solid, high-contrasting colors like text on white paper. Most scanners have difficulty with handwriting, pencil, and colored or lined paper. Just like a photocopier, lightening and darkening the image can help. Another cool trick that scanner software can do is sharpen an image. It increases the contrast among subtle colors and lines. Taken to extreme, it looks like CD art.

Advanced graphics programs can convert the image from a raster (lots of dots) to a vector image (lines and points). Raster images do not size-up well, but vector images can be whatever size you need. A drawback of vector is it is not subtle. To get a complicated picture, you need a great many points and lines, which requires a tremendous amount of graphics processing called *rendering*. Consider how many lines and points are processed in the rendering of a Pixar movie. They use true supercomputers to get the job done. Remember, someone has to fix those ultrafast PCs and workstations, someone just like you.

WYSIWYG

14.2.2: What you see is what you get (WYSIWYG or sometimes WYSIWUG) is not a stage name; it is an actual computer industry acronym. It originally applied to print preview features of early applications that did a better than average job of displaying what the printed paper would look like. Later, the same problems occurred in website development applications. Different browsers interpret the codes differently. At some level, the computer needs to tell the printer what the page looks like. This is called Page Description Language (PDL). It has three flavors: Printer Command Language (PCL), PostScript (PS), and graphics device interface (GDI). You will see these as options in printer drivers. If given the choice, go with PS. It is cross-platform and does a great job of displaying images and text accurately. GDI treats everything as a picture, and the computer tells the printer exactly where to put each dot. PCL is the printer language from HP and is the standard among printers today.

Reduce, Reuse, Recycle

2.1.3: Being able to print has advantages. On the flip side, printing is expensive both in terms of money and the environment. The ugly reality is that unless it is special photograph or a life-insurance policy, everything that a printer prints will at some point be disposed of, often in less than a month. The ink is quite toxic, laser printers in particular use a tremendous amount of electricity; and next time you heave a box of paper around, just imagine the logistics of its manufacture, storage, and transportation. That is a lot of energy, resources, and cost for a very temporary thing.

Your clients are almost always ready to save money if not the good Earth. Reusing paper as scrap is an easy cost-saving method. Just make sure the printed stuff on the other side is not sensitive or libelous. From a troubleshooting perspective, know that some printers don't like to use leftover paper. Double-sided printers are expensive initially but greatly reduce paper consumption. The easiest option is to develop a "think before you print" awareness among your customers and employees.

Toner: The Good, the Bad, and the Messy

14.5.3: Most toner cartridges can be sent back to the manufacturer for refurbishing and refilling. Purchasing these used cartridges is a way to save money. The number one rule about cleaning up toner is don't spill it in the first place. It is affected by static electricity. It is powder, the consistency of baking soda. Do not mop it up. Do not sweep it unless it is on a nonporous surface like a linoleum floor. Do use a vacuum cleaner with a HEPA filter. Do test the vacuum on regular dust before vacuuming up the toner.

Common Printer Problems

14.6.2: Printers tend to have a few basic problems. They are not like operating systems with countless possible issues. Here are three quite common problems, symptoms, and solutions.

Paper Pickup Problems

Try the easy solutions first, such as adding new, clean, dry paper. If that doesn't work, check the printer's rubber wheels, called *paper tires*. They get tired and brittle and are not as "grabby" as a result. Professional rubber restorer is a common solution that all techs can use to can breathe new life into lackluster paper tires. Check also the spring tension that holds the paper up to the rubber rollers. The paper itself can be a problem. Some printers are very picky about paper. If you suspect this, then some experimentation is in order. For the A+ exam, remember that cool, dry, and dust-free keywords associated with ideal paper storage. In the real world, printers and paper do not typically live in such luxury.

Tick, Tick, Tick

Repetitive lines or tick marks or any repeated pattern on the printed document means that something is on the rollers. Hopefully, it can be fixed by replacing the toner cartridge. If not, seek your manufacturer's advice on how to clean or fix this problem. Be really sure you follow their directions exactly because the laser has capacitors that can electrocute you even while unplugged from the wall. It may be time to relegate the printer to in-house, non-presentation quality printing.

Fog of Pages

If the pages look like there are patches of fog where the words drift off into whiteness, the toner is running low. Take out the cartridge. Carefully and slowly shake it from side to side to move the toner inside around to evenly distribute it, and then place it back in the printer. Go buy a replacement cartridge. Soon it will be light text, then no text.

Homework

Make a troubleshooting flowchart beginning with "My printer won't print." Take a basic flowchart and write the script. You are on the phone. They are onsite. Remember, don't use jargon or geek-speak, and be polite and patient. To check your work, print a test page, and instead of clicking OK, choose **Troubleshoot**. Go through the Windows decision tree and compare it to your flowchart.

Another great resource is the manufacturer's website. Use their online troubleshooting tools and explore what tips and tricks the manufacturer of your printer offers.

Funwork

Google the phrases *digital printing press*, *astronomy imagining*, *MRI and x-ray images*, or *underground imagining*. Scanners and printers go far beyond the all-in-one. These big-ticket items are serviced by people like you.

More Networking

A+ 220-603 Exam Objectives

Objective 4.1: Identify the fundamental principles of networks

Objective 4.2: Install, configure, optimize and upgrade networks

Objective 4.3: Identify tools, diagnostic procedures and troubleshooting techniques for networks

Key Points

As a remote tech, you will be connecting to many people through different kinds of connections: remote desktop, remote assistance, phone, chat, text, e-mail, even avatars. (An avatar is an animated version of you that speaks with your voice. It is definitely on the far side of creepy, but help desk managers love it.) The point: No matter how cool (or weird) the technology is, it will not work without a proper network. Today's topics relate to Chapter 15 in the IT Essentials v4.0 course.

Ports of Call

15.2.2: You are expected to know which ports common protocols use. Table 6-1 lists the most common networking protocols, their ports, and a brief description. Commit these to memory for the test and for later when you are called on to manually configure firewalls.

Table 6-1   Ports and Protocols

POP	110	E-mail
IMAP	143	E-mail
SMTP	25	E-mail outgoing to a server or between e-mail servers, not from server to client
SSH and Telnet	22 or 23	CLI remote access
FTP	21	Downloading files
TFTP	69	Transferring files
DNS	53	Friendly URL names
DHCP	67	Autoconfigure network settings

Wire Drill

15.3.1: Unshielded twisted pair (UTP) has the basic categories of Category 3 for phones and Category 5 for computer networks. UTP has a catchment area of 100 meters (328 feet), meaning the cables should not exceed this length. TIA/EIA standards allow for 90 m of horizontal run (in the walls and ceilings). This leaves 10 m for patch cables (outside the walls). Patch cables are used to connect devices in a room to the wall jack. There are physical limitations in the walls, access holes, HVAC (heating, venting, and air conditioning), pipes, ducts, lights, fans, and so on. Physical networking is not an easy task. If you need more distance than 100 m, consider connecting a fiber-optic cable to an intermediate distribution facility (IDF). An IDF has its own 50 m Category 5 area it can cover. Fiber-optic cables can be as long as several kilometers.

So why not just use fiber optic to the desktop? You can, but Category 5 is cheap, easy to install, and can easily support 10BASE-T and 100BASE-T wiring configurations. As users' network demands increase (for, among other things, streaming video, gaming, and videoconferencing), we need to support increasing speeds. 1000BASE-T uses all eight wires, and it is advisable to step up the cable to Cat5e, Cat6, or even Cat6A. Cat6 and 6A have more twists to improve protection from crosstalk and line noise.

File Sharing

15.4.2: File sharing uses network file system (NFS) or server message block (SMB) protocols. SMB is used when sharing files among Windows, Mac, and Linux. The service needs to be first installed, then running, then the folder must be shared and files must be present. This assumes the network is correctly set up. If not, file sharing is a moot point.

Browsers

Browsers can be a source of many problems. Popup blockers, foreign languages, Java settings, trusted sights, cookies… the list goes on and on. Most of these can be solved by uninstalling, reinstalling, and then updating the browser. That usually takes much less time than exploring some tiny setting that caused the problem. As a remote technician, this method works especially well. It is also an opportunity to explore alternative browsers such as FireFox, Chrome, and Safari. This start-all-over approach works well with wireless routers, iPods, and even operating systems.

Homework

Reread the networking section (Day 19 and Day 20) in the Essentials section and ask network people questions. If you ask a network person about these basic things, that person might look at you in a strange way. Remember, that what we learn in networking early on is quite different from the reality. Networking pros live in that reality. It is like asking Stephen Hawking to help you with your physics homework. If they start using terms such as *cloud computing*, *variable length*, *classless*, *IPv6*... thank them for their time and find a lesser networking person (maybe someone who installs cabling). PC techs who do this stuff every day are another good resource; networking folks see a much bigger picture and would expect you to understand some things that are not really part of the PC tech's domain.

Spend some time on a PC and practice the **ipconfig** switches **/all**, **/release**, **/renew**, **/repair**, and **/flushdns**.

Funwork

Caution: This is seriously geeky stuff worthy of tape-repaired glasses and vinyl pocket protectors. Google the phrase *DIY WIFI antennas*. Explore the myriad antenna designs. Some range from small curved paper and wire, to coffee cans, all the way to satellite dishes. If you dare, build one of these antennas (directional ones are really interesting) and measure the signal strength compared to the professional ones. See how many service set identifiers (SSID) you can pick up from your neighbors. (Don't go snooping around on people's unsecured networks. Just because you might leave the windows open does not give strangers the right to explore your house.)

Even More Networking

A+ 220-603 Exam Objectives

Objective 4.1: Identify the fundamental principles of networks

Objective 4.2: Install, configure, optimize and upgrade networks

Objective 4.3: Identify tools, diagnostic procedures and troubleshooting techniques for networks

Key Points

Today you will play follow the packet from Chapter 15 of the IT Essentials v4.0 course. Follow the packet and the homework (and funwork); all work toward putting networking concepts into context (and action).

Follow the Packet

15.8: One way to look at a network is to follow the packet. This is an important skill in troubleshooting because at any point along the way, something can go wrong. Table 5-1 follows a file download step by step.

Table 5-1   Follow the Packet

Event	Potential Problems
The user navigates to the URL and clicks **Download**. Data: In the encapsulation model, the file is currently in the data form. Watch this column as the packet becomes encapsulated.	If the DNS is corrupt or not up-to-date, the server's IP address may not be mapped to the user-friendly URL. **ipconfig /flushdns** resets the DNS cache.
Segmentation: The file on the server is divided into several pieces.	The protocol stack (usually TCP/IP) could not be installed or properly bound to the NIC. **ipconfig /all** and NIC properties display the installed and bound protocols.
Packet: Source and destination IP addresses are assigned to each packet.	Network Address Translation (NAT) and Port Address Translation (PAT) issues on the user's end could mislead the server and the packet would be sent to a phantom destination.
Frame: Source and destination MAC addresses are assigned to each packet.	If Address Resolution Protocol (ARP) tables are not built yet, the server will not know who its neighbors are. **arp -a** displays a list of known IPs and MACs of local PCs.

continues

Table 5-1   **Follow the Packet**   *continued*

Event	Potential Problems
Each packet is sent to the NIC.	The NIC could have wrong or missing drivers or theoretically could have any number of resource conflicts, interrupt request (IRQ), direct memory access (DMA), I/O, although today it is highly unlikely. Hooray for plug-and-play! The NIC Properties Advanced tab is where you resolve these issues (if you ever need to).
Bit: The NIC translates the packet into signals (wired, wireless, fiber, audio).	This is generally not a point of failure.
At each hop along the LAN, new source and destination MAC addresses are applied but the source and destination IPs never change.	Visually inspect the cables. Pinched, frayed, knotted, or otherwise abused cables should be highly suspect. Use a cable tester or known working PC to ping through the cable to verify its effectiveness. Better yet, replace it. In a wireless network, you have signal strength and access filters to worry about (for example, WPA/MAC filtering). Intermediate switches and hubs could not be powered or the network cables not connected. Blinking lights indicate network traffic (a good sign). Switches take some time after they turn on to listen to traffic and learn the location and names of the nearby devices. Don't expect a switch to immediately begin working once turned on.
The packets pass through the gateway, and the router chooses the best path to the destination.	The router might not be configured correctly. The gateway IP address on the PC and the LAN interface IP address must be identical (as must the subnet masks). (Note that the identical subnet mask thing isn't really true. But at this level, on the A+ exam, it is.) There are countless other configuration issues at this point, including NAT and PAT, hardware firewalls, and more.
After traveling through countless routers and switches, the packets arrive at the user's PC.	This is the proverbial "cloud" (the same cloud from the funwork in Day 20). It is a collection of Internet service providers (ISP), long-distance communications, switching stations, satellites, and so on that we don't really need to understand as long as it gets where it is going. Remember the postal carrier analogy. Tracert can display the actual path.
The packet flows through the user's LAN as it did on the server's LAN.	Same potential problems exist on any LAN.
The packets are reassembled and checked for accuracy. This is de-encapsulation: taking the 0 and 1 bits transmission and moving up the model (frame, packet, segment, and back into data form).	In a UDP environment like streaming video, lost packets are ignored. This is what makes online videos quick to load but glitchy. In a TCP environment, like downloading a file, lost pieces are unacceptable. A resend is coordinated with the source PC, until all the packets are accounted for.
The OS searches for an appropriate application to read the file's extension, making the download ready to be opened or run by the user.	You can't view the site correctly because of a missing plug-in or can't launch the program because of an unassociated extension. The file could be compressed (zipped) or could be encrypted. Download and install the correct plug-in or player.

Homework

If you have the opportunity, connect a few computers and switches and cables. Ping everything, and then share files using server message block (SMB) (Samba is an open source version) or network file system (NFS). In the real world, this is called network-attached storage (NAS). This is also the basis of home theater servers and web servers (and even game servers). Next, have someone (fellow computer person) "break" your network in three ways. Do this by inserting faults: Unplug something, change NIC settings, mess with the firewalls, and so on. (No peeking.)

Set a timer and see how long it takes for you to find and fix all three faults. Ask your friend for three different faults and try to beat your time. This lab really does give you firsthand experience applying the networking concepts. If you don't have access to PCs, switches, and cables, you can use your Cisco Networking Academy login credentials and download Packet Tracer from http://cisco.netacad.net. Hint: Go through the tutorials first.

Funwork

Google the phrase *Peter Packet*.

Follow the links to the games on the Cisco website. Yes, the very serious Cisco Systems, Inc., does have a fun side, too. These games greatly simplify networking concepts and are highly entertaining.

Another great resource is a video at http://www.warriorsofthe.net.

Security and Wireless

A+ 220-603 Exam Objectives

Objective 4.1: Identify the fundamental principles of networks

Objective 4.2: Install, configure, optimize and upgrade networks

Objective 4.3: Identify tools, diagnostic procedures and troubleshooting techniques for networks

Objective 5.1: Identify the fundamental principles of security

Objective 5.2: Install, configure, optimize and upgrade security

Objective 5.3: Identify tools, diagnostic procedures and troubleshooting techniques for security issues

Objective 5.4: Perform preventive maintenance for security

Key Points

Wireless computing and security are hot topics in the PC world. CompTIA knows this, and so should you. Today is all about securing wireless connections, with topics that relate to Chapters 9, 15, and 16 of the IT Essentials v4.0 course.

Firewalls

16.2.3: A good security plan uses layered defenses, including hardware and software firewalls. Firewalls work in three ways:

- **Packer filtering:** Packet filtering is the most common and straightforward. Firewalls that use packet filtering either block or allow packets by using basic criteria, such as source or destination IP address, ports, or protocols. The disadvantage of packet filtering is that it is not subtle. It is a reliable but inflexible gate guard. Sometimes, legitimate packets get filtered because they are different.

- **Proxy filters:** Advocates for a kinder, gentler network community allow packets of all persuasions to enter or leave and use more sophisticated rules. These proxy filters are really more concerned about network intrusion rather than internal issues.

- **Stateful packet inspection:** Stateful packet inspection looks for unfamiliar packets and hides the bodies. Once a rogue packet enters the target network, the hacker will never hear from it again.

Hardware firewalls are expensive and difficult to set up and configure, but they don't impact the individual PC's performance. Plus, the hardware firewall can support an entire network.

Hash

16.2: Secure Hash Algorithm (SHA) and message digest algorithm 5 (MD5) are like checksums in that a number is generated by the actual message. A checksum counts the number of bits in a packet and inserts that number in the packet as a reference. The receiving PC reads the checksum number and counts the bits in the packet. If the number of bits and the checksum number are not equal then something has been lost or changed. SHA and MD5 work the same way, but the algorithms are much more complicated. They verify that nothing was lost or altered in the transmission.

Encryption

9.3.3: Symmetric encryption is like two people having identical keys to a house. In fact, the term *key* is used to refer to the password. It would be foolish to give the key to your house to anyone who wants to deliver a package. Keep in mind that the point of encryption is to prevent others not involved in the transaction to see what is in the box. So what do you do with the box? You can't leave it outside. You can't give away your key to strangers. Enter asymmetric encryption. Let's build a foyer that is locked both at the front door and internally to the rest of the house. The public key gets the package into the foyer and away from prying eyes. The private key that only you hold gets the box further into your house. It is not a perfect system, but it is better than nothing.

Troubleshooting Wireless Networks

15.5.1: Even wireless networks have wires. An unfortunate troubleshooting tip: End users sometimes don't understand that some devices (for example, network interface cards) draw power from the PC, whereas others require a power supply. Another wire in wireless networks is the Ethernet to set up the Integrated Services Router (ISR). The ISR is the small residential router that connects a home network to a high-speed Internet service provider (ISP). The physical cable is required for security. Otherwise, a great way to attack a wireless network is to get in (wirelessly), reset to factory settings, and then reprogram the router to suit your needs.

Sometimes, range is a problem. Range extenders work well, but too much range exposes your customers to Internet theft or worse. Your customers could be blamed for bad or illegal behavior of those stealing the access, not good for business. You should always be able to "see" your router. The command syntax **ping** *ethernet interface IP address* will tell you if your router is still there and functioning. Sometimes, ISRs need a reboot; just unplug and plug in the power cord. To reset the ISR, press and hold the reset button while plugging in the power. Then let go of the Reset button. This technique may vary between manufacturers.

Usually, IP addresses are assigned via a DHCP server on the ISR. Printers should be static and entered in the DCHP server as reserved. This means that the ISR always gives the reserved IP address to the MAC of the printer. This is the method used for any device that needs a static IP (for example, VoIP phones, servers, and computers that share printers or files). A periodic look at your DHCP server or a network traffic analyzer is good practice to see whether others are using your network.

Homework

If you have not played with or set up a wireless router and wireless NICs, do so. It is very eye-opening and gives all of these concepts and alphabet soup acronyms a place, an order, and a reason. Start with a hardwired connection to an ISR that has a digital subscriber line (DSL), fiber, or cable-connected ISP. Configure it to give out IP addresses. Set up another PC with a wireless NIC and configure it to see the router and to see the Internet. Use all your tools, like ping, ipconfig, network connections, and TCP/IP properties. Add wireless protected access (WPA) and other features, and become familiar with all the features. Chances are good you will need to do this for a customer one day (and because you are taking the Remote Tech exam, you will likely be helping this future customer over the phone).

Funwork

Your customer, a traveling salesperson, is bent on getting WiMAX on his laptop. He travels take him to Boston, Lisbon (Spain), San Francisco, and Phoenix. Find out whether WiMAX is the best option for him. If not, explain why not. Use those good customer service skills and "write" him an e-mail explaining the benefits and drawbacks of WiMAX. If you think he would be better served with another technology, explain why. This might seem like a writing prompt from a high school English class, but this is a very real scenario.

Customer Service

A+ 220-603 Exam Objectives

Objective 6.1: Use good communication skills, including listening and tact/discretion, when communicating with customers and colleagues

Objective 6.2: Use job-related professional behavior including notation of privacy, confidentiality and respect for the customer and customers' property

Key Points

Providing good customer service is about more than just fixing the customer's computer problem. Always remember the following points when interacting with customers:

- Use clear, concise, and direct statements.
- Allow the customer to complete statements; avoid interrupting.
- Clarify customer statements; ask pertinent questions.
- Avoid using jargon, abbreviations, and acronyms.
- Listen to customers.
- Maintain a positive attitude and tone of voice.
- Avoid arguing with customers or becoming defensive.
- Do not minimize customers' problems.
- Avoid being judgmental or insulting or calling the customer names.
- Avoid distractions and interruptions when talking with customers.

A Geekspeak Translation Guide

10.2.1: The remote technician interacts with the public. Here are some examples of how to speak customer.

Geekspeak:

The semi-knowledgeable customer put an HDD in the computer and could not find it in the BIOS. The jumper on the new drive was not set correctly on the PATA HDD. The old one is still master and the new one is set for CS. Customer must to change them both to CS and plug the new HDD in the end to make it master. Now they are able to see both in the BIOS.

Translation for the customer:

Let me see if I heard you correctly. In the BIOS, you set both primary drive 0 and 1 to auto. You said that the old drive's jumper is set to master, and the new one cable select. You did a great job installing this hard drive. Is the computer off and unplugged? Great, let's set both hard drives to cable select and put the old drive in the far end of the cable and the new one in the middle. Turn it on and enter the BIOS again. Now you should see both in the BIOS.

Geekspeak:

The update did not support the drivers for the touchpad on the laptop. Keyboard commands or a USB mouse navigated to the Device Manager. The driver was rolled back, and the laptop restarted.

Translation for the customer:

It is a great idea to enable automatic updates like you did. Strangely, this update didn't agree with your touchpad. No worries. It works just fine now because the touchpad thinks it was never updated. We'll take a wait-and-see approach to see whether the next update has the same problem.

Geekspeak:

The Vista UAC drives the customer crazy.

Translation for the customer:

We can turn off the Vista UAC, but it does make the PC more susceptible to attack. What is the primary use of this PC? Maybe we can beef up your security in other ways and turn off that annoying Allow or Cancel popup.

Homework

Read the article "How Customer Service Works" on the HowStuffWorks.com website (http://money.howstuffworks.com/customer-service.htm).

Funwork

The following is an "action-packed" techno thriller, so to speak. As the story unfolds, you will be asked, "How did you do that?" Your job is to use your knowledge of PCs and operating systems to fill in the commands, techniques, and procedures to complete the story. Good luck!

A mean-spirited computer technician has been fired, and he maliciously encrypted his most valuable work on his XP Professional desktop PC. He corrupted the boot files so that his PC simply will not boot. He planned to negotiate with his former employer by holding the data and the entire contents of the HDD hostage. He didn't "steal" anything, because his work is still physically on the computer at the office. In his ranting, he let his IT bravado get the best of him. He unwisely alluded to a backup plan. There is, evidently, some sort of virus named killer.bat ready to deploy in the scheduled tasks upon boot that only he can stop. He is demanding $10,000 in exchange for the key and password. (This might seem farfetched, but it is more real than you think!)

This is where you come in. The employer would rather pay you $5000 instead of bowing to this manipulative ex-employee. This is your chance to prove your worth. You are able to get a command prompt (How did you do that?) and can see all the files regardless of that fact that some were marked hidden and system (How did you do that?).

The CD burner requires Windows apps, which requires a full boot, and a jump drive is not recognized in the command-line interface (CLI). However, after installing an identical SATA drive (How did you do that?), you are ready to copy everything over to the new drive minus the read-only and encrypted key support. You enter the command, and the data is now on a new drive without killer.bat. (Check out Part III, Day 12, "Command Prompt: That Old Time Religion," and Day 8," Speaking Fluent XP," and see how you did that.) Then you took that drive to another PC that had proper AV and data forensics. You were able to isolate the encrypted files and some e-mail that will likely be used as evidence against the ex-employee in court. (Go online and find out how you did that.) Then because those e-mails were discovered, this is now a criminal investigation, so you hand the whole thing over to the police.

Contrary to popular belief, law-enforcement agencies have "backdoor" keys to most encryption software. After all, it is in the encryption manufacturer's best interest to work with law enforcement lest they be charged as an accessory to a crime. It usually takes law enforcement, using super computers, just a few short minutes to crack a key. If this sounds like the kind of work you would be interested in, these jobs really are out there.

220-603 Review Day

This is a light day in preparation for your test tomorrow. Enjoy it and relax.

By Any Other Name

The computer industry is full of different names for the same thing. These synonyms are cumbersome and challenging for the new techie. The following list contains some of the synonyms found in the IT industry and on the A+ exams. People will argue that there are subtle differences among these terms and phrases, but it is a good place to start:

- Fault isolation = troubleshooting.

- Load = copy to RAM = run = execute = launch = double-click.

- Mini stereo plug = headphone jack = 3.5TSR.

- PC = IBM clone = computer = system = machine.

- Component = device = part = field replaceable unit (FRU).

- RS232 = DB9 = DE9 = serial port.

- Documentation = release notes = ReadMe files.

- Card = I/O card = adapter card = expansion card = PC card.

- Control Panel icon = applet = configuration application = configuration utility.

- 9x = 95a, 95b, 98a, 98b, Millennium Edition (Me).

- 2K = 2000.

- Pins = contacts = channels = width = conductors.

- Bits per second = bps = b/s.

- Throughput = transfer rate = network speed. (Bandwidth is a measure of ideal speed, not the throughput actually realized.)

- Mini ATX = micro ATX = flex ATX.

- S/PDIF = SPDIF = digital audio interface.

- PCIX (peripheral component interconnect extended) is *not* PCIExpress (PCIe).

Brain Dumps

Practice the following brain dumps:

- PC layered model

- Motherboard map

- OSI and TCP/IP models

- TIA/EIA 568 A and B (wire color arrangements)

- XP boot sequence

- Laser-printer process

- General troubleshooting process

Write Your Own Practice Questions

One of the best kept secrets of academic success is to outthink the teacher. After a few tests, you should know what kinds of questions that teacher, or CompTIA in this case, asks. You have seen a real test and probably several practice tests. Write down the questions as you think they will appear on your exam. This is a skill that is honed and refined over the years. Once you master this, schooling of any kind gets much, much easier. With a little practice, you can do this, too. Answer your own questions and review them right before you enter the room for your exam tomorrow.

Homework

It's time to make your "cheat sheet" study sheet and remake it a dozen times or until you can do it all from memory. The following is a start:

- A good fuse has 0 ohms of resistance, and a blown fuse has an infinite amount of resistance.

- Customers might not always be right, but you must always treat them with respect.

- The manufacturer's website is the best place to find the most up-to-date drivers, software, and documentation.

- Gather information from the customer first, then the PC.

Funwork

Do *something* away from the computer that is fun and a little different from your usual routine: Go out with an old friend you haven't seen in a while. Or take in a movie you wouldn't normally see. Or perhaps visit a museum that you have never been to. Maybe go to a concert featuring music that's not your usual taste. Go to dinner somewhere exotic.

Go to bed early.

220-603 Exam Day

It is easy to see yourself as 90 minutes away from the end. This is a tempting but dangerous trap. Remember, you are a professional. A professional finishes what was begun. A professional puts forth the same effort at the end as the beginning. A professional gets it done correctly, every time.

Before the Exam

Before the exam, sleep well and eat well. Do not eat sugary or starchy foods the morning of the exam. Review your "cheat sheet." As soon as they hand you scratch paper and a pen, write down all your brain dumps, tables, mnemonics, charts, diagrams, religious prayers, whatever you like. Be sure to give your notes back to them at the end of the exam.

During the Exam

During the exam, remember: One question at a time; that is, read the darn question (RTDQ). Don't let distracters do their job. Don't read too much into the questions. Always eliminate obviously wrong answers when stuck on a difficult question. This ups your odds if you have to guess. Do not hurry toward the end. You will have plenty of time to be excited afterward. Focus on each question, one at a time. Remember how much effort you put into preparing for this exam and the money you invested in your education and the test! You want it to be money and time well spent. If you are a slow test taker, keep an eye on the clock.

After the Exam

After the exam, write down the questions (someplace away from the exam center) that you remember stumped you. Look up the answers right away. You'll feel better knowing the answers. Go enjoy the rest of your day. You deserve it.

You will get your test scores as soon as you finish, but it will take few weeks to a month to get the actual certificate. Be sure and frame that certificate and hang it on the I-Love-Me wall behind your desk. For good measure, tuck the score sheets behind the certificate in the frame just in case you need to prove something later. Along with the certificate, you will receive a plastic card for your wallet.

The computer industry is constantly growing and changing. There is a never-ending supply of new and interesting technologies. Keep learning. Get on a tech RSS feed, subscribe to a periodic e-mail newsletter, join a Linux or Mac users group, participate in forums, and attend a conference. CompTIA conferences are really quite good. Remember, you are an IT professional. It is your responsibility to maintain your knowledge and skills. It is a big and fast-moving field. Enjoy the ride. Good luck!

Part IV

Taking the Bench Technician Exam 220-604

Elbow Deep in Hardware

A+ 220-604 Exam Objective

Objective 1.1: Install, configure, optimize and upgrade personal computer components

Key Points

Depot, or bench, technicians (also called benchies) do not typically interact with customers or concern themselves much with operating systems. A depot technician's bench is a lot like an intensive care unit in a hospital. Devices come in broken and either get a new lease on life or are deemed organ donors (and then recycled).

Just because you work behind the scenes doesn't mean your job is less valuable. You would not want a fast-talking salesperson to fix cars, nor would you want the oil-covered, master mechanic trying to win hearts and minds of strangers. Here is something else to consider. Just about every IT company you can name was started by a bench tech just like you. Dream big, but for now focus on the second half of your A+ exam.

Today you will cover topics from Chapters 1 and 11 of the IT Essentials v4.0 course. The next four days you are going to live, eat, breath, and sleep chips, slots, sockets, charts, and drives. After all, 45% of the Bench Tech exam (220-604) is hardware. Roll up those sleeves!

Seriously SCSI

11.3.6: It is time to learn all the gritty detail about small computer system interface (SCSI). Far too many people believe that *SCSI* is synonymous with *server*. The fact is that after 20 years of development and countless versions, SCSI is still half as fast and twice the price of serial advanced technology attachment (SATA), not to mention the fact that SATA drives are so easy to install that an end user could do it.

The three most common problems found in SCSI arrays are

- Wrong family (type)
- Wrong device number (ID)
- No termination

Every device in a SCSI array must be the same SCSI type. A 68-bit-wide cable will not connect to an 80-pin drive, a narrow 8-bit interface will not play with a 16-bit-wide one. Rule of thumb, like processors and motherboards, confirm the compatibility before you buy.

Wide means it is 16 bits of parallel data. Narrow is 8 bits and is a newer SCSI that is similar to SATA in that it is serial. Unless otherwise specified, it is an 8-bit (narrow) bus.

The 80-pin cables include power in the cable, like SATA drives. The 50- and 68-pin interfaces require a Molex power cable. Something to seriously consider when building a SCSI system is the wattage of the power supply and the number of Molex plugs. The 50-pin cables use Centronics plugs, like the printer end of a parallel cable.

Single-ended (SE) cable lengths are 1.5 to 6 meters (5 feet to almost 20 feet). These lengths are not a problem for internal devices, but these distances can be limiting for external printers, scanners, and other bulky external devices that probably out not take up premium desk space.

High-voltage differential (HVD) cables are the other extreme. They can go up to 70 m (230 feet), but have speed limitations. At that length, it is time to look at networking options.

The happy compromise is low-voltage differential (LVD). For most applications, 12 m (39 feet) is just fine. Notice that the cables with 80 pins support 15 devices. Table 14-1 lists SCSI types and their details. Note that the oldest SCSI technologies are listed first.

Table 14-1   SCSI Comparison Chart

SCSI Type	Speed	Pins	Number of Devices
SCSI-1	5 MBps	50 or 68	7
Fast SCSI (SCSI-2)	10 MBps	50 or 68	7
Fast Wide SCSI (SCSI-2)	20 MBps	68 or 80	15
Ultra SCSI (SCSI-3)	20 MBps	50 or 68	7
Wide Ultra SCSI (SCSI-3)	40 MBps	68 or 80	7 or 15
Ultra 2 SCSI (SCSI-4)	40 MBps	50 or 68	7
Wide Ultra 2 SCSI (SCSI-4)	80 MBps	68 or 80	15
Ultra 3 SCSI (Ultra160/m)	80 MBps	50 or 68	15
Wide Ultra 3 SCSI (Ultra160/m)	160 MBps	68 or 80	15
Wide Ultra 320 SCSI	320 MBps	68 or 80	15

Legacy Expansion Slots

11.4: Table 14-2 shows what you need to know about older expansion slots.

Table 14-2   Legacy Expansion Slots

Expansion Slot	Need to Know (In Order of Importance)
ISA	16 bit, 8.3 MHz, supports plug-and-play, and is usually colored black.
PCIX	64-bit version of PCI. Currently much less common than PCIe.
MCA	Micro Channel Architecture, manufactured by IBM.
EISA	Extended ISA wider bus (32 bit), longer slot.
VESA	(VL-Bus) If AGP is the father of a PCIe video card, its grandfather is VESA.

Old-School D Plugs

1.5: Serial and parallel ports use D plugs. The *D* refers to the trapezoid shape of the grounded housing that surrounds the pins. The number of pins range from 9 pins, as in DE9, to 50 pins of the DD specification. The three that are likely to be on the Bench Technician exam are DA15 (otherwise known as the joystick port), DB25 parallel (if female) or serial (if male), and the DE9 standard serial port. These ports are found when a computer is connected to cash registers, robots, chip programming consoles, exotic or old printers, and other far from typical end-user devices. Note that the VGA port and joystick port are both 15-pin D plugs. The difference (besides usage) is that the joystick has two rows, and the VGA has three rows of five pins.

The name DB9 (sometimes with an *M* at the end to designate male) has given way to the name *RS232* or just *serial.*

IEEE 1284 vintage parallel ports come in three flavors: standard parallel port (SPP), enhanced parallel port (EPP), and extended capabilities port (ECP). SPP is unidirectional (one way) and slower. EPP is bidirectional and uses a direct memory access (DMA) to increase speed. ECP is faster still, bidirectional (two way), and the current standard parallel port. A standard parallel printer cord has a Centronics port on the printer end and a DB25 on the other.

Game controllers today are almost always USB. This was not always the case. Older sound cards often have a 15-pin female port (DA15) designed for game controllers, lovingly referred to as joysticks. VGA ports are also 15-pin female ports, but they are arranged in three rows of five, whereas the DA15 has two rows and looks like a shorter parallel port.

D plugs and the VGA port have threaded screws that can secure the plug to the port. Good news: They won't fall out. The bad news: If the computer is shoved against a wall, the secured port will snap and break the actual motherboard inside. If they are plugged in but not tightened, they will simply become unplugged if force is applied to them (and so must be reconnected). A broken motherboard is often the economic death of a PC. It is a shame to see a serial port cause the death of an otherwise good machine.

Absolute Power Supplies

11.3.1: Occasionally, you will find an oddly shaped PC, such as a really small, shoebox-shaped PC or flat U1 or U2 rack-mounted servers. These devices don't fit a regular ATX power supply, or motherboard. In addition to the wattage and number of DC plugs on the power supply, several unique form factors provide power to these exotic case configurations. Table 14-3 lists these.

Table 14-3   Oddly Shaped Power Supplies

Power Supply	Supports
TFX12V	Low-profile ATX
LFX12V	Low-profile BTX
SFX12V	FlexATX
CFX12V	Micro BTX (L shaped)

Homework

Download a copy of all the acronyms used on the A+ exams from the CompTIA website. It is a part of the objectives downloads.

Funwork

Walk up to an IT old-timer and say, "I remember a time when people used floppy disks and a 10/100 NIC was awesome." Bring a comfy chair because the old-timer will likely counter, "Oh yeah, I remember a time when…." These legacy guys love to sit around, perform backups, watch status bars, and reminisce about the good old days. Ask them about old printers, coaxial network cables, 3-n-300 NICs, D plugs. Let them spend half an hour telling you how it once was.

Yes, it is as painful as you imagine, but also enlightening and useful. Consider who writes the questions for the A+ exam. It is important to hear the old pro's perspective on things because that is the angle from which the test is written.

Listen to the vocabulary, diction, acronyms, and verbs. Match what you know with what they know. That overlap is where the test focuses. Question them and find out what is important in their point of view. Find out why "this or that" outdated concept or technology is still *so* crucial to understand. These guys really are a font of knowledge. Be respectful, and remember many of them saw the dawn of our field. They get lots of cool points for being there. Once you have had your fill of Leave It to Geezer, have someone text you with something really important to do. Otherwise, you might be stuck there until you, too, are an IT old-timer.

AMD, Intel, and You

A+ 220-604 Exam Objective

Objective 1.1: Install, configure, optimize and upgrade personal computer components

Key Points

Today you will cover topics from Chapter 5 and Chapter 11 of the IT Essentials v4.0 course. If you are a true hardware person, you really need to memorize all the CPU families and compatibilities from Day 31. You will explore a much more detailed version of that chart today. It is tedious work, but at least you don't have all the operating system (OS) files and network protocols to memorize.

What's Under the Hood?

5.5.3: It is tempting to immediately open the case and look inside. But quite often, this voids warrantees, increases risk of electrostatic discharge (ESD), and (oddly) it is not very helpful when determining the exact hardware in the PC. It is difficult to tell what kind of CPU is installed while staring at the fan and heat sink. Just like a surgeon runs tests and gathers data before picking up a scalpel, you should know what is inside before you go looking.

The BIOS is a good place to find more detailed information about the hardware, especially about how much RAM is installed in the slots. That information proves useful in RAM upgrades.

System Information and Device Manager are two tools you will use often. A newbie will look for Device Manager in the Control Panel only to spend more time trying to figure out where Microsoft put it in that particular version of Windows. You will eventually find it buried even deeper, hidden beneath several tabs. Now you are a pro and will have none of that. You go straight to the **Start > Run** and enter **devmgmt.msc** any time you get a question like, "Exactly what kind of processor does this computer have?," "Does the computer recognize the IR keyboard yet?," and "Where do I go to reinstall or roll back a driver?" All these questions can be answered in the Device Manager.

The second tool the pros use is System Information. Go to **Start > Run** and enter **msinfo32.exe**. You can answer the following questions in the System Information applet: "What is the I/O address of my system clock?," (as if you'd ever need to know) and "What is assigned to IRQ 13? Or 113 for that matter?," (Did you know that there are actually a lot more than 16 interrupt requests (IRQ) on modern PCs?)

NOTE: The reason IRQs are less important today is the devices themselves are much more sophisticated than they once were. In fact, many devices share IRQs. Modern system buses allow devices to directly communicate with each other, thus freeing up the CPU. This is called bus mastering.

There are more applicable uses for System Information, like, "Exactly what is the name and model of the NIC?," or "Does this problem affect *every* PC that uses this driver and that video card?" You can connect to remote computers right from the System Information utility and see the same kind of detailed info about their systems. Talk about saving time, what if the other PC is in Hong Kong? System Information is an information-gathering tool only. In Device Manager, you can add, remove, troubleshoot, disable, and enable devices. System Information provides you with more details than any sane person should know about a PC.

Another useful command is **Start > Run** (and then enter **dxdiag.exe**). It automatically updates the DirectX on the OS and provides you with detailed diagnostic information about sound and video interfaces.

A Bag of Chips

11.3.3: A brief history: AMD and Intel have long battled for market share. Gamers and hacker wannabes enjoy the underdog, bad-boy image of AMD, and the business world loves the Intel/Windows (Wintel) desktop combo. The latter makes up the vast majority of PCs. The fact is that all these machines are really quite good. Stiff competition in the CPU world, increases in speed, and decreases in size and power consumption have created some really great chips. CPU research and development arrived at a physical limit of about 4 GHz in 2002. Enter: the dual-core chip. This is not to be confused with a multiprocessor, where the motherboard supports two, four, or more CPUs. Dual core means one CPU chip, two set pipelines, two executable units, and one shared cache.

The reason that 32-bit CPUs can only address 4 GB of RAM is because the number of addresses available is only 2^{32} (4.3 billion, or about 4 GB). You can manually edit your BOOT.INI file to include the following physical address extension (PAE):

> multi(0)disk(0)rdisk(0)partition(1)\WINDOWS="Microsoft Windows XP Professional"
> /noexecute=optin /fastdetect /usepmtimer/PAE

This PAE allows for up to 64 GB of RAM. And although 64-bit processors can address 2^{64} bytes of RAM (which is, well, a very large number), no current OS can support that amount of RAM.

Upgrading the CPU

11.4.2: The A+ exam loves questions about upgrading the CPU. There are four conditions to consider:

- The new CPU must have the same socket as the old.

- It must be compatible with the current chipset on the motherboard.

- The new chip must accept power in the range that the current power supply and motherboard provide.

- The CPU must operate with the existing RAM.

If the front side bus (FSB) of the new CPU is faster than the RAM, it may be time to upgrade the RAM, too. In the real world, it usually makes more sense to upgrade the CPU, motherboard, and the RAM at the same time, to maximize the performance and guarantee the interoperability of the "trinity."

When handling CPUs, you are holding wires that are literally nanometers apart from each other. Any static electric discharge will short out at that close a distance. It is imperative to use antistatic straps and magnetically shielded bags when handling and storing CPUs. Inserting CPUs must be done using the zero-insertion-force (ZIF) lever. CPUs and sockets must be oriented exactly right.

Once the ZIF arm secures the CPU into the socket, put a small dot of thermal grease onto the face. Use a small amount; you don't want it to squish out the sides when the heat sink is installed. Keep the thermal grease off of you. It is not human friendly. Now, for the most important but easiest step, plug the fan into the motherboard.

Homework

This might seem like a short day. It isn't. A site called Tom's Hardware is an outstanding resource for all things PC. Imagine a chart with all the processors, models, code names, clock speeds, FSB widths, cache amounts (L1, L2, and L3), transistor numbers, voltage, temperature ranges, and packages (form factors). As if by providence, it conveniently covers processors from 1994 through summer 2006, which is essentially the scope of the 2006 A+ exam objectives.

Go to http://www.tomshardware.com/reviews/cpu-charts-summer-2006,1304-2.html or Google "Tom's Hardware CPU chart 1994 - 2006."

These charts might intimidate you at first glance. Don't be. It is like going to a family reunion and meeting hundreds of new people, all of whom seem to know you. For the bench tech, these CPUs, sockets, code names, FSBs, and clock speeds are your new family. Go introduce yourself.

Let's get a game plan, by looking at the branching charts first, before you tackle the monster tables. The following tables should help organize your understanding, and you should begin to see patterns among the families of processors and sockets. Table 13-1 shows AMD and Intel sockets.

Table 13-1   Identifying Intel and AMD Sockets

Sockets	Memorizing Tricks
Socket 370	Only Intel uses 3xx and 4xx.
Socket 423	Only Intel uses 3xx and 4xx.
Socket 478	Only Intel uses 3xx and 4xx.
Socket 775 Core and Netburst	Core and Netburst are Intel exclusively (you may see this as LGA775).
Slot A	A as in AMD.
Socket A	A as in AMD.
Socket AM2	AM as in AMD.

continues

Table 13-1   Identifying Intel and AMD Sockets   *continued*

Sockets	Memorizing Tricks
Socket 754	754 is lower that Intel's more popular 775.
Socket 939	Only AMD uses 9xx.
Socket 940	Only AMD uses 9xx.

The 7xx is the only real overlap. Just remember that Intel, who dominates the market, is a higher number 775 than AMD (which is at 754).

Don't focus so much on the transistor size (nanometers [nm]); size isn't really a CPU compatibility issue at the technician level. You can come back to that later. Focus instead on other parts of this chart. Table 13-2 maps sockets to FSB speeds. Remember the FSB is the speed of the CPU's front door.

Table 13-2   Sockets to Front Side Bus Speeds

Sockets	FSB Speeds
Socket 370	66–133 MHz
Socket 423	100 MHz
Socket 478	100–200 MHz
Socket 775	133–266 MHz
Slot A	100 MHz
Socket A	100–200 MHz
Socket AM2	200 MHz
Socket 754	200 MHz
Socket 939	200 MHz
Socket 940	200 MHz

Now associate the code names to the sockets. Intel chooses code names from rivers and cities in the Pacific Northwest (with just a few exceptions). AMD likes astronomy, horses, hammers, and international cities. Code names are used to group resources and employees and to launch disinformation campaigns used to throw off corporate espionage. (An interesting topic for some day *after* your exam.)

Table 13-3   Sockets to Code Names

Sockets	Code Names
Socket 370	Tualatin, "tu-WALL-e-tin"
Socket 423	Willamette, "will-AM-et"

Table 13-3   Sockets to Code Names *continued*

Sockets	Code Names
Socket 478	Willamette Northwood Prestonia Gallatin "GALL-e-tin" Prescott
Socket 775 Netburst	Gallatin Prescott Prescot Smithfiled Cedar Mill Presler
Socket 775 Core	Conroe (You can spell *core* from Conroe, or if you are not a fan, you can remember it spells *no core*.)
Slot A	Pluto Orion
Socket A	Thunderbird Morgan Spitfire Palomino Thorton Thoroughbred Thoroughbred Applebred Barton
Socket AM2	Manilla Orleans Windsor
Socket 754	Paris Clawhammer Newcastle Palermo Oakville
Socket 939	Clawhammer Newcastle Winchester Venice Manchester Toledo San Diego
Socket 940	Sledgehammer

Now associate the brand names with the sockets. Hint: Table 13-4 is important. You should really focus on this one.

Table 13-4   Sockets to Brand Names

Sockets	Brand Names
Socket 370	Celeron Pentium 3
Socket 423	Pentium 4
Socket 478	Celeron Celeron D Pentium 4 Pentium 4 EE
Socket 775 Netburst	Celeron Celeron D Pentium 4 Pentium 4 EE Pentium D
Socket 775 Core	The very popular line Core Duo begins here.
Slot A	Pluto Orion
Socket A	Athlon Athlon XP Duron Sempron
Socket AM2	Sempron 64 Athlon 64 Athlon 64 FX Athlon 64 X2
Socket 754	Sepron (32 bit) Athlon 64
Socket 939	Athlon 64 Athlon 64 FX Athlon 64 X2
Socket 940	Athlon 64 FX

Associate the clock speed with sockets, as shown in Table 13-5. This should give you a feel for the families, their relative age, and capabilities. Note that processor speed is typically measured in megahertz (MHz). Even though it is really 2.2 GHz, it is still written as 2200 MHz.

Table 13-5   Sockets to Clock Speeds

Sockets	Clock Speeds
Socket 370	533–1400 MHz
Socket 423	1300–2000 MHz
Socket 478	1400–3800 MHz
Socket 775 Netburst	2530–3800 MHz
Socket 775 Core	1866–2933 MHz
Slot A	500–1000 MHz
Socket A	650–2250 MHz
Socket AM2	1600–2000 MHz
Socket 754	1400–2400 MHz
Socket 939	1800–2800 MHz
Socket 940	2200–2400 MHz

Can you answer the following questions: "Can you put an Athlon 64 X2 in socket 940?" (No), "How about in a 939?" (Yes), "What options do I have when upgrading from a Celeron in a 478 socket?" Believe it or not, benchies need to be able to answer these kinds of questions. You might also want to research some of the sockets and processors that are newer and so not on this chart. Now that you speak CPUs and sockets, go learn about the Socket AM3, Intel's Core Duo families of processors, socket T (LGA775), and socket B (LGA1366). A truly certified geek (which you will soon be) keeps up on these specs and gets excited about newly announced FSBs or entire new socket lines. Too geeky for you? There is always fashion school.

Funwork

After all that heady work today, Google "computer songs and poems." A particularly popular one is "Dr. Seuss's Computer Crash." Who said computer geeks don't have a sense of humor?

The Right Tool for the Right Job

A+ 220-604 Exam Objective

Objective 1.2: Identify tools, diagnostic procedures and troubleshooting techniques for personal computer components

Key Points

Besides not needing to wear the happy face for customers, as a bench tech you have the luxury of having every conceivable tool and probe, diagnostic kit, and cleaning supply at your disposal. Your tool box should look like a mad scientist's and should probably be on wheels. Having access to these tools comes with the responsibility to learn the names of each. Unfortunately, you can't call something "the whippy, reach-around-underneath, three-prong, grabber thingy." You will lose cool points among your fellow benchies. Topics from Chapters 1, 2, and 11 of the IT Essentials v4.0 course are covered today.

Tools

11.2.2: For the A+ Bench Tech exam (220-604), you need to be familiar with a variety of tools, including those seldom used tools (a #0 Philips head, for example). You also need to be familiar with weird names for common tools like the hemostat (a fancy name for long tweezers that close and lock) and tools of yesteryears like the integrated circuit (IC) puller that removed old BIOS chips. The following is the list of tools to which the bench tech should have access:

- Standard flathead (minus) screwdriver, including large, small, and a set of really small drivers.

- Phillips-head (plus) screwdriver, including #0, #1, and #2. (You probably don't need #3 unless you are building bridges or tanks.)

- 5-in-1 screwdriver. (This is a multipurpose driver that has interchangeable Phillips and standard heads and hex drivers.)

- Tweezers/hemostat.

- Part retriever (the aforementioned whippy, reach-around-underneath, three-prong, grabber thingy).

- Needle-nosed pliers.

- Diagonal wire cutters. (Old timers refer to these as diags, pronounced "dikes.")

- Wire strippers.

- Hex wrench set (metric 2 mm though 6 mm and fractional 5/64", 3/32", 7/64", 1/8", 9/64", and 5/32").

- Allen wrench set, metric and fractional.

- Star head driver (size T10h through T40h).

- Tri-head drivers, including #1, #2, #3, and #.

- Square head drivers, including #0, #1, #2, and #3.

- Torx screwdriver T8 through T27.

- Digital multimeter. (A good multimeter is your new best friend.)

- Small mirror. (Often, you can use a mirror to read behind and under obstructing components that otherwise would need to be removed, increasing risk to the machine and wasting valuable time.)

- Dust brush. (Most brush material conducts electricity, so don't brush anything while the PC is on.)

- Small brush. (Toothbrushes work well to clean contacts. Buy new.)

- Vacuum with HEPA filter.

- Rubbing alcohol that is greater than 70% isopropyl.

- Cotton swabs (perfect for cleaning ball mice and hard-to-reach places in printers, but cotton swabs tend to leave small amounts of cotton on rough edges and corners).

- LCD cleaning solution or wipes. (Never, *never* use a paper towel on a soft LCD screen.)

- Mild detergent solution or wipes (for the outside of the case).

- Glass cleaner (for CRT monitor screens, your safety glasses, and your hands after you've picked up toner).

- Paper towels (only for general cleanup, not for inside the PC).

- Soft, lint-free cloth.

- Cable ties/spiral wrap.

- Scissors. (Electrician scissors are short, stout, and work very well.)

- Small flashlight. (Head-mounted lights are nice but look a little goofy.)

- Electric tape. (You want lots, and get good quality and many colors. Colors are useful in wire identification.)

- Extra jumpers, case, and drive mount screws. (You will tend to collect these over the years; just keep them in a small box or container.)

- Pencil or pen. (Watch out when using pencils. The graphite conducts electricity and shorts out components. In fact, the military uses special bombs that rain graphite on radar and electronics systems because of its conductive nature.)

- Magnifying glass (to read the tiny printing on boards).

- A journal or notebook. (Sometimes, a voice or video recorder is a convenient, hands-free method of documenting your work.)

- Compressed air. (Always used right side up.)

- Antistatic wrist strap (Use a wrist strap whenever inside the PC, but never use one when inside power supplies, batteries, monitors, and printers. Yes, bench techs sometimes go inside field replaceable units [FRU].)

- Specialized testers like cable testers, loopback plugs, and POST cards.

- Knife. (A locking blade is strongly recommend.)

- Box cutter. (Expendable razor-sharp blades are a must for any benchie. Get one with a locking blade.)

- RJ-11, RJ-13, and RJ-45 crimping tool (RJ-11 for phone, RJ-13 for modular phone, like in an office, and RJ-45 for network cables).

- IC insertion/extraction tool (for adding and removing chips).

- Solder iron. (Get a good one for $300+. Poor-quality soldering irons are really frustrating.)

- Solder supplies, including solder, flux, small vice and/or mounted clips, sponge, and so on.

CAUTION: Solder almost always contains lead, and if ingested (even wiping your eyes with your hands), it will have profoundly negative effects on your cognition. Age already provides more than enough mind mellowing. Do not help it along. Also, do not breathe the soldering fumes.

Multimeters and Electricity

1.3.2: Multimeter is truly a go-to tool for techs of all sorts. Get a good and tough one because they don't bounce well and false readings are dangerous. Arguably, Fluke makes an excellent multimeter.

The following is a list of straightforward statements that you should know regarding multimeters and electricity for the A+ exam:

- Power (the ability to do something) is measured in watts (W).

- Voltage is electrical potential (pressure) on the circuit.

- Amps are the current (flow) of electrons.

- Resistance slows down the current and gives off heat. (That is why computers are hot.)

- P = IE, meaning power (P) is equal to amps (I) multiplied by volts (E).

- V = IR, meaning voltage (V) equals amps (I) multiplied by resistance (R).

- Alternating current (AC) goes long distance and cycles ~115 volts at 60 hertz; 250 volts at 50 hertz in Europe. (Other combinations exist elsewhere.)

- The power outlet in a wall is measured in AC.

- Direct current (DC) maintains a constant voltage (no cycles, no long distance).

- Inside the PC, electricity is measured in DC.

- Resistors are measured in ohms.

- Capacitors are measured in Farads.

- Continuity sends the signal through one lead, and the other lead listens for it. When it hears the signal, it beeps, verifying that they share a common connection. Don't send current through sensitive electronics. It is mainly used for wire identification.

- A good fuse reads few if any ohms.

- A bad fuse reads infinite ohms (because the wire inside is broken).

- A good speaker reads 8 ohms (although sometimes they are suppose to read 4 ohms).

- A bad speaker reads any other amount of ohms, usually 0 ohms (shorted out) or infinite ohms (separated).

- A simple circuit includes a power supply, a load, and connections between them in a circle (hence the word *circuit*).

Connecting Devices Properly

11.6: Until you have spent quality time inside a computer, it is difficult to know how much force to use when seating cards, dual inline memory modules (DIMM), zero-insertion-force (ZIF), parallel advanced technology attachment (PATA) cables, jumpers, and the like. If you have not already done so, spend some time inside a dead PC that you don't plan on using again. Most computer repair instructors have some. There is almost always a dead PC in a consignment store. It is impractical to test physical skills like this on the A+ exam, but be prepared for multiple-choice/multiple-answer (MCMA) questions that include an improperly seated or oriented card, board, card, cable, port, and so on.

Known-Good Devices

2.2.3: One method of bench troubleshooting is to isolate the fault down to a hunch and then replace that component with a "known-good" one. For example: The PC simply won't start (no lights, no vibrations, no life at all). Your hunch is that the problem is with the power supply. Have a known-good power supply nearby and swap it out. If the PC turns on with lights, vibrations, and signs of life, you have saved time and correctly identified the problem.

Be sure to keep your known-good devices. Don't accidently give them away with the PC. Some techs spray paint or otherwise identify their known-good components with bright colors to avoid doing just that. The known-good technique works well on standard devices, such as monitors, printers, fans, HDDs, FDDs, optical drives, and even some common RAM and motherboards.

Homework

Review the wire colors, voltages, and power supplies from Day 31, "Hardware Concepts: Part 1 of 2."

Go price shopping online and design your perfect tool set. You will begin to associate the name with the picture, and so you can use the right name for the right tool. Your tool set should include everything listed today. Don't forget a great big toolbox on wheels. All these tools and supplies cost a lot more than you might think. Over the years, you find the "right" tools, the ones that "just fit." Then you will understand the bench tech's reluctance to lend out tools. As a newbie, be very respectful when borrowing tools.

Funwork

There are "blackbox" diagnostic devices called POST cards that connect to an expansion slot or port. In a perfect world, they tell you exactly what is wrong with the hardware. There is a wide range of both price and effectiveness among POST cards. Go read reviews and learn how they work.

An Ounce of Prevention

A+ 220-604 Exam Objective

Objective 1.3: Perform preventive maintenance of personal computer components

Key Points

After yesterday, you deserve an easy day. Today you will cover cooling the CPU and graphics processing unit (GPU), and will later review driver and firmware updates. Parts of Chapters 2 and 11 of the IT Essentials v4.0 course are covered today. Enjoy your easy day.

What's Hot and What's Not

11.5.2: The following are some cooling-related best practices found on the A+ exam:

- Don't cover or enclose the case vents with paper, excessive cords, blankets, or unventilated drawers or closets. The hot exhaust needs to escape.

- Make sure all the expansion slot covers or "expansion brackets" "blanks" or "back plates" are in place. It forces the air to flow though the case properly and maximizes heat transfer. Believe it or not, mice and snakes are drawn to the warmth of a PC. Don't leave a door open for them.

- In dusty environments, use filters that cover the air intakes to keep dirt and dust from coating the heat sink. Observe and replace filters.

- Tighten loose screws. Replace missing screws. You really don't need a screw rattling around causing shorts inside the PC. There are two sizes of screws. Case screws are larger than drive mounting screws.

- Cable management inside and outside the case improves airflow, increases safety of the PC, reduces trip hazards, and just looks better. Spiral wrap or cable ties are great for bundling and organizing cables.

- GPUs frequently have their own fan.

- HDDs can also have dedicated fans.

- Do not stick anything in the blades. Some fans are deceptively strong and will hurt the object or damage the fan.

- Additional slot fans (that take the space of an expansion card) can be added to increase airflow.

- Water cooling is an option but it has its own problems, including reservoir level, leaks, air in the lines, and mold.

- Underclocking reduces heat, but it also reduces performance.

Cleaning Solutions

2.3.4: The A+ Bench Technician exam will likely ask you about what cleaning products to use and when. The following is a list of cleaning best practices:

- Make sure the PC is off (remove any batteries from laptops).

- Remove any peripherals, because they might have their own power supply.

- Spray mild detergent onto the lint-free cloth, not onto the PC directly.

- Never use abrasive or lint-laden materials, like paper towels, on soft LCD screens, lenses, CDs, scanners, print or optical readers, anything that could get scratched or is sensitive to dust from the rag. Use very light pressure, especially on LCDs.

- Monitors and most PC components are best served with antistatic materials. Use them if you have the option.

- A solution of >70% isopropyl alcohol is used for cleaning electrical contacts.

- Never use solvents or glass cleaner (which often include ammonia) on an LCD screen.

Homework

Spend some more time with the CPU chart in Part IV, Day 13, "AMD, Intel, and You." Don't forget that anything made by Intel and AMD since 1994 is fair game for the A+ Bench Technician exam.

Use MSINFO32.EXE or DEVMGMT.MSC to determine the exact driver version of your basic adapter cards: video, sound, USB, NIC, and so on. Go to the manufacturer's website and see whether there are any updates for your cards. Remember if the new driver causes problems, just use the rollback feature in the Device Manager.

Funwork

Design a point-of-sale (POS) computer system with a thermal printer for receipts and a laser scanner that reads barcodes. Make sure it includes an application that can understand barcodes. If you want a challenge, find a scale that communicates with your PC for weighing produce. Don't forget that many products use RFID in addition to barcodes. Redundancy and reliability is important here as it this is a mission critical computer. Can you design a cheaper system than commercially produced POSs? Don't forget the credit card reader and software to run all of the devices. There is an entire industry within the computer repair world dedicated to creating and supporting POSs. Check out the portable (handheld) POS systems.

Batteries and LCDs

A+ 220-604 Exam Objective

Objective 2.1: Identify the fundamental principles of using laptops and portable devices

Key Points

Today you will review information about batteries, LCD screens, and video memory, all from Chapter 13 of the IT Essentials v4.0 course. Portable devices and laptops are "frequent flyers" at repair shops. There are very few customer replaceable units (CRU) on portable devices, so fixing them is really a bench tech's job. Fortunately, because of the portable nature of the devices, they ship well.

Portable Power

13.3.1: Practically every portable device uses a battery. They are fundamental and are a good source of A+ exam questions. The following is a list of battery-related best practices for the bench tech:

- Unplug the battery before doing any physical work on a laptop or portable device.

- Any battery, from a hearing-aid battery to a deep cell marine battery, is tested with an auto-ranging digital multimeter set to volts DC.

- Portable device batteries typically have more than two leads (like a standard battery) that supply different voltages. The battery should explain what each lead is supposed to read. If not, check the manual or online.

- A charged battery is 5% to 10% over the value printed on the battery.

- A dead battery is about 20% less than the number printed on the battery.

WARNING: A dead battery is far from 0 volts. It just does not have enough power to run the device. Be mindful that it still produces electricity and can be dangerous to other electronics or itself if shorted between the leads. Large "dead" batteries, such as an uninterruptible power, can be dangerous to you, as well. Even a laptop running 20 volts at 3 amps is something you will remember for a long time.

- NiCd (nickel cadmium) and NiMH (nickel metal hydride) batteries need to be occasionally exercised to prevent a memory. A memory means that the battery charges and powers a device but dies quickly. To exercise a battery, drain it down as low as possible (slowly and safely), and then charge it a little higher than normal. Repeat this cycle several times, and then charge it normally and use it.

- Just like in a laptop, if the portable device will be unpowered for a long time (a month or more), drain and remove the battery. Running the device until it is "dead" is enough.

- Unplug chargers from the wall when not in use. The transformers draw current even when not charging anything. If they are warm to the touch, that is the dispersed energy. It is common to have many of these chargers around a residence. The wasted electricity can be quite significant over time.

Crystal Clear

13.2: There are three main parts to the liquid crystal display (LCD):

- A flat, lighted fluorescent or LED panel.

- A field of twisting crystals.

- A "tough" membrane. Note that practically anything will scratch an LCD; even mean looks can ruin an LCD screen.

Just as with a cathode-ray tube (CRT), magnets and electromagnetic interference (EMI) need to be far away. Liquid crystals are very "excitable." It is possible to short out the electronics by too much static electricity/magnetism.

A standard LCD monitor is usually cheaper to replace than fix. LCD screens are in so many devices today that in many cases it is cost-effective to replace the screen or backlight. High-end phones and MP3 players, digital cameras, expensive laptops, dashboard displays, ATMs, point-of-sale systems, watches, and even fish finders that use sonar can be very pricey and warrant repair over replacement.

An LCD screen that is dark and can be seen only from an angle means the backlight is either not powered or is broken. If it takes a long time for the screen to get bright or some places on the screen are brighter (or darker) than others, plan on replacing the backlight. Extreme temperatures, both hot and cold, have a similar effect.

If the LCD screen is pixilated, check the video source first. Often, streamed video and even digital subscriber line (DSL), fiber, and cable Internet service provider (ISP) connections can fail to provide a proper high-definition (HD) signal. If the source is the problem, try downloading the file entirely and running it locally.

If the screen flickers or randomly changes color, check the physical connection; it might be loose. On a laptop, this is no easy task. The ribbon cable that connects the LCD to the motherboard is hidden in one of the hinges. Know before you go. Read up on the repair of that specific laptop before you pick up a screwdriver. If the screen just flickers (no color change), the problem might be the inverter that powers the backlight, not necessarily the light or cable.

If there are fantastic modern art designs with lines and radiant divisions like a cracked windshield, the screen is cracked and needs to be replaced. If the screen is still bright, the backlight is not broken.

Are there just a few persistent specks? That is called a *stuck pixel* or *pixel death*. An individual or small group of crystals has quit working. Live with it or replace the screen.

If the screen is black and shows no life, check obvious things first (such as whether the laptop is actually turned on). Is it set to project out the video graphics array (VGA), digital visual interface (DVI), or high definition media interface (HDMI) port rather than the LCD? Is it in sleep mode? These seem pretty obvious, but they make good exam questions.

Video Sharing

13.3.4: Remember the drawback to integrated video cards? They use the system memory, and the south bridge ties up critical resources that should be used for other things (for instance, the CPU). If your customer (or you) is price shopping for a bargain-basement laptop, make sure that it has good graphics. It should have its own VRAM, and preferably have a brand name such as NVIDIA or ATI. You will pay more at the outset, but your eyes will not tire as quickly, and you will get better overall performance out of your laptop.

On many shared-memory laptops, you can manually dedicate an amount of shared RAM to the graphics processing unit (GPU) in the BIOS. The disadvantage of this sharing is that it robs the OS of RAM. Solution: If you have a shared-memory laptop, add more RAM (up to 4 GB, which is the max on 32-bit, multicore systems) and allocate 128 to 256 GB to video.

Homework

Review Day 27, "Laptops and Portable Devices: Part 1 of 2," especially the section on batteries. It is an A+ exam favorite.

Funwork

The HowStuffWorks website (http://www.howstuffworks.com) and Lab Rats Episode 18 (http://labrats.tv) have a great explanation of how LCDs and plasma screens work. Read the article and watch the video. The article is a great review, and the video is fun to watch.

Go online and watch some videos about replacing cracked screens and backlights.

Swapping Drives

A+ 220-604 Exam Objective

Objective 2.2: Install, configure, optimize and upgrade laptops and portable devices

Key Points

Today you will spend some time in Chapter 6 of the IT Essentials v4.0 course covering hot-swappable devices and flash storage in real-world terms. Anyone who has ever dropped a traditional HDD appreciates the invention of flash memory and its brain child, the solid-state drive (SSD).

Hot Swappable and Not Swappable

6.4.2: Mistaking a device that is not hot swappable for one that is can let out the magic blue smoke that makes it work. It is really important to know which devices are hot swappable and which are not so that you do not destroy both the device and the motherboard. Table 9-1 reviews what is and what isn't hot swappable for all PCs, not just for laptops.

Table 9-1   **Drive Swapability Comparison**

Hot Swappable	Not Swappable
SATA drives	PATA drives
Modern SCSI array drives	RAM
FireWire	PCI, PCIe, PCIX, AGP, ISA
USB	PS/2
PCMCIA	Serial
HDMi, DVI, VGA	Parallel

Laptop Hard Drives

6.3.4: A laptop HDD is a slimmed-down version of a PC HDD. It measures 2.5 inches across and functions exactly like a PC hard drive. It is removed and installed by access panels and usually has a couple of screws that discourage end users' techie ambitions. Almost all laptop hard drives today are serial advanced technology attachment (SATA), and some are external storage devices that connect thought USB or FireWire. Other laptop storage devices and external attachments include ExpressCards, PC cards, and PCMCIA.

SSDs are essentially drop proof. Rated at thousands of gravities (the amount of force exerted on an object), they are simply not going to break like the spinning platters and moving arms of the traditional HDD sometimes do. This explains the survivability of flash drives and MP3 players that use such technology. It comes at a cost. There is a finite number of times the media can be rewritten. You really do not need to defrag an SSD because of the solid-state nature. Regardless of fragmentation, the drive will access it about the same as if it were completely contiguous. More, those countless reads and writes by defrag will greatly age an SSD.

Homework

Review PC cards and PCMCIA from Day 27, "Laptops and Portable Devices: Part 1 of 2."

It's been a few days. Go review the CPU charts from Part IV, Day 13, "AMD, Intel, and You."

Go online and familiarize yourself with CPUs that are designed for laptops (such as Intel's Centrino and Atom, and AMD's mobile versions of Athlon, Sempron, and Turion).

Funwork

Shop around, read reviews, and go find your dream laptop. Does your dream laptop use a distributed, cloud-computing, integrated worldwide wireless Internet service provider (ISP) connection? Or do you like the more secure feeling of knowing that your documents live on your laptop? Is your laptop a glorified personal digital assistant (PDA), just a way to work while away from your killer PC at home? Is it light? Is it tough? Does it have a big heavy battery that lasts a week, or a skinny device that fits in your pocket? Is it a Mac or a PC? Did it come as a DIY kit? Is it covered with peace stickers or sleek and sophisticated? Portable computing is an exciting and rapidly changing frontier. Familiarize yourself and learn the trends.

Troubleshooting Portable Devices

A+ 220-604 Exam Objective

Objective 2.3: Identify tools, diagnostic procedures and troubleshooting techniques for laptops and portable devices

Key Points

Today you will cover troubleshooting portable devices. You will focus on topics from Chapters 6 and 11 of the IT Essentials v4.0 course.

The lines between laptops and cell phones are very blurry. Basically, if it is sold by a telco, it is a phone. If not, it's a PC. Cell phones have a CPU, RAM, motherboard (called a main board) storage, input/output ports, USB, FireWire, Bluetooth, WIFI, and, of course, radio (RF) to communicate with a cell tower. Keyboards, styluses, touch screens, and even dual- and tri-core chips are available now on phones. Cell phones have a flash-based operating system, store data, and run applications. So really, little differentiates a computer from a cell phone.

What exactly is a "smart phone?" It is a somewhat outdated term that roughly means a 3G phone, a cell phone with lots of extras. Do not confuse what the A+ exam calls a smart phone for a personal digital assistant (PDA). A PDA does not have calling or texting features. Instead, it is a dedicated scheduler, contact manager, calendar, diary, grocery-list maker, and so on. Another difference is that PDAs are thought of as belonging to and synced with a PC. In contrast, a cell phone is considered a standalone device that can connect to and share files with a PC. A BlackBerry would be considered a smart phone on the A+ exam.

Troubleshooting Cell Phones

6.7.2: The following is a list of CP-related best practices and troubleshooting methods:

- Because of the small size of the touch screens, a stylus is often included. When the touch-screen input and the LCD output do not match, run the stylus calibration tool. It asks you to touch the screen in various places and adjusts the input to match those coordinates.

- When you have an unresponsive phone, check obvious things such as the battery, screen lock, or cracks on the screen. The SIMM card could be missing or inserted incorrectly. It is possible for the service provider to lock/disable a phone in case it is stolen. (For this reason, it is advisable to verify ownership of the phone before fixing it.)

- Before you donate, return, or recycle a phone, press the master reset button, which is usually located inside by the SIMM card and battery.

- Update the "OS" or master code by flashing the firmware. Note that this is the method by which phones are "unlocked." There are legal issues involved in changing the network to which a phone is registered. There are legitimate reasons for flashing a cell phone's firmware. Make sure you have a good (and legal) reason to flash the firmware on a registered phone, such as the following:

  — You work at a service provider's licensed repair center or legitimate refurbishing facility.

  — A legitimate upgrade was made available by the manufacture or service provider.

  — The firmware is corrupt.

  — The main board was just replaced.

Function over Form Factors

6.3.1: Desktops have rules regarding size, height, voltage, cooling, and so on. These standards or form factors are absent in the laptop and portable device world. The relentless pursuit of smaller and more powerful, efficient, brighter, and tougher devices means every portable device you open is bound to be different. The following are best practices found on the A+ exam regarding fixing laptops and portable devices:

- Always look online for directions and how-to regarding your procedure every time, on every laptop. Preferably, use the manufacturer's site; otherwise, use reputable forums and repair sites. Subtle design changes among even similar cell phones and laptops and PDAs often lead to very different steps. Follow them carefully.

- Draw a quick sketch of the device and punch the screws through the paper where they go in the drawing. The reason is twofold. One, there are no standards regarding screw placement and mounting points inside any portable device. Some have very creative combinations of screws that range in length, diameter, and thread count. It is imperative they go back in the same hole. The second reason is if they are punched through the paper they will not roll around your work area.

TIP: If you drop one of these minuscule screws on the floor, lay a flashlight flat on the floor and shine it across the area where you think it fell. Even the smallest object casts a rather long shadow in the horizontal light. Turning off surrounding and overhead light helps you see the shadow contrast.

Quirky Qwerty

11.4.6: A user complains of a keyboard malfunction. You might be tempted to label it a PEBCAK error (problem exists between customer and keyboard). Often it is. However, if the keyboard types incorrect characters, it could be one of several issues. Laptops typically overlay a 10-key keypad over the QWERTY keyboard. The Num Lock key toggles between normal keyboard and the 10-key keypad. When entering passwords, this and Caps Lock can be most frustrating.

The Keyboard option in the Control Panel allows for exotic keyboard support. Dvorak is another way to arrange the keys on a keyboard in a way that is more ergonomically correct. You can change this in Regional and Language Options in the Control Panel.

Language packs and special characters are also another source of strange keyboard issues. Languages are handled in the Control Panel. New language packs are found on the OS CD and are available from MS online, too. Word and other word processors have autocorrect features that automatically respell commonly misspelled words. Occasionally, the programming makes unwanted changes. Although that is beyond the scope of the A+ exam, it is a common customer question.

If the keyboard does not type anything, check the physical layer first. Older systems that use PS/2 ports for the keyboard and mouse are easy to switch accidentally. They are usually color coded or otherwise indicated by icon (so that you can determine which is for the keyboard and which is for the mouse). In the absence of any indication of which is for the mouse and which is for the keyboard, know that the keyboard is the one closest to the motherboard. PS/2 input devices are not hot swappable. You will need to restart the PC for them to work.

Wireless keyboards are nice but pose another layer of problems. If they use infrared (IR), the keyboard and receiver need to be lined up like a remote control and TV. The range of radio frequency (RF) coverage varies by make and model. When working with wireless devices, consider the needs of the presenter in an auditorium versus the needs of an office worker. Wireless keyboards can also interfere with each other. If someone can move your arrow and his own, too, use the dip switches or jumpers inside to change the frequency to avoid that kind of interference. Some wireless keyboard/mice systems use a button to activate. Look for this when troubleshooting such systems. A final note about wireless devices: They eat batteries. Check there first when troubleshooting. Also consider rechargeable batteries (Earth first and all).

Homework

Use Help feature built in to Windows to troubleshoot the following problems. Run the tool multiple times and explore the many divergent paths in this troubleshooting tree:

- A touchpad does not move the arrow.

- A laptop keyboard types the wrong characters.

- The speakers do not make sound.

- An external monitor connected to a laptop that does not display anything.

Funwork

You would think it is common sense by now, but people will still come to you with a dead flash drive and ask you to recover data. They did not heed warnings about using the Safely Remove Hardware button from the taskbar. Are they really out of luck? Go online and see what options they have. There are techniques and programs that can revive or retrieve the data (although success is still rare).

Projectors and Cameras

A+ 220-604 Exam Objective

Objective 2.3: Identify tools, diagnostic procedures and troubleshooting techniques for laptops and portable devices

Key Points

Today your focus is on projectors and cameras. It is hard to imagine a computer world void of these optical wonders. In fact, there is an increased focus on these technologies on the A+ exam because of growing consumer demand and lower prices. Consider the huge growth of home theater systems that really exemplify the convergence of our industry. On-demand, server-based files are downloaded or streamed to client systems around the globe. Those computers, game systems, DVRs, and media center edition operating systems process and store the data. Video and sound cards flow precision signals to crystal-clear speakers, monitors, and projectors. How cool is that, considering the VHS tape ruled supreme just 15 short years ago?

Like laptops and inkjet printers, it is easy for a simple problem like a dead projector bulb to spell the financial death of the entire projector. The upside is a growing refurbished market for cameras and projectors. It is your job to breathe life back into these digital miracles. The topics in this chapter relate to Chapter 1, Chapter 6, and Chapter 11 of the IT Essentials v4.0 course.

Troubleshooting Cameras

11.3.7: Single-lens reflex (SLR) cameras and expensive standard digital cameras are usually worth fixing. The SLR uses an optical viewfinder and proper 35 millimeter optics. In a standard digital camera, the LCD panel acts as the finder with smaller, lower-quality optics. As a bench tech, you are mostly interested in the digital side of digital cameras. If the problem is the camera (shutter, f-stop, lenses, and so on), you should probably turn that over to a repair shop.

Customer replaceable units (CRU) include memory sticks, batteries, and attachable lenses. Field replaceable units (FRU) include LCD display, backlight, firmware, ports, and communication with the computer. Start with the battery. Check all hardware, check the physical connections, and replace any broken or shorted wires. Check and, if necessary, flash the firmware (OS). At the application layer, test the camera using all the settings options (including the flash).

If the user is experiencing a problem downloading the pictures and videos, treat the camera like any other peripheral. Is the camera powered, turned on, and connected to the PC? Are the drivers for the port correctly installed (DEVMGMT.MSC)? Are the drivers for the camera installed correctly (from CD, from the manufacturer's website, or from third-party collections)? Are the applications used to download pictures installed and configured correctly?

Fixing cameras is a specialty repair field. If you are serious about doing this, you should spend time apprenticing at a shop that specializes in camera repair.

Measuring Memory and Speed: When Size Matters

6.3.4: When customers ask, "How big is this memory card?," they are not concerned about the physical dimensions or even bytes. We computer geeks know that "memory" is RAM, dynamic and volatile. Customers purchasing a camera know memory as flash, static (like USB) or solid-state drives that we call storage. Marketing people take the blame for this confusion. Still, we do not want to parse words with customers, especially when commissions and repeat business is on the line. Customers expect an answer in terms they understand.

Digital cameras are rated in megapixels. Flash storage is measured in bytes. The resolution (number of megapixels) and the size of the field of view determine the size of the JPG file. These are approximate values, but they should give you some ballpark answer either to a customer or on the A+ exam. Of course, the short answer is the more storage, the more megapixels, the better. Music and video take up considerable room. A typical popular music MP3 song is roughly 4 minutes and takes about 4.3 MB of space at a standard 128 kbps compression. Video MPG4 using the standard H.264 compression is measured in minutes. The quality and resolution of photos and video greatly affect the size of the files. These file sizes and limitations hold true for any storage device, iPod, cell phone, or camera, even for HDDs. Table 7-1 gives you and your customers a feel for file size and capacity.

Table 7-1 Flash Memory in Real-World Terms

File Type and Quality	512-MB Memory Card	1-GB Memory Card	2-GB Memory Card
3-megapixel JPG	500	1000	2000
6-megapixel JGP	180	320	640
12-megapixel JPG	80	160	320
128-kbps compressed MP3	120	240	480
H.264 compressed MPG4	70 min	140 min	280 min

Storage cards are measured in access speed, just like optical drives: n x 1.5 MBps = access speed. "N" is the rating. For example: 40X means 40 x 1500000 bytes per second = 6 MBps access speed. Why is this important? Speed and quality go hand in hand with multimedia. How often have we opted not to watch a video online because it was loading too slowly, or was too poor a quality to see what was going on? Table 7-2 lists common speeds of flash storage.

Table 7-2   Flash Memory Access Speed

Rating	Speed
40X	6 MBps
66X	10 MBps
80X	12 MBps
133X	20 MBps
266X	40 MBps

Troubleshooting Projectors

1.7: Thin film transfer (TFT) projectors are essentially a good LCD screen that uses a bright projector light rather than a fluorescent or LED backlight. Digital light processing (DLP) uses tiny mirrors to reflect the image onto the lenses. Most projectors, especially those in the $1000 and up price range, are fixable. On projectors, the only customer replaceable unit (CRU) is the bulb. It is important to never touch the bulb except where the directions tell you to. A bench technician can replace the power supply, cards, LCD screen, or DLP unit. as you would on any computer or monitor. As you do for cell phones, read up on the exact make and model. Know before you go.

The following is a list of potential problems when connecting a computer to a projector:

- The cable could have a short, broken wire, bent pin, or just might not be connected. (Don't overlook the obvious, especially on an exam question.)

- If it is a laptop, it might not be sending signals out the auxiliary video port. Look for the function key that switches video modes.

- Projectors often have multiple inputs. Using the projector menus, make sure it is set correctly to receive signal.

- Either the projector or the computer (or both) could be in a power-saving mode.

- The bulb could be blown.

- XP has many options regarding how to use an additional monitor or projector. It could be a reproduction of the current desktop. It can also be an extension of the existing desktop. You can tell the display settings to extend your monitor to the right or left (or above or below).

Homework

Memorize Table 7-1, "Flash Memory in Real-World Terms," and Table 7-2, "Flash Memory Access Speed."

If you have access to a "dead" projector or camera, open it up and familiarize yourself with the components. Use online documentation to identify the parts with the correct terms. Remember that the exam uses accurate terminology. It is called a DLP unit, not the reflective mirror thingy.

Funwork

Go "shopping" for a midrange SLR camera. Get as close to $1000 as you can while maximizing quality. Don't forget extra memory cards, batteries, a car charger, and a good-quality waterproof case to protect everything. It is likely you will do this in the future for real. Your company, friends, and family will be seeking your opinion before making their purchases. Know your stuff so that you can advise them well.

The Big World of Printers and Scanners

A+ 220-604 Exam Objectives

Objective 3.1: Identify the fundamental principles of using printers and scanners

Objective 3.2: Install, configure, optimize and upgrade printers and scanners

Key Points

Printers are great for business. Everyone wants them, and they always need to be fixed. There are many good careers just doing printers and scanners. Photocopiers are in reality just large laser all-in-one printers complete with onboard print servers. Scanners are pretty straightforward. Keep them clean, oil moving parts, and set DPI to 300 when using optical character recognition (OCR).

Printers are not so simple. End users famously mistreat printers. One wrong transparency and the insides are laminated. Spill a soda inside and the rollers are sticky, smell like cola, and attract ants. Holiday and birthday cards with sequins and ribbons get wound around and stuck in gears and axels. Paperclips, staples, tape… the list goes on, and it is not pretty. Printers, unsung heroes of the office, work tirelessly, faithfully, and one day fall down dead. Everyone stands around opening panel doors and scratching their heads wondering what happened. All they were doing was saving money by printing on *both* sides of the paper towel. What could go wrong with that? That's when they call you. Today is all about Chapter 14 of the IT Essentials v4.0 course.

Safety First

14.1: Trip hazards and lifting injuries are unfortunate risks in the computer-repair world. Add to that rollers, drive belts, very high voltages, high temperatures, poisonous inks and cleaners, and really messy toner. It is no wonder that most people wisely consider the entire printer a field replaceable unit (FRU). The seasoned benchie, on the other hand, knows there is a world inside printers that remains largely unexplored.

Normally, you are told "always wear the antistatic wrist strap." Good advice, but it should be a little more nuanced than that. You must be cognizant about exactly what you are doing while working on printers. If you are exploring power-supply or electrophotostatic (EP) drum issues, you and the printer avoid sharing any electrical connection (in other words, no wrist strap). When you are working with the integrated circuit (IC) boards and RAM, you should wear the strap. Be mindful of the moving parts when wearing the strap. If the cord or clip gets in between rollers, it will likely break the rollers and give you quite a fright as it pulls your wrist toward them. Do not wear any loose clothing (or long sleeves), neckties, or jewelry. Wear safety glasses. It is an awful but poignant thought: Ink and toner are very difficult to get out of your eyes (or lungs for that matter).

As if these dangers are not enough, printers have sharp metal edges and hot surfaces (both electrically "hot" and temperature hot). Get in the habit of touching surfaces with the back of your hand first. If they are electrified or actually hot, your reflexes will jerk you hand closed and toward you, releasing you from the object. Plus, burns on the back of your fingers are much more fun than on your fingertips or palms. One trick techs use is placing electrical tape on sharp edges or electrically "hot" or "live" surfaces. But, don't cover moving or high-temperature surfaces with tape; it will melt. (Be sure to remove the tape when you are done.)

Table 6-1 lists printer devices and supplies that you should be able to identify for the Bench Tech exam.

Table 6-1   Bench Tech Printer Terms

Term or Part	Explanation
Guide rails	Guides or rails the direct moving parts much like the metal guide that assists sliding drawers.
Platen	Another name for roller, although it can sometimes refer to the glass on the flatbed scanner. Really, it means an object that presses paper, fabric, metal, or other flat material against a screen or form to transfer an image or to cut like a cookie cutter.
Automatic document feeder (ADF)	ADFs are notorious for jams because they often forces thin or oddly shaped paper around a very tight roller.
Electrophotostatic (EP) drum	The EP drum is the "roller" that is charged with ^300VDC. The laser "draws" the image on to the EP drum by reducing the charge where the laser touches.
Corona wire	The corona wire coats the EP drum and the paper with a layer of ions (either positive or negative depending on the system).
Paper pickup tire	Rubber "fingers" that pull up paper from the tray. These get dry and lose their effectiveness over time. Clean and recondition them periodically.
Rubber roller reconditioner	This is used to restore the "grippiness" of the rubber paper handlers.
Heat stable cleaner	This is a cleaner and degreaser for surfaces that get hot. Do not use this while the surface is still hot, unless your skin is fireproof. Use this on belts, rollers, platens, anything that moves and gets hot.
Degreaser solvent	This removes toner, ink, and general grime, but it also hurts the plastic. Definitely keep it off of rubber. In general, use it sparingly and make sure the container used to store this does not leak.

Printer RAM and Firmware

14.3.1: If users on a network complain that only half of their document printed, it might be that the shared printer does not have enough memory and it is relying on the PCs to hold the document in their queue. The RAM on a network printer should more than exceed the size of the documents it receives. Keep in mind peak printing times require even more RAM. Keep in mind that adding RAM can increase performance, especially when printing picture-intensive documents, but it will not improve the speed at which documents are processed. Most printing speed problems are fixed with additional patience, not more RAM.

Firmware updates for printer are rare, but they do exist, and they can greatly improve performance. Like any firmware upgrade, check the manufacturer's website, and double-check that it is the correct file before downloading. You wouldn't tell your color laser printer to think it is suddenly a desktop inkjet. Download the file and follow the directions from the manufacturer. In a troubleshooting situation, make sure documentation supports your decision to update the firmware. The manufacturer will often state that a firmware upgrade fixes a specific list of problems. If your problem is not mentioned, do not update the firmware. You might accidently update (and upgrade) your problems, too.

Scanner Software

14.4.2: Many applications work with scanners. Once an image is scanned, it is usually modified or at the very least saved as a JPG or GIF by an application. The application can do several common tasks, which you need to be familiar with for the A+ exam. Scanners can resize the picture, for example. Going smaller is easy, but bigger tends to get grainy. Keeping the aspect ratio (usually by holding the Shift while dragging the edge of the picture) will prevent distortion. Scanners love dark, solid, high-contrasting colors, like text on white paper. Most scanners have difficulty with handwriting, pencil, and colored or lined paper. Just like a photocopier, lightening and darkening the image can help. Another cool trick that scanner software can do is sharpen an image. It increases the contrast among subtle colors and lines. Taken to extreme, it looks like CD art.

Advanced graphics programs can convert the image from a raster (lots of dots) to a vector image (lines and points). Raster images do not size-up well, but vector images can be whatever size you need. A drawback of vector is it is not subtle. To get a complicated picture, you need a great many points and lines, which requires a tremendous amount of graphics processing called *rendering*. Consider how many lines and points are processed in the rendering of a Pixar movie. They use true supercomputers to get the job done. Remember, someone has to fix those ultrafast PCs and workstations, someone just like you.

WYSIWYG

14.2.2: What you see is what you get (WYSIWYG or sometimes WYSIWUG) is not a stage name; it is an actual computer industry acronym. It originally applied to print preview features of early applications that did a better than average job of displaying what the printed paper would look like. Later, the same problems occurred in website development applications. Different browsers interpret the codes differently. At some level, the computer needs to tell the printer what the page looks like. This is called Page Description Language (PDL). It has three flavors: Printer Command Language (PCL), PostScript (PS), and graphics device interface (GDI). You will see these as options in printer drivers. If given the choice, go with PS. It is cross-platform and does a great job of displaying images and text accurately. GDI treats everything as a picture, and the computer tells the printer exactly where to put each dot. PCL is the printer language from HP and is the standard among printers today.

Print Servers

14.3: Basically, there are two options for sharing a printer. You can dedicate a networked PC to manage a local connection to a printer and share it across a network. Advantages of print servers are they are easy to set up and allow for user permissions, but they require an extra whole computer to run all the time to make the printer available.

Option two is a network printer. A network printer is the same as building a network server into the printer and plugging the network right into the printer. The advantages are it is really easy to set up and you have no need for additional hardware. The disadvantage is that it is less manageable with regard to user and permission options.

Homework

Memorize the six steps of the laser printing process from Day 22, "Printers."

Most of what you need to know about printers for the Bench Technician exam was covered in the Essentials exam. Take this easy day and review printers and scanners (Day 22 and Day 21, "Scanners") in the Essentials section.

Funwork

Manufacturers often issue new drivers to support their products on new operating systems. They do not do this forever. As a product approaches its end of service date, the company must consider the cost of creating a new driver, including testing and everything that goes into that process. At some point, the company determines that it is not worthwhile to spend the resources and essentially forces customers to purchase new products. Uber-techs have a way to combat this.

Printer manufacturers are in many ways like car manufacturers. Every year, every model gets a fresh new look, but the basic machine rarely changes. In their defense, these manufacturers are following the two golden rules of techies: Keep it simple, silly! (KISS), and "If it ain't broke...." Plus, it is too expensive to R&D a whole new way of printing every year.

The printer drivers are associated with the basic machine called a printer engine, not any specific make and model. That is good news for serious techs. If third-party sites don't have a driver for the new OS, try a driver written for the new OS that supports your printer engine. Go down this road much further and you will find that many manufacturers share printer engines, not unlike auto manufacturers share common distributors for parts. Go online and find out what printer engine your printer uses and see how many other printers share common hardware.

Printers and Scanners on Your Own Terms

A+ 220-604 Exam Objectives

Objective 3.3: Identify tools, diagnostic methods and troubleshooting procedures for printers and scanners

Objective 3.4: Perform preventive maintenance of printer and scanner problems

Key Points

Troubleshooting printers is sometimes more fun than troubleshooting computers. Operating systems are so heady and theoretical that fixing them can seem like a religious ritual. Printers and scanners exist in the physical world. You can see and touch them. It is often easy to see the problem, watch it happen, and then replace parts until the printer or scanner works again. Today you will spend a lot of time in Chapter 14 and a little in Chapter 2 of the IT Essentials v4.0 course.

Got Ink?

14.6.1: When troubleshooting printers, always check the easy stuff first. Make sure the printer is powered and connected to a PC. Check that the printer has paper and ink or toner. If you see error codes, address those. You might have to restart the printer and the PC. It is surprising how often printer drivers fail or become corrupt. A simple driver delete and reinstall is a magic bullet for many printer issues.

In the case of network printers, you also need to check the TCP/IP settings. The IP address that PC sends the print job must actually be the IP address of the printer. This might seem obvious, but a printer set for Dynamic Host Configuration Protocol (DHCP) can lose the assigned IP address. Either reserve the printer's IP address in the DHCP server or set a static address on the printer.

Error Codes

14.4.1: As a bench tech, you will likely see many of the same brands and models of printers. Certainly over time, you will become more familiar with popular printers. Table 5-1 contains the more common error codes found in HP LaserJet printers. It is more important to focus on the kinds of problems and solutions more so than memorizing the codes in this table.

Table 5-1   HP LaserJet Error Codes

Code	Meaning	Solutions
00	Ready.	No problems.
02	Warming up.	Just give it a minute to warm up.
04	Self test.	Run power-on self test (POST) and some self diagnostics.
06	Config or demo.	Print a test page right from the printer.
09	I/O reset.	The connection to the computer is not correct. Check the network, USB, FireWire, Bluetooth, infrared (IR), serial or parallel connection configurations.
11	Out of paper.	Add paper.
12	There is a panel or door still waiting to be shut.	Shut the panel or door. If everything is closed, it could be a fault sensor.
13	Paper jam.	Open the door, remove the toner cartridge, and look for and carefully remove the paper (watch for hot surfaces).
16	Toner low.	Remove the toner cartridge. Shake (the cartridge) from side to side. Reinstall the cartridge and order new toner.
18	MIO.	Missing I/O or cannot detect the network or computer.
20	Insufficient memory.	Turn off the printer, unplug the network or computer connection, turn it back on, and plan to purchase more RAM soon.

Serious Solutions for Serious Bench Techs

14.6: This section describes troubleshooting techniques and solutions that only a bench tech should do. Because you have the tools and the space to do these, they fall under your exam material. Enjoy!

Serious Solutions: Laser Printers

Laser printers are the business-PC and increasingly home-use gold standard. They are usually worth fixing and can last a long time. It is your job to keep them lasting and performing year after year. Table 5-2 lists laser-printer problems and solutions that only bench techs should perform.

Table 5-2   Serious Laser-Printer Problems

Symptom	Cause	Solution
Ink smudges off of the paper. In reality, the toner failed to fuse to the paper.	The fixing film over the fuser is broken or ripped.	Replace the fuser sleeve (which contains the fixing film).
Vertical lines on the paper.	Worn-out wiper blade is not removing all the remaining toner (like tired windshield wipers leave streaks).	Replace the wiper blade (and the windshield wipers).

Table 5-2   Serious Laser-Printer Problems

Symptom	Cause	Solution
Horizontal lines or repetitive "tick" marks.	The electrophotostatic (EP) drum is damaged or dirty.	Attempt to clean, but plan on replacing the EP drum (watch out for heat).

Serious Solutions: Inkjet Printers

For the end user and field and remote techs, the inkjet printer is a field replaceable unit (FRU). For you, it is a charity case challenge. Be mindful of the price of replacement versus your price per hour. Some inkjets cost less than $30. Table 5-3 lists inkjet printer problems and solutions.

Table 5-3   Serious InkJet Printer Problems

Symptom	Cause	Solution
Ink carriage will not come out of hiding.	The carriage parks itself off to one side. Any of the following could be the problem if it won't move: ■ Jammed paper ■ Broken or loose drive belt ■ Unplugged or broken ribbon cable	Remove jammed paper. Tighten/replace drive belt. Replace ribbon cable (doing so might require replacing the carriage assembly, too).
Fuzzy or auras surround objects.	The print heads are not aligned.	Run print head alignment diagnostic on printer.
Blotches, spatters, missing or weird color.	Ink heads are dirty or leaking.	Clean the ink head. Run self-cleaning diagnostic. Replace ink cartridges if necessary. Run color calibration.

Serious Solutions for Paper Problems

Table 5-4 lists printer problems that haunt all printers and their solutions.

Table 5-4   Serious Printer Paper Problems

Symptom	Cause	Solution
Multiple sheets of paper are drawn from the paper tray simultaneously (major paper jam).	Paper separator failed to grab the remaining sheets and only let the one get picked up by the tire.	Recondition or replace separation pad.
No sheets are drawn from the paper tray.	Paper could have static, or the environment could be humid. The spring that pushes the paper up could be tired. The tire could be old and not grippy.	Use new paper. (Try different brands; some printers seem to be brand picky.) Recondition or replace the tire.

Cleaning the Bench Tech Way

14.5.3: Printers get dirty. They need to be cleaned. It is a dirty job, and you are the person to do it. This section describes procedures for cleaning printers. Pay careful attention to this; you might see it on the exam.

Cleaning Inkjet Printers

When cleaning inkjet printers, follow these steps:

Step 1   Turn off the power and unplug the printer.

Step 2   Use compressed air or a vacuum to remove the dust.

Step 3   Spray >70% isopropyl rubbing alcohol on a soft, lint-free cloth, and wipe the guide rails.

Step 4   Lubricate the guide rails with silicon spray or lightweight oil. Note: Always use lubricants sparingly in a printer. Too much gets on the paper, which gets on the paper pickup tire, which then slips, which causes jams, and so on.

Step 5   Lubricate all gears the same way, sparingly.

Step 6   Use another alcohol-dampened soft, lint-free cloth to clean the platen. Turn the platen to clean all the parts.

Step 7   Remove and clean the print heads on the cartridges with a cotton swab and >70% isopropyl rubbing alcohol.

Cleaning Laser Printers

When cleaning laser printers, follow these steps:

Step 1   Turn off and unplug the printer.

Step 2   After letting the printer cool down, use compressed air or a vacuum to remove the dust.

Step 3   Use compressed air to blow out dust from around the EP drum and corona wire.

Step 4   Use a cotton swab and >70% isopropyl rubbing alcohol to clean the corona wire extra well.

Step 5   Remove and gently shake the toner cartridge and replace.

Dot-Matrix Printers

When cleaning dot-matrix printers, follow these steps:

Step 1   Turn off and unplug the printer.

Step 2   Slide the print head to the middle of the platen and remove the head.

Step 3   Clean the pins with a cotton swab (no rubbing alcohol).

Step 4   Check the tension of the printer carriage belt (and, usually, tighten it).

Paper Sizes: Letter, Legal, and A4

14.6: Paper size is a constant issue when printing cards, notes, signs, and other oddly shaped documents. Even when printing normal documents, the printer needs to be told what size paper to use. Letter is used in the United States to print 8.5 by 11-inch documents. The European A4 paper size is 8.25 by 11.75 inches (actually 210 mm by 297 mm), close but more than enough to seriously change the format on the print job. Legal paper is several inches longer than letter and A4 and can cause problems when accidentally printing legal-length documents on standard-sized paper.

Reduce, Reuse, Recycle

2.1.3: Being able to print has advantages. On the flip side, printing is expensive both in terms of money and the environment. The ugly reality is that unless it is special photograph or a life-insurance policy, everything that a printer prints will at some point be disposed of, often in less than a month. The ink is quite toxic, laser printers in particular use a tremendous amount of electricity; and next time you heave a box of paper around, just imagine the logistics of its manufacture, storage, and transportation. That is a lot of energy, resources, and cost for a very temporary thing.

Your clients are almost always ready to save money if not the good Earth. Reusing paper as scrap is an easy cost-saving method. Just make sure the printed stuff on the other side is not sensitive or libelous. From a troubleshooting perspective, know that some printers don't like to use leftover paper. Double-sided printers are expensive initially but greatly reduce paper consumption. The easiest option is to develop a "think before you print" awareness among your customers and employees.

Toner: The Good, the Bad, and the Messy

14.5.3: Most toner cartridges can be sent back to the manufacturer for refurbishing and refilling. Purchasing these used cartridges is a way to save money. The number one rule about cleaning up toner is don't spill it in the first place. It is affected by static electricity. It is powder, the consistency of baking soda. Do not mop it up. Do not sweep it unless it is on a nonporous surface like a linoleum floor. Do use a vacuum cleaner with a HEPA filter. Do test the vacuum on regular dust before vacuuming up the toner.

Homework

Right-click an installed printer icon in the Printers applet in the Control Panel. Print a test page, and then click **No** to indicate that it didn't print. Doing so launches the Printer Troubleshooting Wizard. Answer the questions and follow the troubleshooting flowchart. Map it out as you go along. Go back through the wizard and answer the question differently. Each time you do this, you will fill in more of the flowchart. Take that flowchart with you and review it before your Bench Tech exam.

Pick an exam topic that still scares you a little, tear it in small pieces, and learn each piece. Divide and conquer. Ask your forums and friends. Go own that knowledge. You have a test in less than a week.

Funwork

Ever seen a newspaper printing press? How about a magazine printer? An architect's plotter? Imagine the printer that made this book. How do they scan wall-sized works of art for museum posters? How do they scan inside bodies, brains, and molecules? Someone is responsible for maintaining these truly amazing machines. As a bench tech, you are exactly the person to do that. Go explore the many and various kinds of printers and scanners. Remember, for every exotic or common, huge or minuscule, complex or simple printer or scanner, there is a job and a career.

Alphabet Soup

Key Points

Today is the day you will spend some time with the A+ exam's acronyms. The Bench Tech exam in particular is notorious for tripping people up by using so many acronyms. It is a dry day, but really important. Consider this: If the exam uses an acronym that you do not recognize, let alone understand, what chance do you have of answering the question correctly? Today you are working on your defensive game. Troubleshooting and fixing things is your offensive game. Offense (doing something) is always more fun, but everyone knows that defense wins games. If your brain still hurts from CPUs, portable devices, and printers, deal with it because you are a few days away from being a certified professional, and professionals never complain (at least not in public).

Acronym List

Table 4-1 is a reduced, annotated list of acronyms customized for the Bench Tech exam. The complete list is online at the CompTIA website (http://www.comptia.org). Notice that Table 4-1 has no logical order. It is not alphabetic, nor grouped by topic. This is no accident. It is important for you to see these acronyms out of order. As you have seen on the Essentials exam, each question is a different topic and a different set of terms and acronyms. This can be jarring, and this disorganized list helps you get used seeing these acronyms out order and out of context. If you think you know all of them already, cover the right columns and challenge yourself.

Table 4-1   **Alphabet Soup**

Acronym	Long Names	Notes
NTFS	new technology file system	Preferred file system for MS operating systems.
MIDI	musical instrument digital interface	An analog-to-digital conversion for musical instruments.
ESDI	enhanced small device (or disk) interface	Old drive bus, like PATA.
VESA	Video Electronics Standards Association	A predecessor of SVGA.
Mb	megabit	1,000,000 bits.
LED	light emitting diode	A small light bulb used to indicate the status of a port or device.
GDI	graphics device interface	A kind of printer driver.
WLAN	wireless local area network	A general term for a wireless network.
IRQ	interrupt request	A priority list of devices that can request the attention of the CPU.
EVGA	extended video graphics adapter/array	A better version of VGA.

continues

Table 4-1   **Alphabet Soup**   *continued*

Acronym	Long Names	Notes
EVDO	evolution data optimized or evolution data only	A cell phone protocol based on code-division multiple access (CDMA).
ASR	automated system recovery	A method of repairing an OS in the event of failure. It must be set up while the OS works.
FAT	file allocation table	The map of an HDD used to retrieve data by the controller.
MBR	master boot record	Boot files that are copied into RAM at startup.
IrDA	Infrared Data Association	The standards organization the governs IR technologies.
FAT32	32-bit file allocation table	The file allocation table used in Windows 9x.
EIDE	enhanced integrated drive electronics	A better version of IDE, ATA, PATA that allows for more channels and can support faster communications and more drives.
SPDIF	Sony-Philips digital interface format	Digital audio port.
OEM	original equipment manufacturer	Customized OS made for a specific PC model.
CRIMM	continuity-rambus inline memory module	Proprietary RAMBUS form factor.
FPM S DRAM	fast page-mode symmetric (or synchronous) dynamic random access memory	A faster form of RAM but not as fast as DDR.
ISO	Industry Standards Organization	One of the standards organization that decides protocols and creates definitions for interoperability among technology companies' devices.
PATA	parallel advanced technology attachment	Also called IDE or ATA.
MPEG	Moving Picture Experts Group	Movie file.
LPT	line printer terminal	Parallel printer port.
BIOS	basic input/output system	Stores boot, drives, and integrated device configurations.
FAT16	16-bit file allocation table	The file allocation table used in Windows 3.1 and early editions of 95.
CD	compact disc	Can refer to +/-R, +/-RW, and ROM.
LPT1	line printer terminal 1	The first parallel printer port.
AT	advanced technology	Very old motherboard form factor.
PCI	peripheral component interconnect	Common expansion slot.
CD-RW	compact disc-rewritable	CD can be burned over and over.
ERD	emergency repair disk	Used to restore an OS.
WEP	Wired Equivalent Privacy	A wireless encryption protocol, better than WAP but not as good as WPA.
CRT	cathode-ray tube	Big heavy monitors, not LCD.

Table 4-1   Alphabet Soup   *continued*

Acronym	Long Names	Notes
GB	gigabyte	1,000,000 bytes. (Actually, it is 1,073,741,824 when calculated properly.)
SP	service pack	SP1, SP2, and SP3.
ROM	read only memory	Unchangeable.
HDMI	high definition media (or multimedia) interface	High-quality video and audio interface.
LAN	local area network	A group of computers and network devices that share resources and exist in a relatively small geographic area like a building or campus.
DVD-RW	digital video disc-rewritable	Read and write (R/W) the disk many times (approximately 1000 times).
UTP	unshielded twisted pair	Standard network cable.
GUI	graphical user interface	Desktops, icons, mouse arrows, and other graphically oriented objects and tools that enable users to interact with a PC.
ATA	advanced technology attachment	Same as IDE and PATA expansion bus.
RIMM	RAMBUS inline memory module	Proprietary competitor of DIMM RAM.
FPM	fast page-mode	Improved performance SD RAM.
HCL	hardware compatibility list	The online list of hardware that is approved by Windows.
FDD	floppy disk drive	3.5-inch-wide 1.44-MB removable, read/write media.
ATX	advanced technology extended	The basis of modern motherboards.
DVD-RAM	digital versatile disc-random access memory	A DVD that is used primarily for security camera footage because of good R/W abilities.
IDE	integrated drive electronics	Same as ATA and PATA.
KB	kilobyte	1000 bytes. (Actually, 1024 when properly calculated.)
MMX	multimedia extensions	Handles some multimedia tasks to free up CPU resources.
RS-232	recommended standard 232	Serial port.
BNC	Bayonet-Neill-Concelman or British naval connector	Twist-push-lock style connector used for antennas and some fiber cables.
ESD	electrostatic discharge	Static electricity.
DIN	Deutsche Industrie Norm	The German standards organization. They made the standards for DIN and mini-DIN ports. Round collar and symmetrical pins, PS/2 mice, and keyboards use mini-DIN connectors.

continues

Table 4-1   **Alphabet Soup**   *continued*

Acronym	Long Names	Notes
Kb	kilobit	1000 bits. (Actually, 1024 bits when calculated properly.)
URL	uniform resource locator	http://anything.somewhere.out/there/on/the/web.
RF	radio frequency	2.4 GHz, for example.
IEEE	Institute of Electrical and Electronics Engineers	One of the standards organization that decides protocols and creates definitions for interoperability among technology companies' devices.
LPX	low profile extended	Expansion cards that use shorter plates to fit in low-profile cases.
MCA	micro channel architecture	Very old bus.
COM1	communication port 1	Usually the first serial port.
DDR SDRAM	double data-rate symmetric (or synchronous) dynamic random access memory	Common RAM in modern PCs.
IR	infrared	A point-to-point wireless technology that uses a spectrum just outside of our visual perception. (Think flashlight signals that we can't quite see.)
SPGA	staggered pin grid array	A zigzag pin arrangement, like the stars on the American flag.
PDA	personal digital assistant	Think of this as a BlackBerry with no calling, texting, or e-mail ability; just calendar, diary, notes, and so on.
AGP	accelerated graphics port	Old-school good video card.
SDRAM	symmetric (or synchronous) dynamic random access memory	Basic RAM used in older PCs.
DB-25	serial communications D-shell connector, 25 pins	There is a more common parallel port that uses DB-25. The parallel port DB-25 is female and sometimes purple.
DC	direct current	Electricity used inside electronics, not wall power.
AC	alternating current	Wall power.
TCP/IP	Transmission Control Protocol/Internet Protocol	The standard protocol used in networking.
DIMM	dual inline memory module	Common RAM form factor.
NLX	new low-profile extended	Low-profile motherboard.
DIP	dual inline package	Basic removable IC chip. Old BIOSs were stored on these chips.
SSID	service set identifier	Broadcasted name of a wireless network.
DB-9	9 pin D shell connector	Standard serial port.
DRAM	dynamic random access memory	Has no power or memory. Basis of modern RAM.

Table 4-1   Alphabet Soup

Acronym	Long Names	Notes
DVD	digital video (or versatile) disc	Can refer to +/-R, +/-RW, and ROM.
DVD-R	digital video disc-recordable	DVD that once written is forever read only.
SIMM	single inline memory module	Old RAM chips that need to be installed in pairs.
POST	power-on self test	A set of tests that check basic hardware function and configuration on startup.
ACPI	advanced configuration and power interface	An old technology that allows the OS to control system power settings. Current operating systems use Advanced Power Management.
WIFI	wireless fidelity	A general term for a wireless network.
SLI	scalable link interface or system level integration or scanline interleave mode	Coupling video cards to increase processing power.
SoDIMM	small outline dual inline memory module	Small RAM for laptops.
CPU	central processing unit	The main IC chip in the computer.
CMOS	complementary metal-oxide semiconductor	The chip that holds the BIOS info.
DVI	digital visual (or video) interface	Common video connection.
AMD	advanced micro devices	CPU manufacturer.
ECC	error correction code	Checks for errors in RAM.
ECP	extended capabilities port	A bidirectional fast parallel port.
EDO SDRAM	extended data out symmetric (or synchronous) dynamic random access memory	Older RAM replaced by DDR.
MHz	megahertz	1,000,000 cycles per second.
SGRAM	synchronous graphics random access memory	A style of RAM used on video cards.
EEPROM	electrically erasable programmable read-only memory	Flash memory.
WUXGA	wide ultra extended graphics array	A widescreen, 1920 x 1200, 16:9, version of UXGA.
DDR	double data-rate	DDR 2 and DDR 3 also exist.
EGA	enhanced graphics adapter	A predecessor of VGA.
SD card	secure digital card	A security-enabled flash memory card. Do not confuse the SD with SD RAM.
CGA	color/graphics adapter	As opposed to monochrome, seriously old video card/port.
EISA	extended industry standard architecture	Better version of ISA but still obsolete.
SOHO	small office/home office	A home or small office environment that supports a small group of users.

continues

Table 4-1   Alphabet Soup   *continued*

Acronym	Long Names	Notes
RDRAM	RAMBUS dynamic random	A proprietary RAM made by RAMBUS, inc. access memory.
DVD-ROM	digital video disc-read only memory	
EPP	enhanced parallel port	Bidirectional parallel printer port.
DOS	disk operating system	The basis for command prompt.
PCL	printer control language	A kind of printer driver.
RJ	registered jack	Refers to all rectangular jacks (like phone cables).
WPA	Wireless Protected Access	Better wireless encryption protocol, even better: WPA2.
ZIP	zigzag inline package	A pin arrangement on very rare RAM chips. A zip file is a collection of files that are grouped and compressed. Zip drives are old removable drives.
RJ-11	registered jack function 11	Standard telephone jack.
RTC	real-time clock	The steady beat that the PC uses to time and coordinate communications.
SATA	serial advanced technology attachment	Current standard drive interface.
CD-ROM	compact disc-read-only memory	CD was pressed at a factory, not burned by a user.
RAID	redundant array of independent discs	A fault-tolerant set of HDDs.
SXGA	super extended graphic array	1280 × 1024 32-bit color.
Tb	Terabit	1,000,000,000,000 bits.
UDMA	ultra direct memory access	A wider faster version of direct memory access.
PIN	personal identification number	An identification code used like a password.
GHz	gigahertz	1000 cycles per second.
ISP	Internet service provider	A company that connects a computer or a LAN to the Internet.
SFC	system file checker	A utility that looks for corrupt system files.
UDF	universal disk format	A formatting used on optical disks.
FRU	field replaceable unit	A part or device that is replaced not fixed.
RAMBUS	trademarked term, not an acronym	Proprietary competitor of DIMM RAM.
I/O	input/output	Describes any transfer of data either in and out of the PC or in and out of the CPU.
Micro DIMM	micro dual inline memory module	RAM form factor for subcompact laptops.

Table 4-1   Alphabet Soup

Acronym	Long Names	Notes
RISC	reduced instruction set computer	A CPU that uses fewer instructions to complete tasks.
EMI	electromagnetic interference	Any interference on a wire or wireless communications.
VGA	video graphics array	If referring to a resolution, it is 640 x 480, 8-bit color. If referring to the VGA port, it is a DE15F, meaning D plug, size E, 15-pin, female, standard VGA port.
SRAM	static random access memory	No power is no problem; memory stays.
BTX	balanced technology extended	Newer version of an ATX motherboards.
MMC	Microsoft Management Console Multimedia card	The standard utility interface for Windows operating systems. An older form of Secure Digital Card that is a flash storage device used in cameras, portable devices, and laptops. Tip: Use contextual clues in the question to determine the meaning of MMC.
SCSI ID	small computer system interface identifier	The number assigned to a SCSI drive.
MP3	Moving Picture Experts Group	Audio file.
PGA	pin grid array	Describes the arrangement of pins on a chip and socket.
RGB	red green blue	Another name for analog video ports.
IP	internet protocol	The common Layer 3 protocol on the Internet, as in TCP/IP.
EFS	encrypting file system	A file system that uses a key to encrypt every file on the drive.
NIC	network interface card	An interface between a PC and a network.
FCC	Federal Communications Commission	The governing body that coordinates and regulates many computer industry policies, including radio spectrum usage.
PnP	plug and play	Autoconfiguration and driver installation initiated by connecting a device.
RJ-45	registered jack-45	Standard NIC jack.
DDR RAM	double data-rate random access memory	A faster version of SDRAM.
SEC	single edge connector	Slot-style CPUs.
UART	universal asynchronous receiver transmitter	The process by which parallel communication is converted into serial or from serial to parallel. Think four lanes of traffic funneled into one lane to avoid construction.
UPS	uninterruptible power supply	Battery backup for equipment and computers.

continues

Table 4-1   **Alphabet Soup**   *continued*

Acronym	Long Names	Notes
MB	megabyte	1,000,000 bytes.
USB	universal serial bus	The standard port to connect a device to a PC.
FAT12	12-bit file allocation table	The file allocation table used on floppy disks.
HDD (also HD)	hard disk drive	The primary storage device in a PC.
NTLDR	new technology loader	A boot file for NT, XP, Vista.
OSR	original equipment manufacturer service release	A service pack or update designed for an OEM OS.
ISA	industry standard architecture	Old, 16-bit expansion bus.
PAN	personal area network	Think Bluetooth.
MSDS	material safety data sheet	Papers that explain the onsite hazardous material.
PCIX	peripheral component interconnect extended	Longer PCI slots.
RAM	random access memory	The primary system memory.
CDFS	compact disc file system	File allocation table used on CDs.
TB	terabyte	1,000,000,000,000 bytes.
XGA	Extended graphics array	1024×768, 32-bit color.
PCIe	peripheral component interconnect express	Faster than PCI.
ST	straight tip	Fiber-optic cable connection that uses a BNC connector.
PCMCIA	Personal Computer Memory Card International Association	An expansion slot for laptops.
DMA	direct memory access	Bypasses the bus and directly accesses the RAM.
LVD	low voltage differential	SCSI technology that extends the max cable length and increases throughput.
SVGA	super video graphics array	800×600, 4-bit color.
PGA2	pin grid array 2	Describes the arrangement of pins on a chip and socket, different from PGA.
SCSI	small computer system interface	An old drive interface.
ZIF	zero-insertion-force	The lever used to secure the CPU.
HPFS	high performance file system	A legacy file system not supported by Microsoft since Windows Me.
WAP	Wireless Application Protocol	A wireless HTTP access on smart phones and PDAs.
OS	operating system	The main software that supports data storage, applications, and users (and hardware and communications).

Table 4-1   Alphabet Soup

Acronym	Long Names	Notes
ENET	Ethernet	IEEE 802.3. It is a group of network technologies that are common in LANs.
PROM	programmable read-only memory	Nonflashable ROM.
PS/2	personal system/2 connector	Old keyboard and mouse ports.
QoS	quality of service	A measure of reliability for networks and ISPs.
STP	shielded twisted pair	Network cable with foil between the PVC jacket and around each of the twisted pairs to help reduce EMI.
LCD	liquid crystal display	A flat-panel monitor.
UXGA	ultra extended graphics array	1600 × 1200, 32-bit color.

Homework

After all that, you deserve a break.

Funwork

Go back to your IT old-timer and ask about some of the acronyms you did not recognize. These terms are tricky, and you really need to know what they mean.

Security and Environment

A+ 220-604 Exam Objectives

Objective 4.1: Identify the names, purposes and characteristics of physical security devices and processes

Objective 4.2: Install hardware security

Objective 5.1: Identify potential hazards & proper safety procedures including power supply, display devices and environment

Key Points

Your top security priority is protecting your customers' equipment. Nothing spells doom for a repair shop like news of theft (identity, data, or physical). Today you will cover topics from Chapter 16 of the IT Essentials v4.0 course. You then review Day 18 and several sections from Days 23 and 17–15 of Part I of this book.

Security Devices

16.2.2: Many gadgets increase security, including fobs, smart cards, fingerprint readers, and so on. You need to know about them for the exam. Also know that the best security starts with your common sense. For example, don't leave PCs logged on; use hardened passwords, and do not write them down; do not open suspicious e-mail attachments; challenge the credentials (but don't be rude) of gas, electric, and other service techs who snoop around your place; and put tools away and lock equipment up at night. These and countless other really basic common-sense tasks really do work. Security gadgets are only as good as the people who implement them.

Fobs

A proper fob and receiver solve the same equation every 60 to 90 seconds. At any given time, they should be at the same step in solving the equation. Authentication is simply comparing the two devices. Remember, in math class your teacher droned, "Always show your work." Imagine two students solving the same problem. Every minute on the dot, they complete the next step in solving that equation. If they passed notes to each other, they could include the output of the step in addition to the message. The equation output should be the same as on the receiver's paper. The note (or packet) is compared by the receiver. If the steps match, the packet is acceptable. Otherwise, it is discarded.

When used for encryption, that step in the equation is used as the key. If a message is intercepted and unencrypted, the key is useless to apply to the next message because by that time the equation output (and new encryption key) is different. A standard key or password is used over and over, and once discovered, that stream of communication is compromised.

The term *fob* has been downgraded some in past years to include any kind of physical chip that is used to compare with the receiving chip (such as a car key and the ignition, or in some cases used as a login tool for an OS). By far, the best biometric device is a retinal scanner, but they are expensive, cumbersome, and frankly a little too sci-fi for most people. DNA scanners are a promising device in the future.

Smart Card Readers

A smart card is usually an ID card with a magnetic strip that is read like a credit card. The information on the card is compared to information in a database, and access is granted if the information matches. Smart card readers work well until they are stolen. Smart cards combined with other forms of security make a tighter, layered system.

Security at Your Fingertips

Physical security is a big part of a bench tech's job. Social-engineering attacks are surprisingly common at repair centers. Picture it from the bad guy's perspective. There are rooms full of computers that are full of personal data. "Yeah, I'm here to pick up my sister's PC. I think it is black, newish (pointing). Yeah, that's the one." A few hundred bucks later, and the PC is his, data and all.

Keep the customer's equipment locked behind a retinal, fingerprint, or palm scanner. Pharmacists and banks have used biometric locks for years. It is also a good idea to have some way of authenticating the person who picks up the computer. Verify the customer by use of a fingerprint or at least verify the credit card number.

Security Cameras

Security cameras are cheap and easy to set up and run on your existing wireless or wired network. Use them. They are a networking device with their own IP address. Always use a combination of visible and unseen cameras. Never disclose the location of unseen cameras to employees. You never know who is planning a social-engineering or insider attack. At the same time, know the laws in your area. Footage is admissible in court, so do not get the footage thrown out of court because it was taken illegally.

Environment

2.1.3: Just a quick review from the Essentials exam: You should know about material safety data sheets (MSDS) and local government procedures for proper disposal of batteries and electronic equipment. Remember that ink and toner are bad for the environment. So, use proper cleaning techniques. Also, laptops are better than PCs for the environment because they draw less power and have less physical material. Refer to Day 17, "Environmental Issues," if you need further review.

Homework

CompTIA takes environmental concerns seriously. They know it is only a matter of time before "green" momentum surpasses the "coolness" of computers and we realize that what has driven the worldwide connectedness and economy is really bad for the environment. They know this, and they want to make sure you know this. Throughout this book, eco-concerns have been pointed out as well as safety issues. Go reread the following sections: Day 18, Day 23, Day 17 (except for the section on customer service). Read carefully Chapters 15 and 16 in the IT Essentials v4.0 course, and call it a night.

Funwork

For the ecologically minded, the bench technician is a real-life hero. By maintaining, refurbishing, and reselling, you are truly the second pillar of "reduce, reuse, recycle." It might not be as visible as saving baby seals or chasing large ships in rubber rafts, but your job actually has much greater impact by reducing the total number of electronic devices and conserving the resources that are spent making new ones. Google the phrase *refurbished electronics*. Explore both the methods and products that are reused. HowStuffWorks.com has a great explanation of the process.

220-604 Review Day

This is a light day in preparation for your test tomorrow. Enjoy it and relax.

By Any Other Name

The computer industry is full of different names for the same thing. These synonyms are cumbersome and challenging for the new techie. The following is list of some of the synonyms found in the IT industry and on the A+ exams. People will argue that there are subtle differences among these terms and phrases, but it is a good place to start:

- Fault isolation = troubleshooting.

- Load = copy to RAM = run = execute = launch = double-click.

- Mini stereo plug = headphone jack = 3.5TSR.

- PC = IBM clone = computer = system = machine.

- Component = device = part = field replaceable unit (FRU).

- RS232 = DB9 = DE9 = serial port.

- Documentation = release notes = ReadMe files.

- Card = I/O card = adapter card = expansion card = PC card.

- Control Panel icon = applet = configuration application = configuration utility.

- 9x = 95a, 95b, 98a, 98b, Millennium Edition (Me).

- 2K = 2000.

- Pins = contacts = channels = width = conductors.

- Bits per second = bps = b/s.

- Throughput = transfer rate = network speed. (Bandwidth is a measure of ideal speed, not the throughput actually realized.)

- Mini ATX = micro ATX = flex ATX.

- S/PDIF = SPDIF = digital audio interface.

- PCIX (peripheral component interconnect extended) is *not* PCIExpress (PCIe).

Brain Dumps

Practice the following brain dumps:

- PC layered model

- Motherboard map

- OSI and TCP/IP models

- TIA/EIA 568 A and B (wire color arrangements)

- XP boot sequence

- Laser-printer process

- General troubleshooting process

Write Your Own Practice Questions

One of the best kept secrets of academic success is to outthink the teacher. After a few tests, you should know what kinds of questions that teacher, or CompTIA in this case, asks. You have seen a real test and probably several practice tests. Write down the questions as you think they will appear on your exam. This is a skill that is honed and refined over the years. Once you master this, schooling of any kind gets much, much easier. With a little practice, you can do this, too. Answer your own questions and review them right before you enter the room for your exam tomorrow.

Homework

It's time to make your "cheat sheet" study sheet and remake it a dozen times or until you can do it all from memory. The following is a start:

- A good fuse has 0 ohms of resistance, and a blown fuse has an infinite amount of resistance.

- Customers might not always be right, but you must always treat them with respect.

- The manufacturer's website is the best place to find the most up-to-date drivers, software, and documentation.

- Gather information from the customer first, then the PC.

Funwork

Do *something* away from the computer that is fun and a little different from your usual routine: Go out with an old friend you haven't seen in a while. Or take in a movie you wouldn't normally see. Or perhaps visit a museum that you have never been to. Maybe go to a concert featuring music that's not your usual taste. Go to dinner somewhere exotic.

Go to bed early.

220-604 Exam Day

It is easy to see yourself as 90 minutes away from the end. This is a tempting but dangerous trap. Remember, you are a professional. A professional finishes what was begun. A professional puts forth the same effort at the end as the beginning. A professional gets it done correctly, every time.

Before the Exam

Before the exam, sleep well and eat well. Do not eat sugary or starchy foods the morning of the exam. Review your "cheat sheet." As soon as they hand you scratch paper and a pen, write down all your brain dumps, tables, mnemonics, charts, diagrams, religious prayers, whatever you like. Be sure to give your notes back to them at the end of the exam.

During the Exam

During the exam, remember: One question at a time; that is, read the darn question (RTDQ). Don't let distracters do their job. Don't read too much into the questions. Always eliminate obviously wrong answers when stuck on a difficult question. This ups your odds if you have to guess. Do not hurry toward the end. You will have plenty of time to be excited afterward. Focus on each question, one at a time. Remember how much effort you put into preparing for this exam and the money you invested in your education and the test! You want it to be money and time well spent.

After the Exam

After the exam, write down the questions (someplace away from the exam center) that you remember stumped you. Look up the answers right away. You'll feel better knowing the answers. Go enjoy the rest of your day. You deserve it.

You will get your test scores as soon as you finish, but it will take few weeks to a month to get the actual certificate. Be sure and frame that certificate and hang it on the I-Love-Me wall behind your desk. For good measure, tuck the score sheets behind the certificate in the frame just in case you need to prove something later. Along with the certificate, you will receive a plastic card for your wallet.

The computer industry is constantly growing and changing. There is a never-ending supply of new and interesting technologies. Keep learning. Get on a tech RSS feed, subscribe to a periodic e-mail newsletter, join a Linux or Mac users group, participate in forums, and attend a conference. CompTIA conferences are really quite good. Remember, you are an IT professional. It is your responsibility to maintain your knowledge and skills. It is a big and fast-moving field. Enjoy the ride. Good luck!

Index

G – H

J - K - L

M